Copyright © 2020 Devon Vasquez

All rights reserved.

ISBN:

A COLLECTION OF DOODLES

Dedicated to me and anyone else who may be interested. Oh and my dog Shortie obviously.

(Any quotes used are NOT my own)

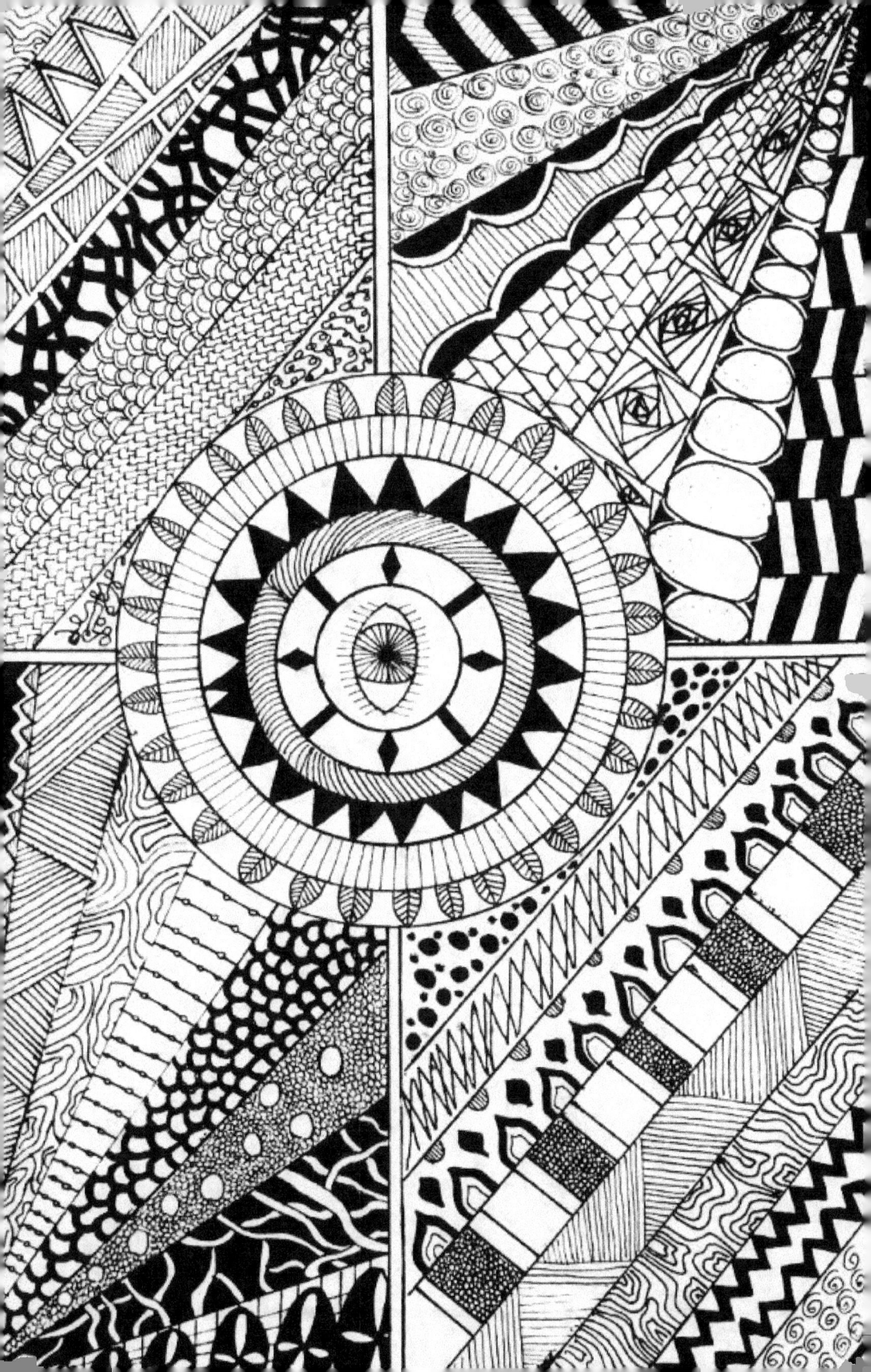

THE COSMIC BARRY
(AKA THE Orbital Nano Jackal - ONJ-457)

Type:
Far-Range Interplanetary Light Annilator

Home Planet:
Tauri NT03 Coil
Permian Period E.Vaporator
17hr Days
1.56x Earth Gravity
5 Moons

Stats:
- Sensors: Avg.
- Weapons: Good
- Shields: Avg
- Crew: 10-20 members
- Speed: Above Avg.
- Cargo space: Very poor

Labels:
- Ushaf Stabilizer Conductor
- Corrosion Block
- Corrosion Block
- Large F-Mainstay Feed For Semi-Pad
- Inverse Z-Repeller
- Fusion X-Gauge
- Outom Cylinder
- Titanium Edge Ignition
- Quad space Valve
- Rhodium Brod Deactivator

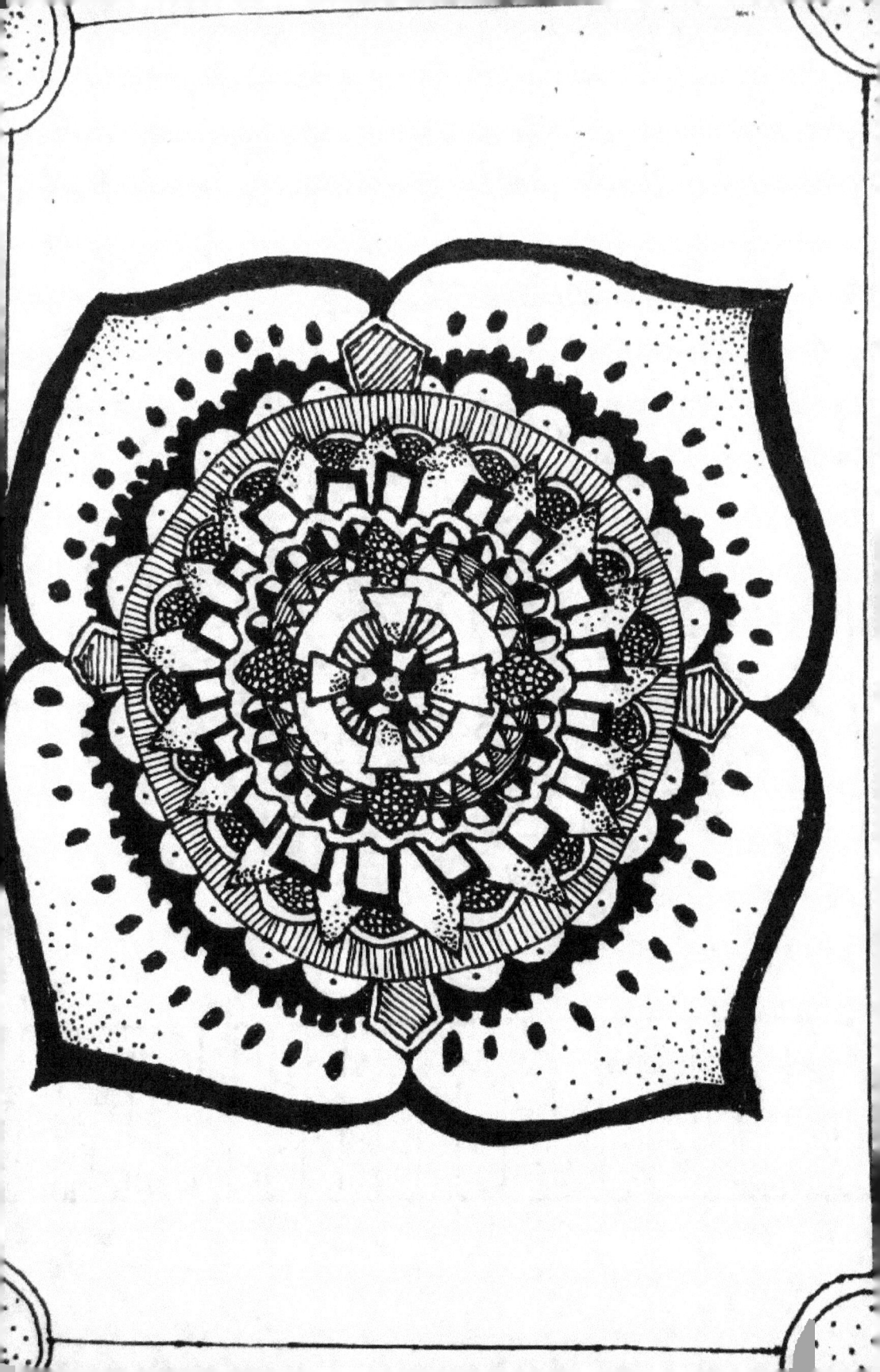

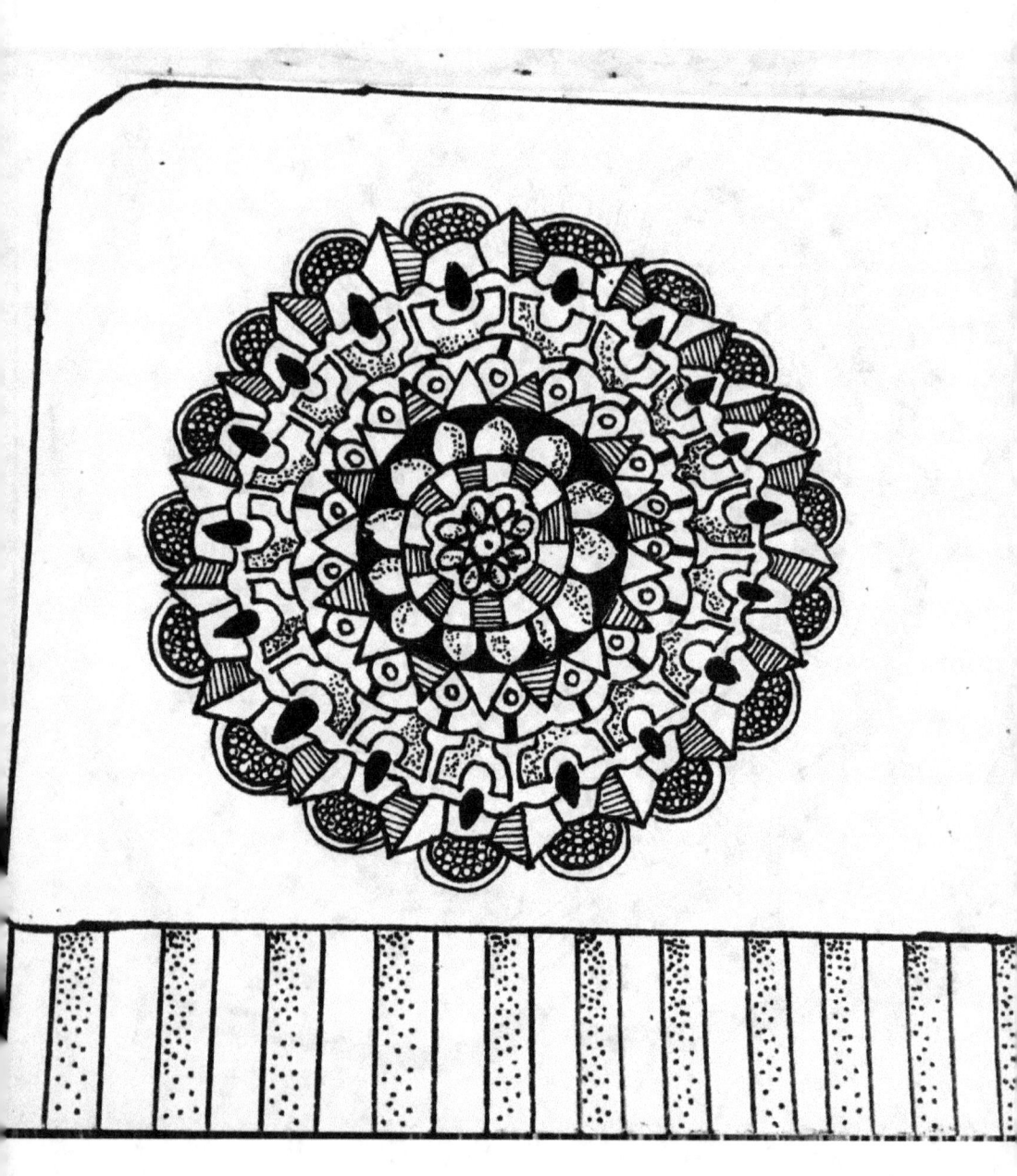

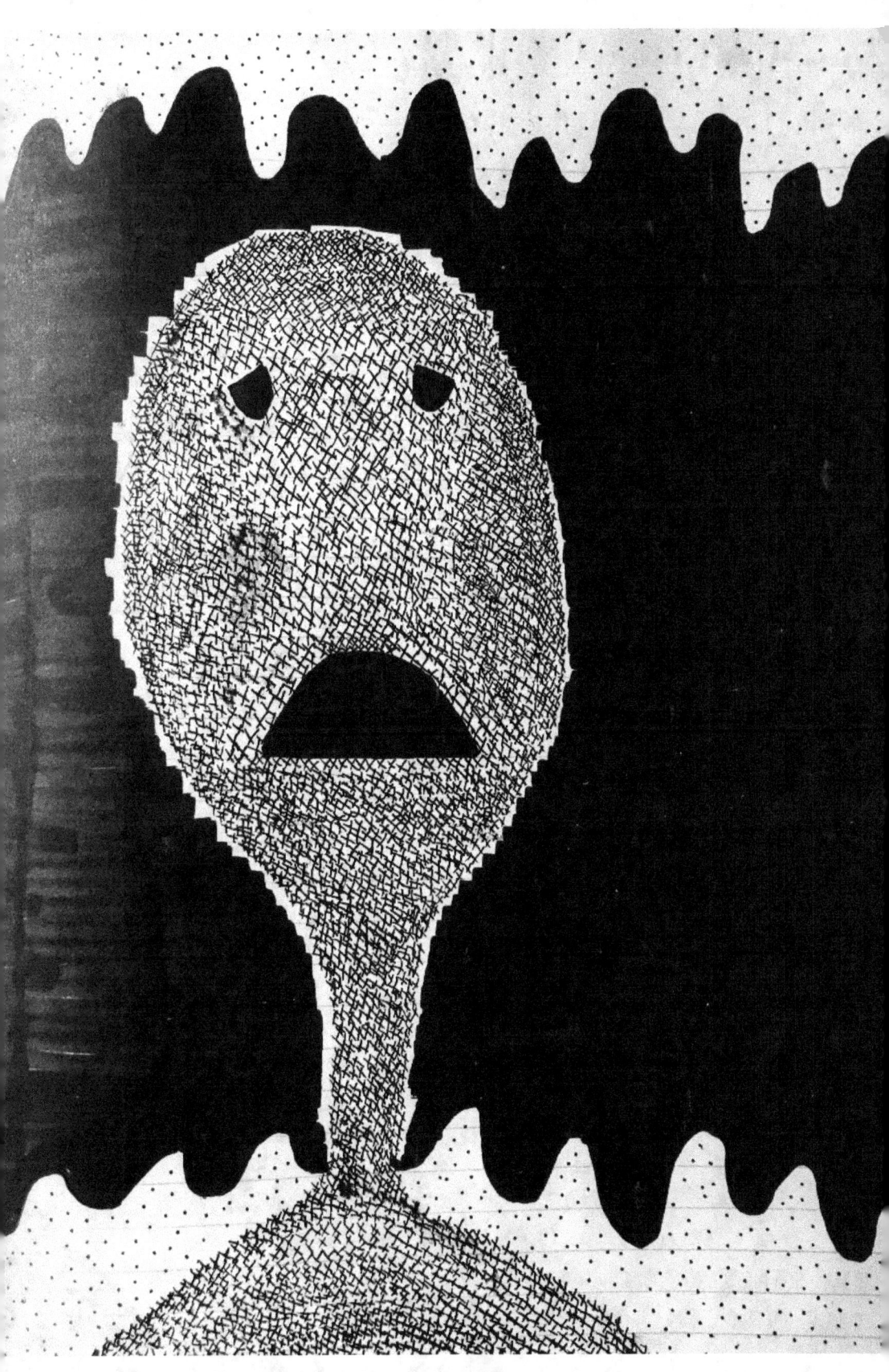

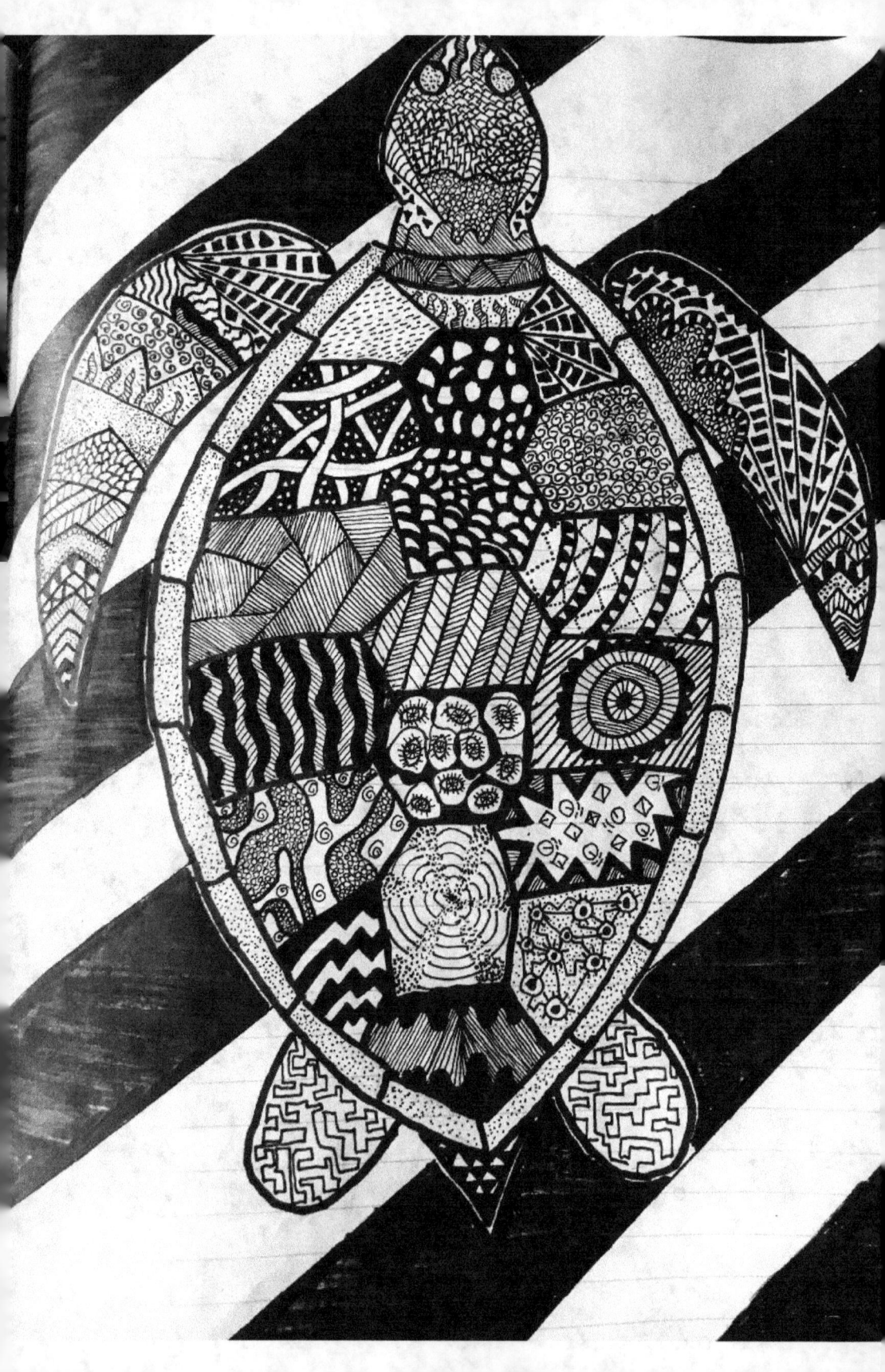

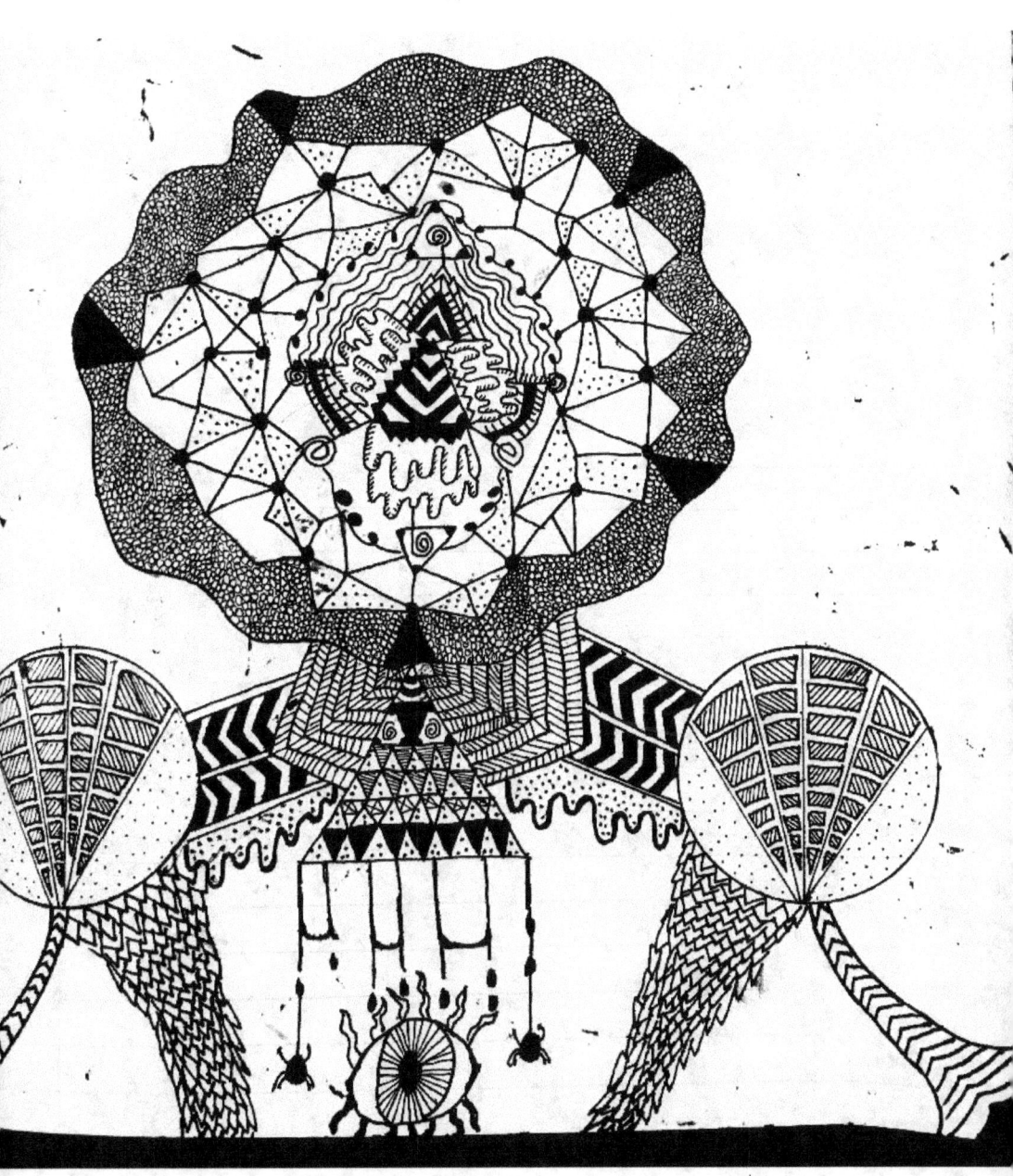

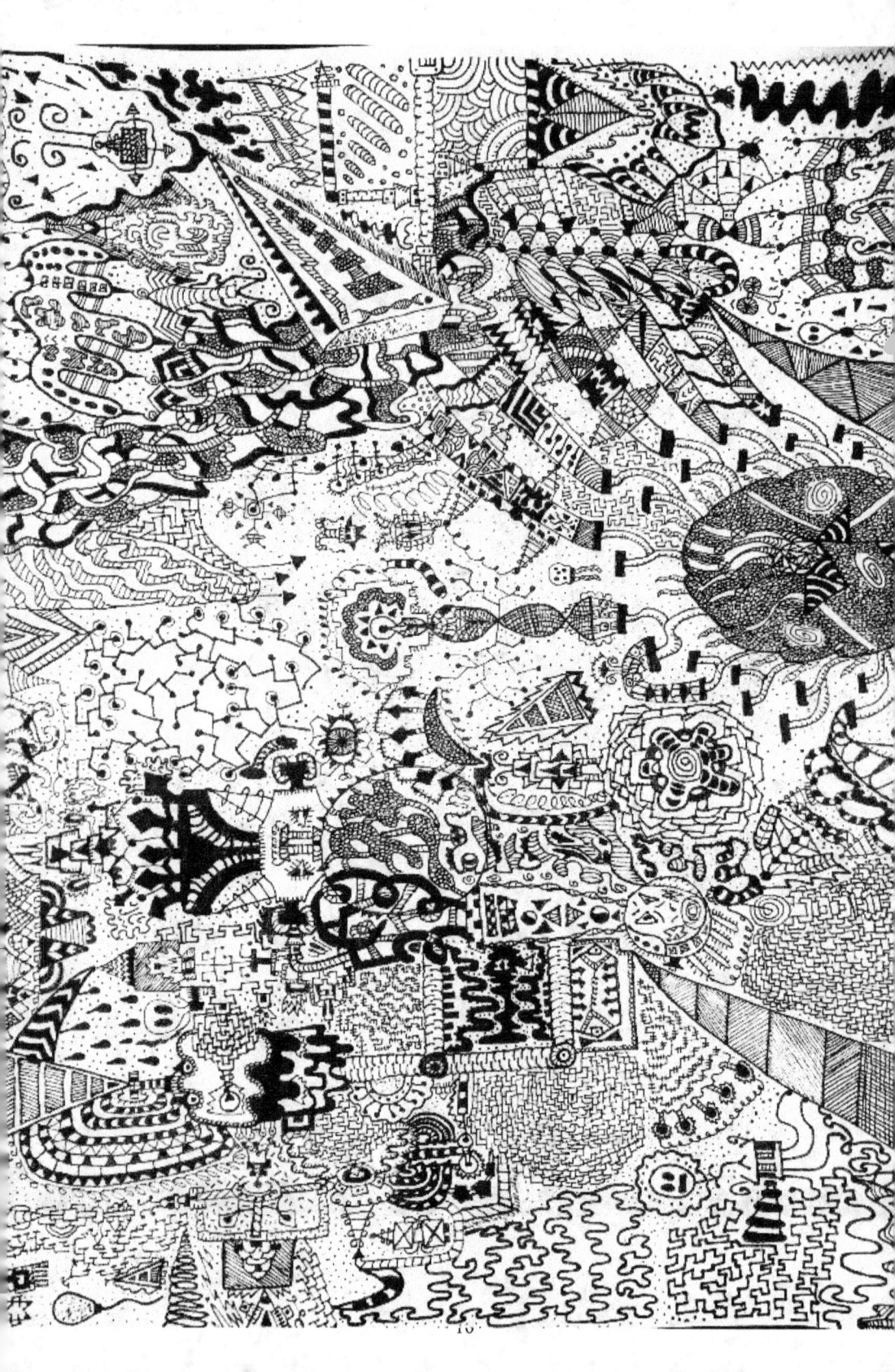

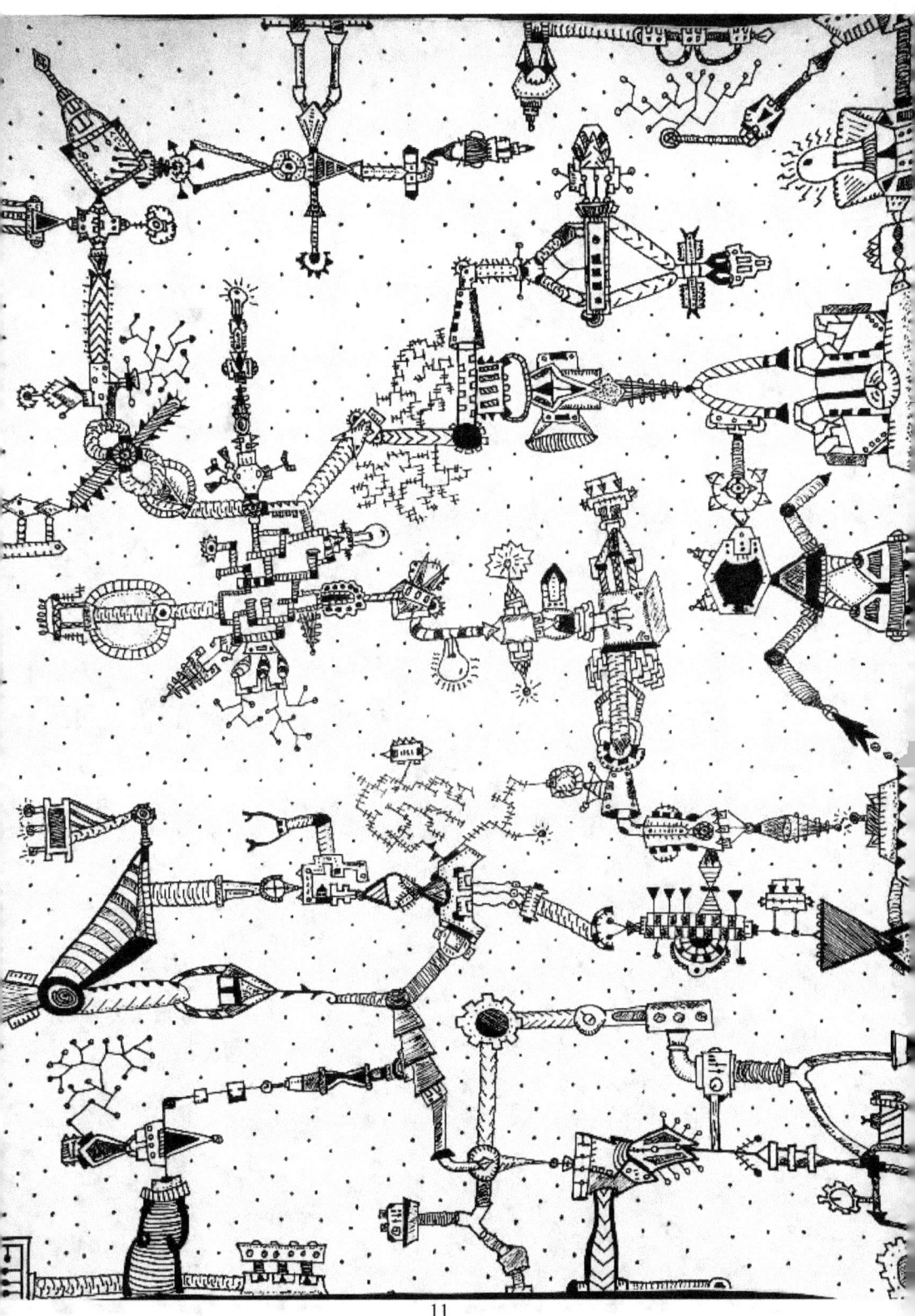

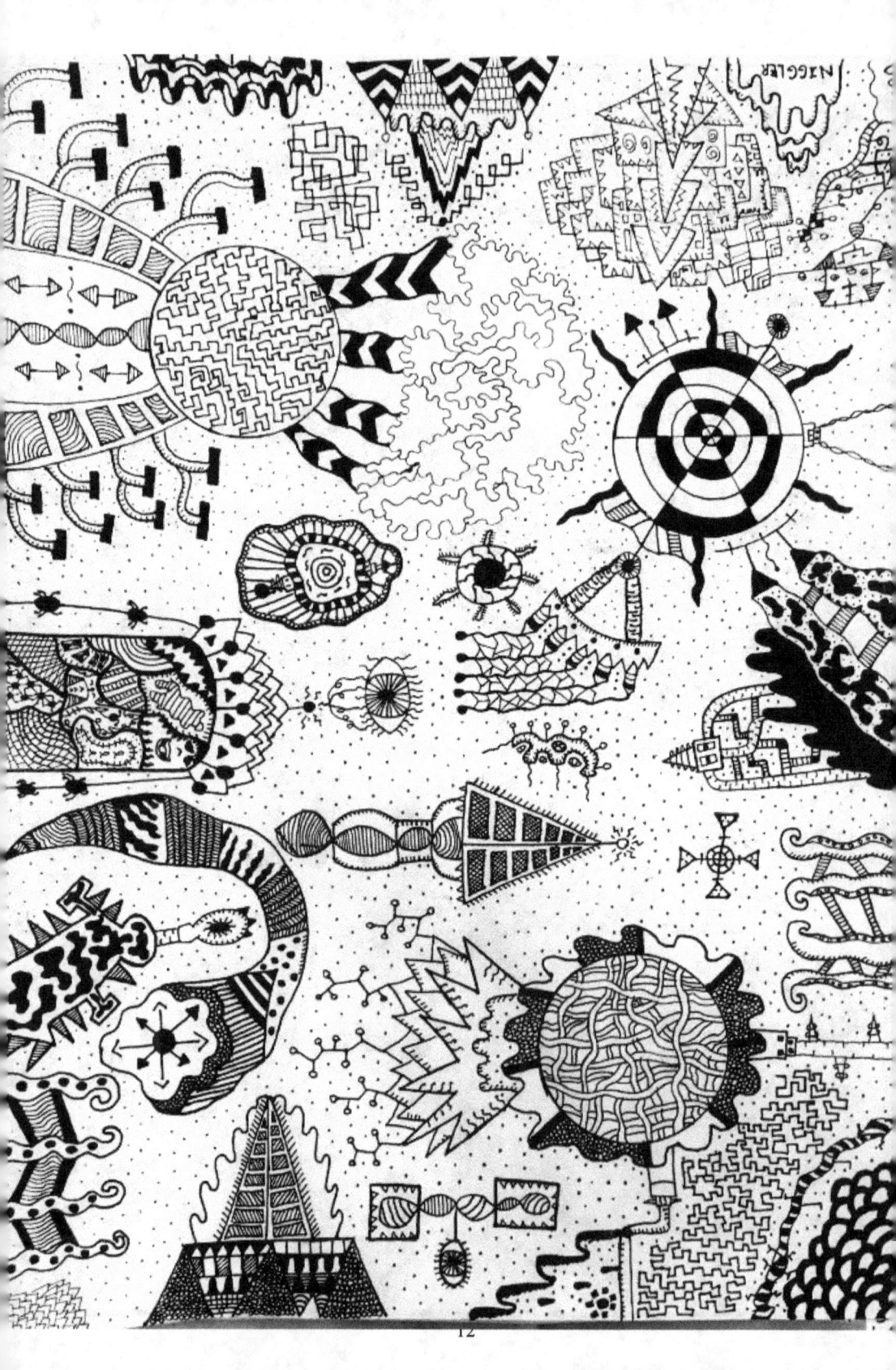

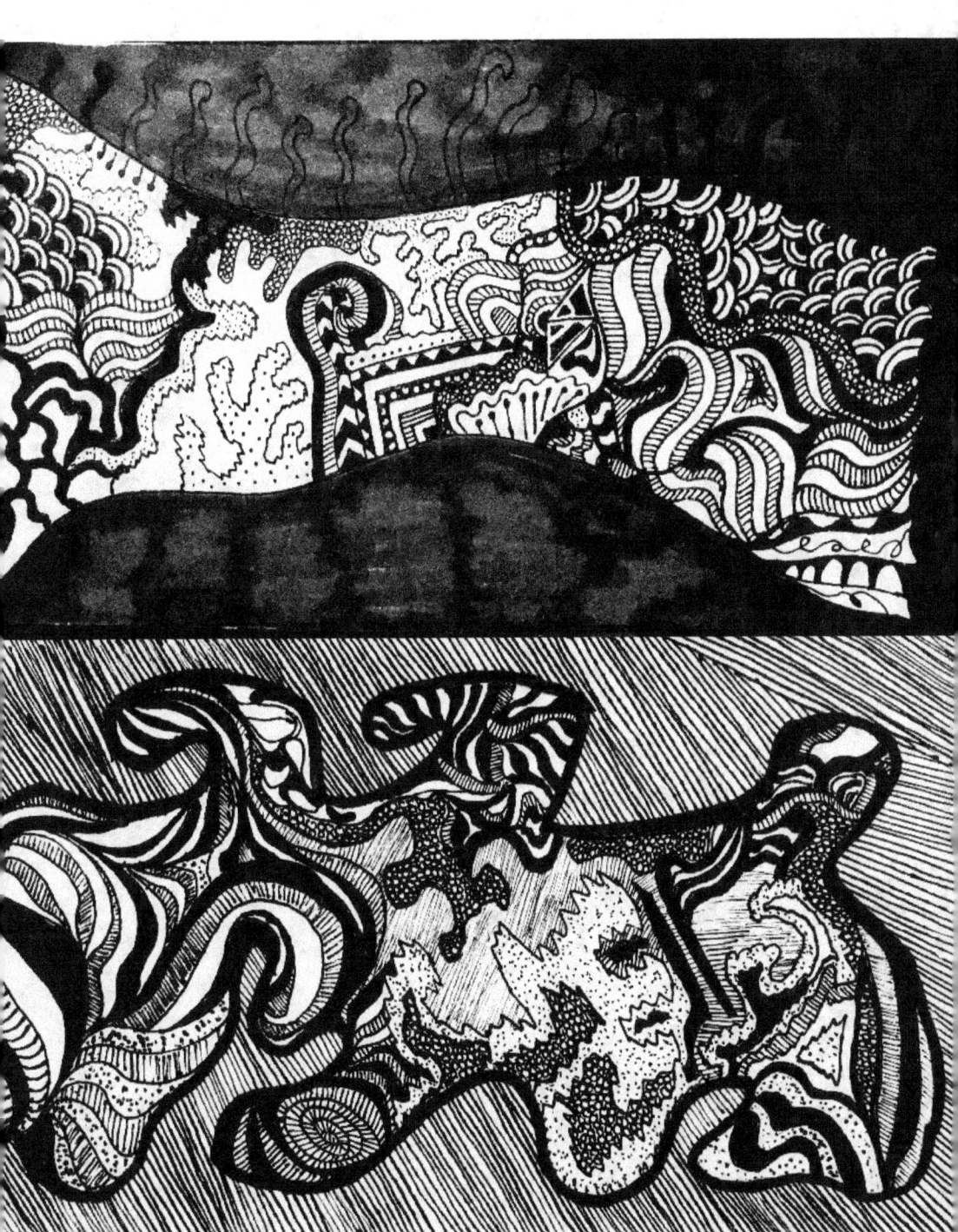

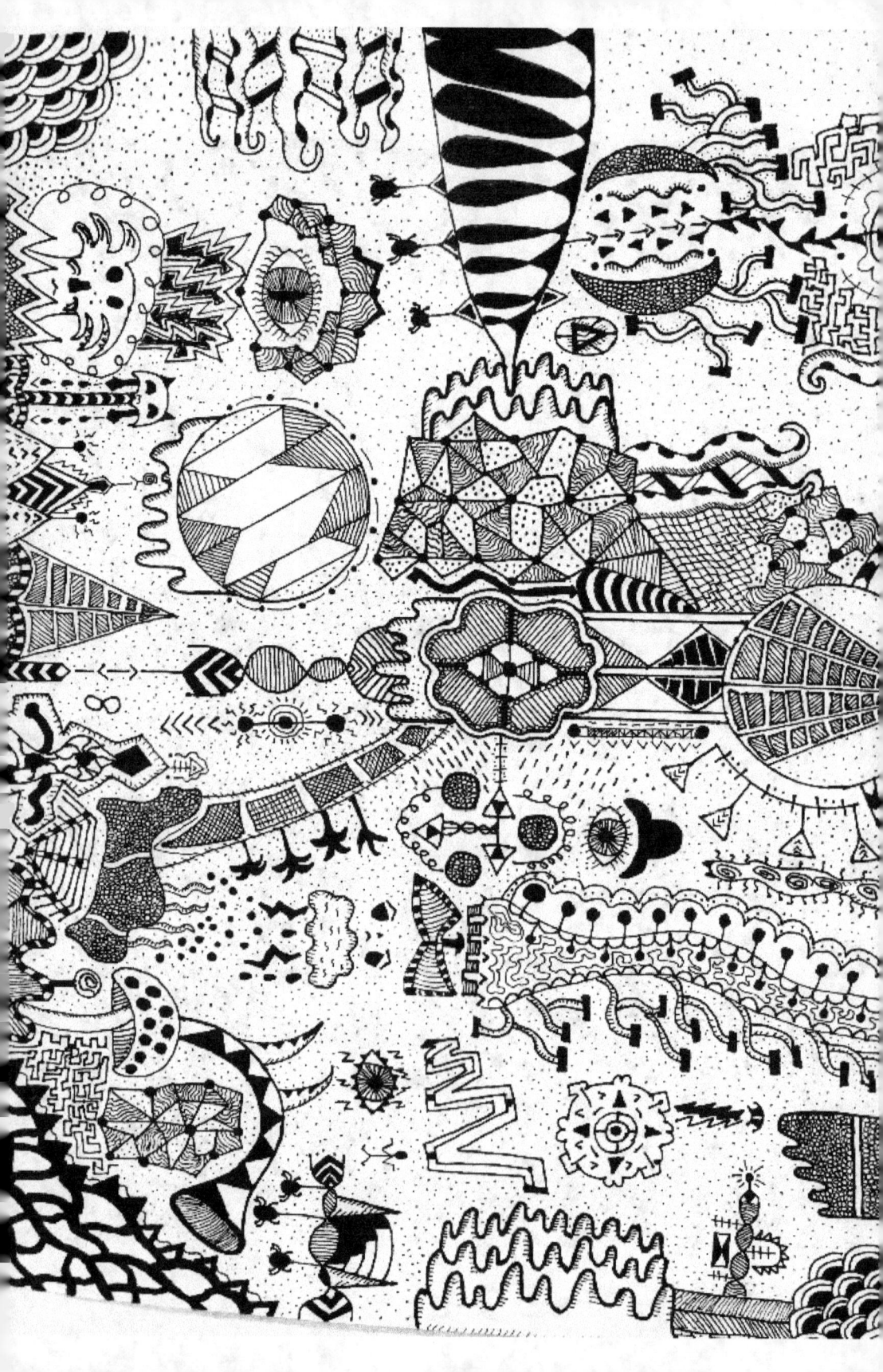

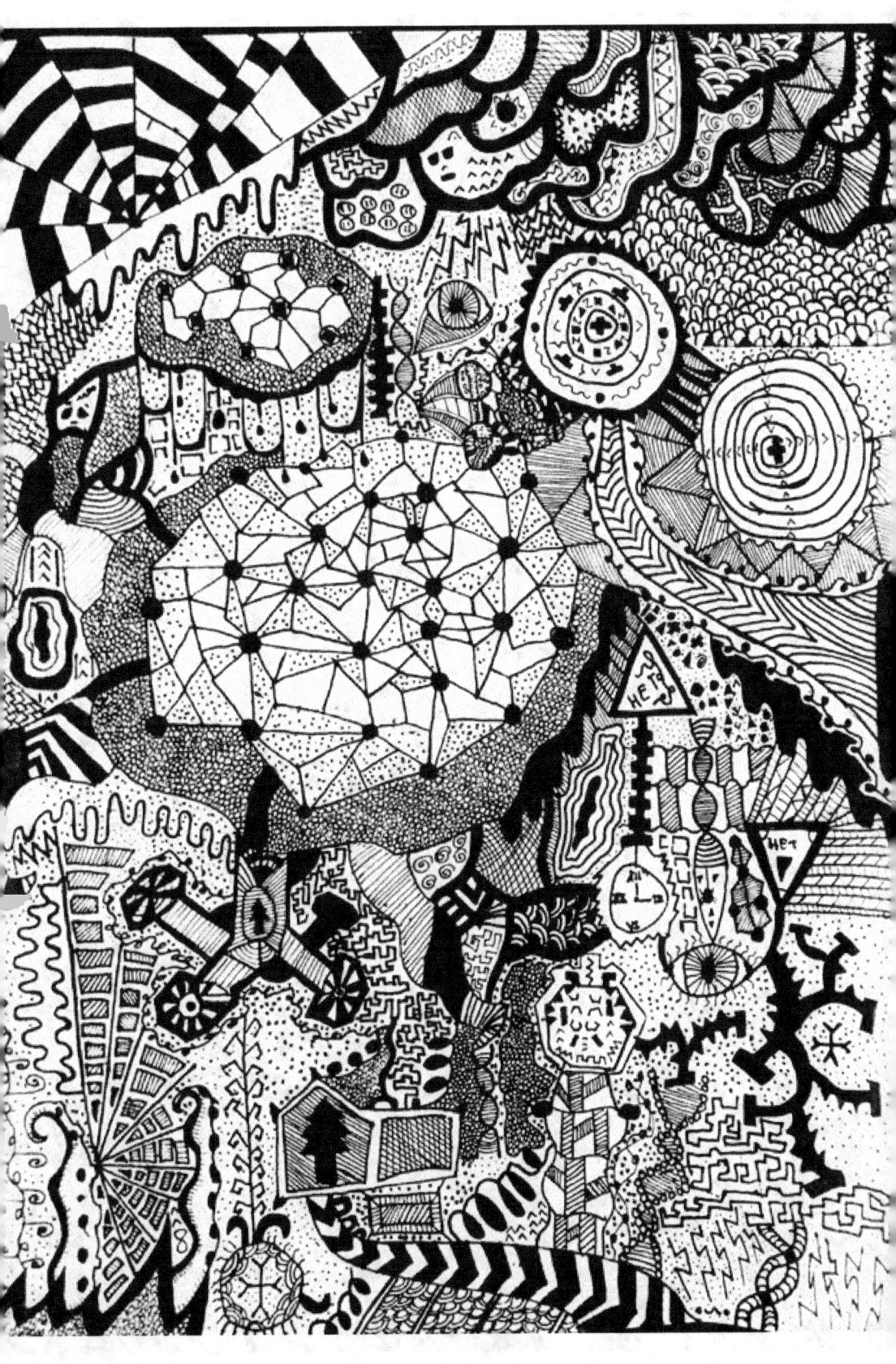

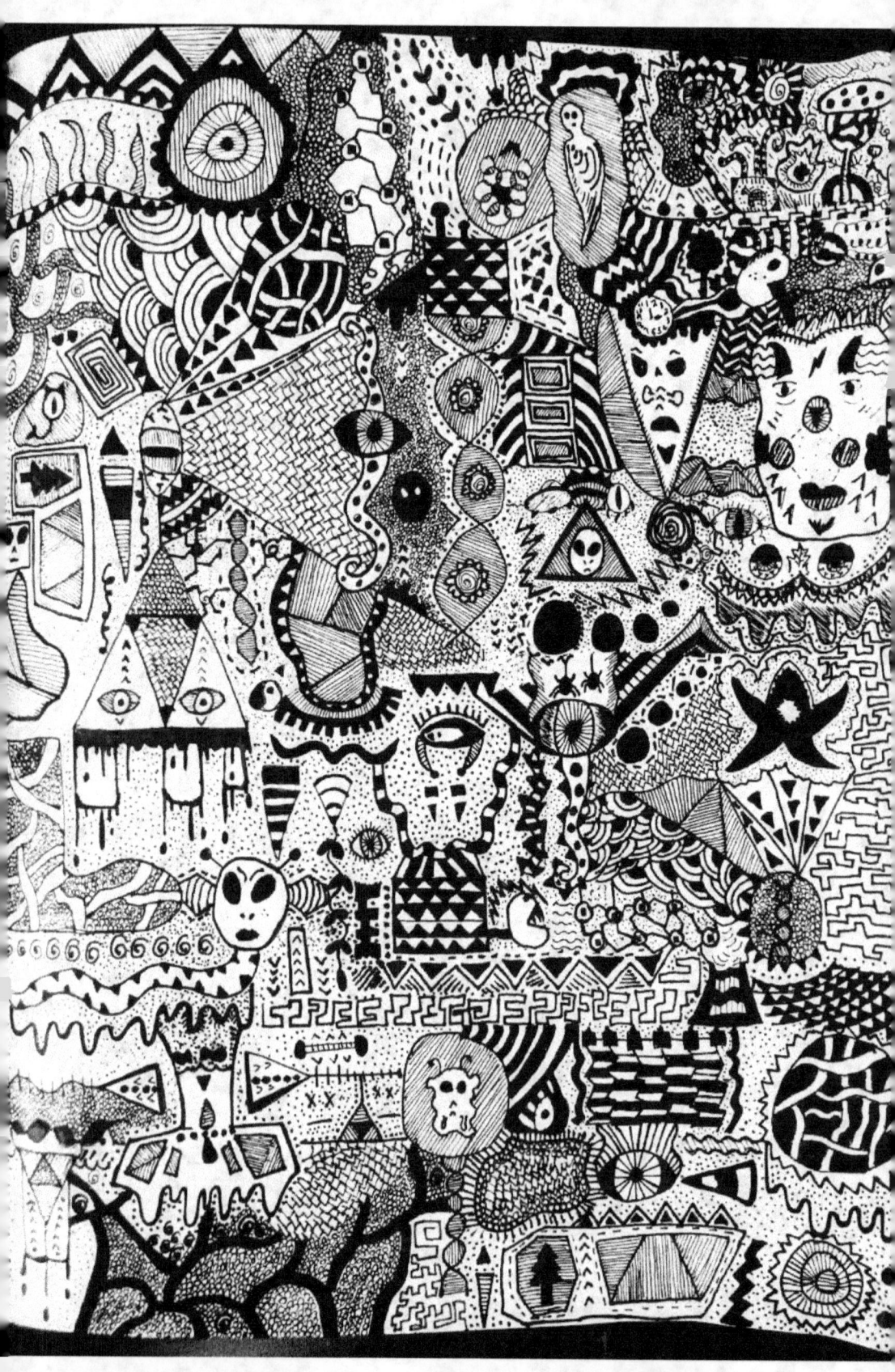

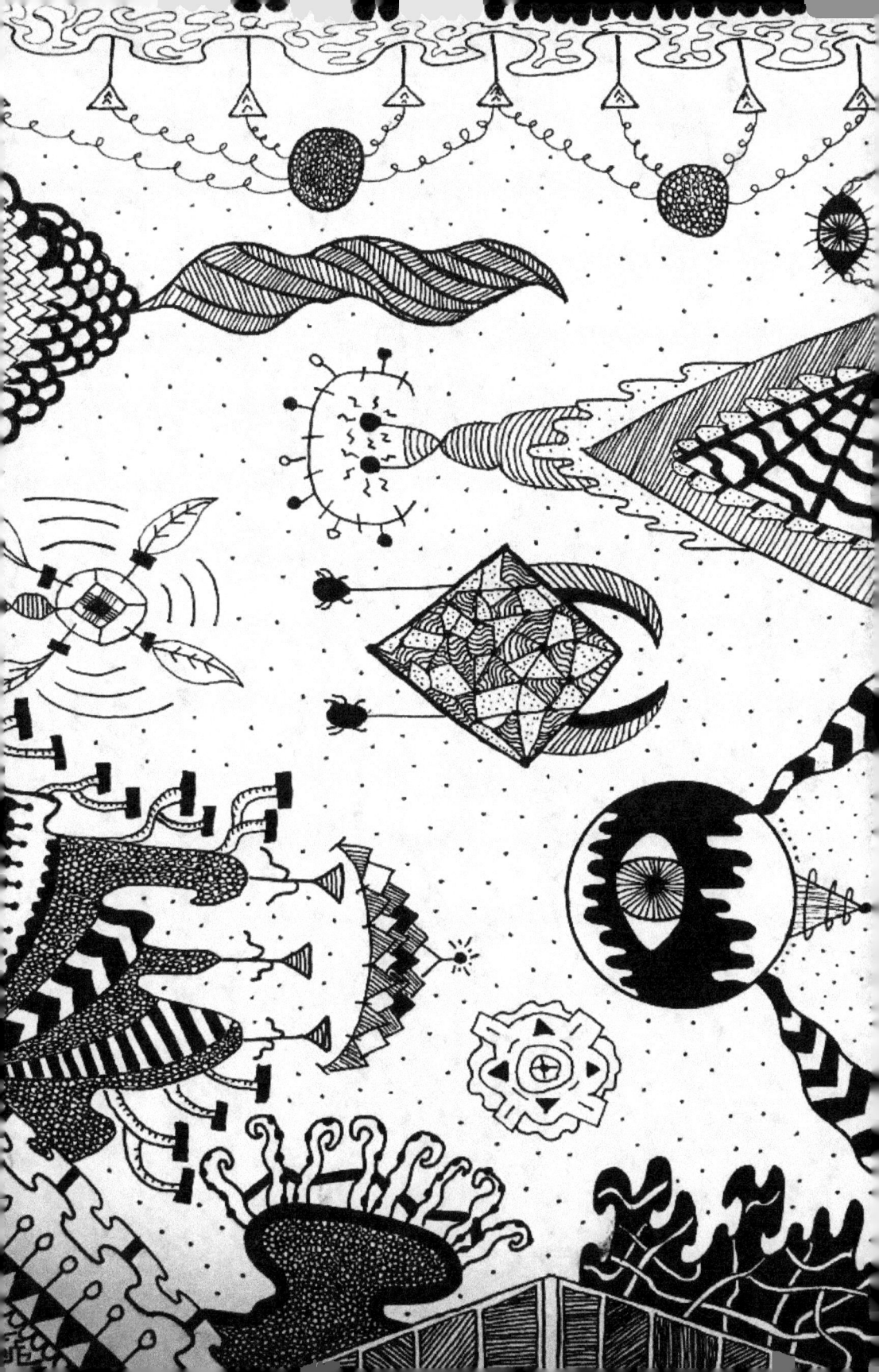

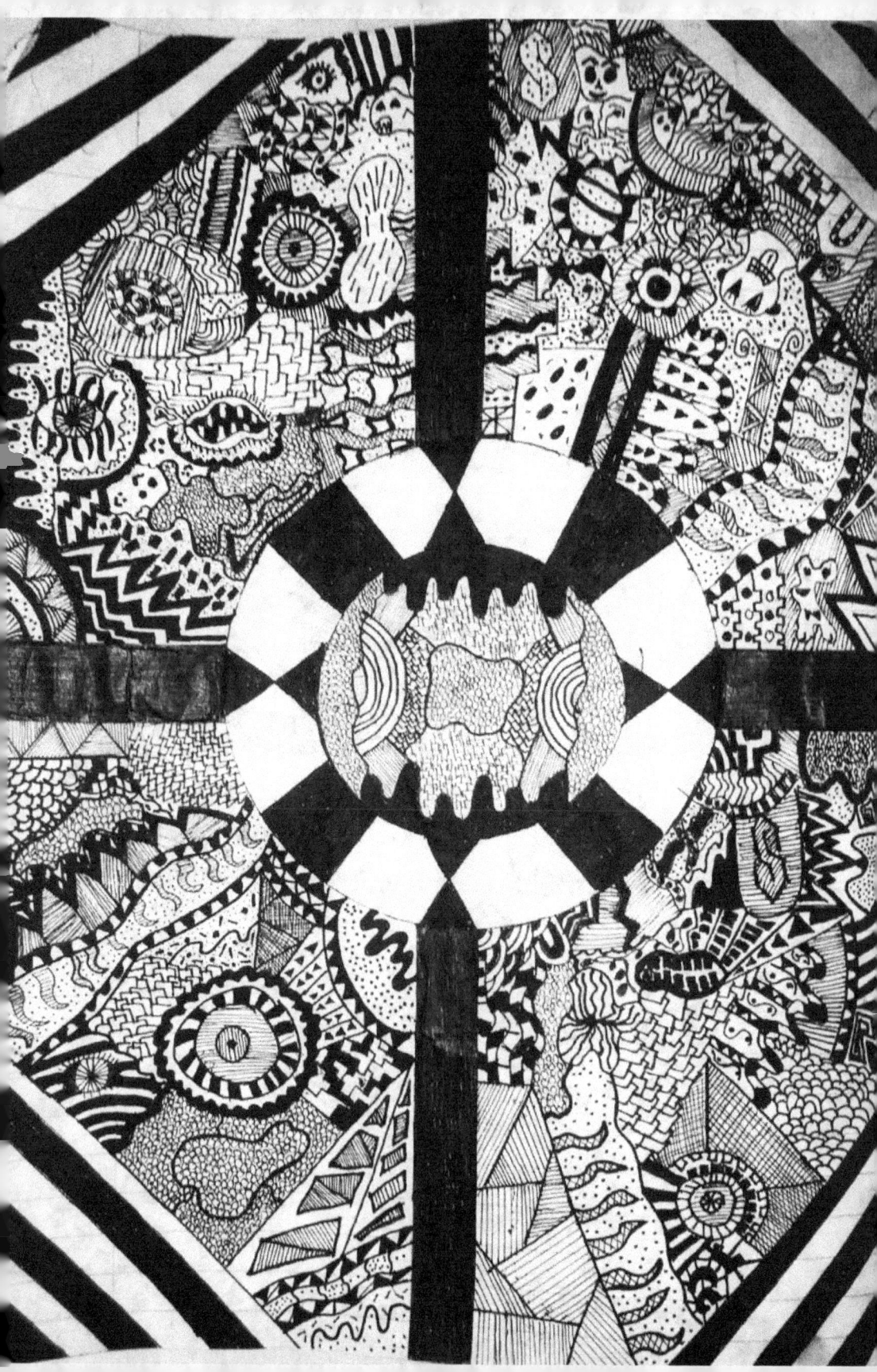

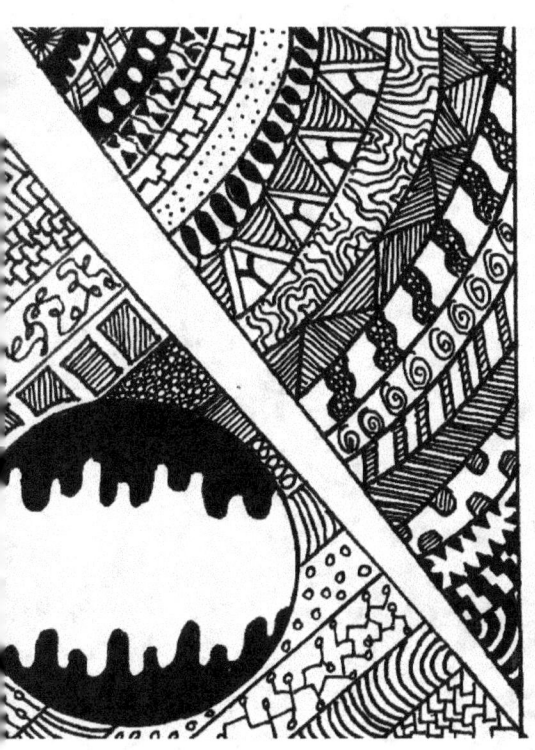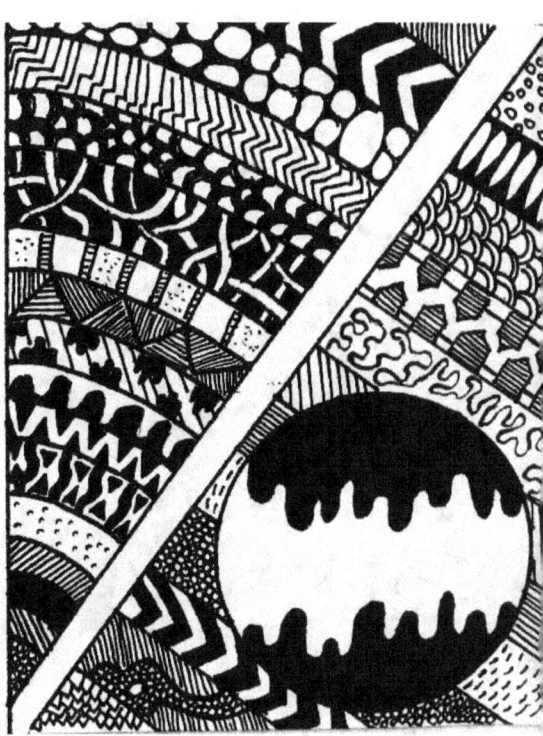

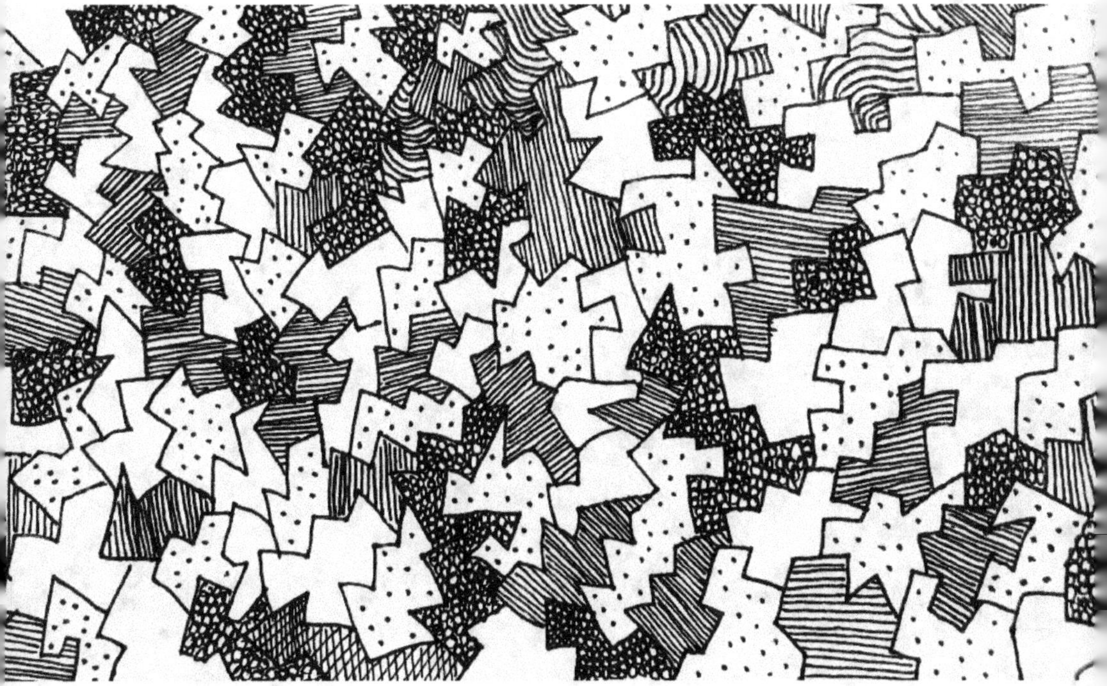

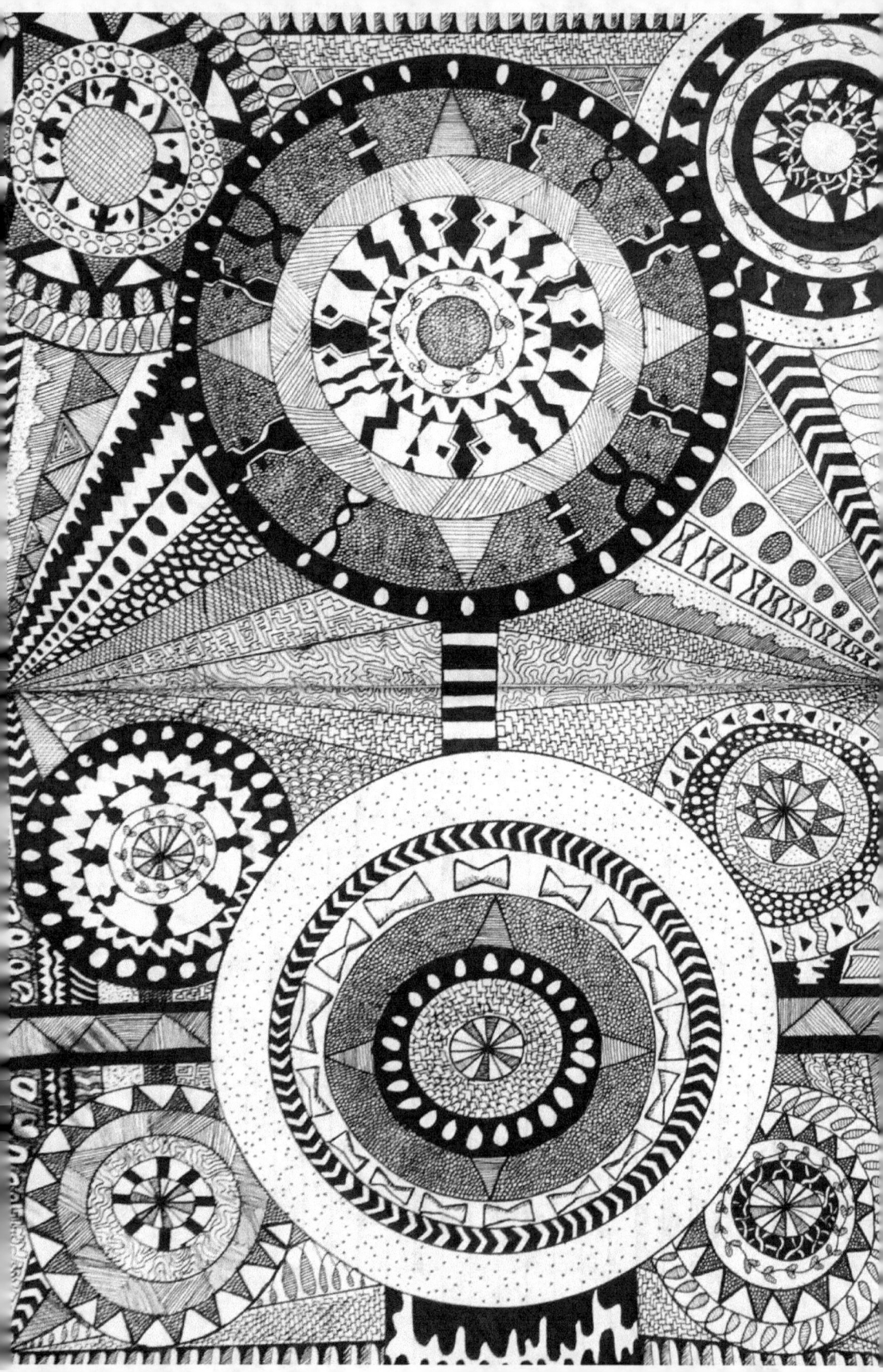

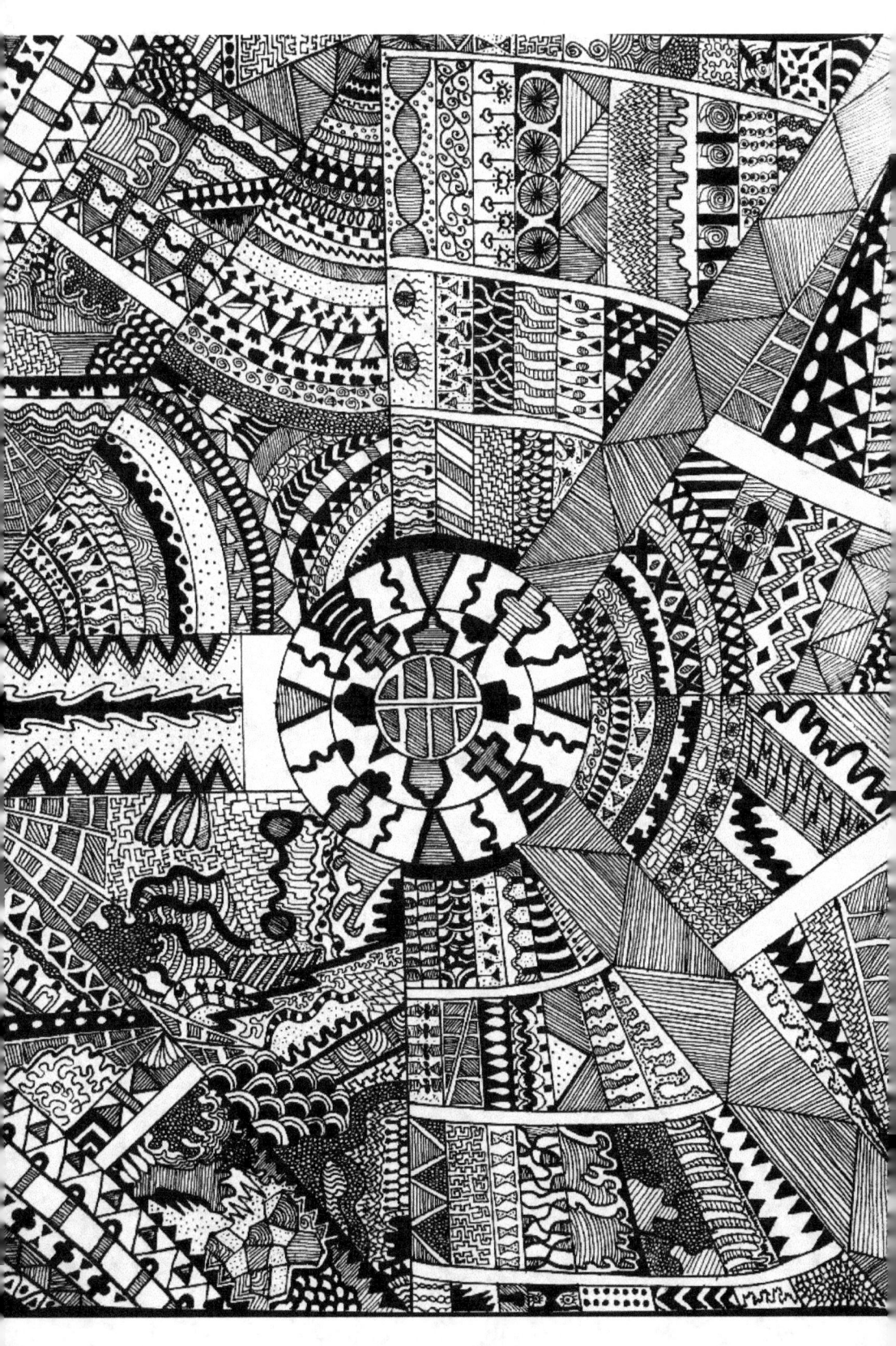

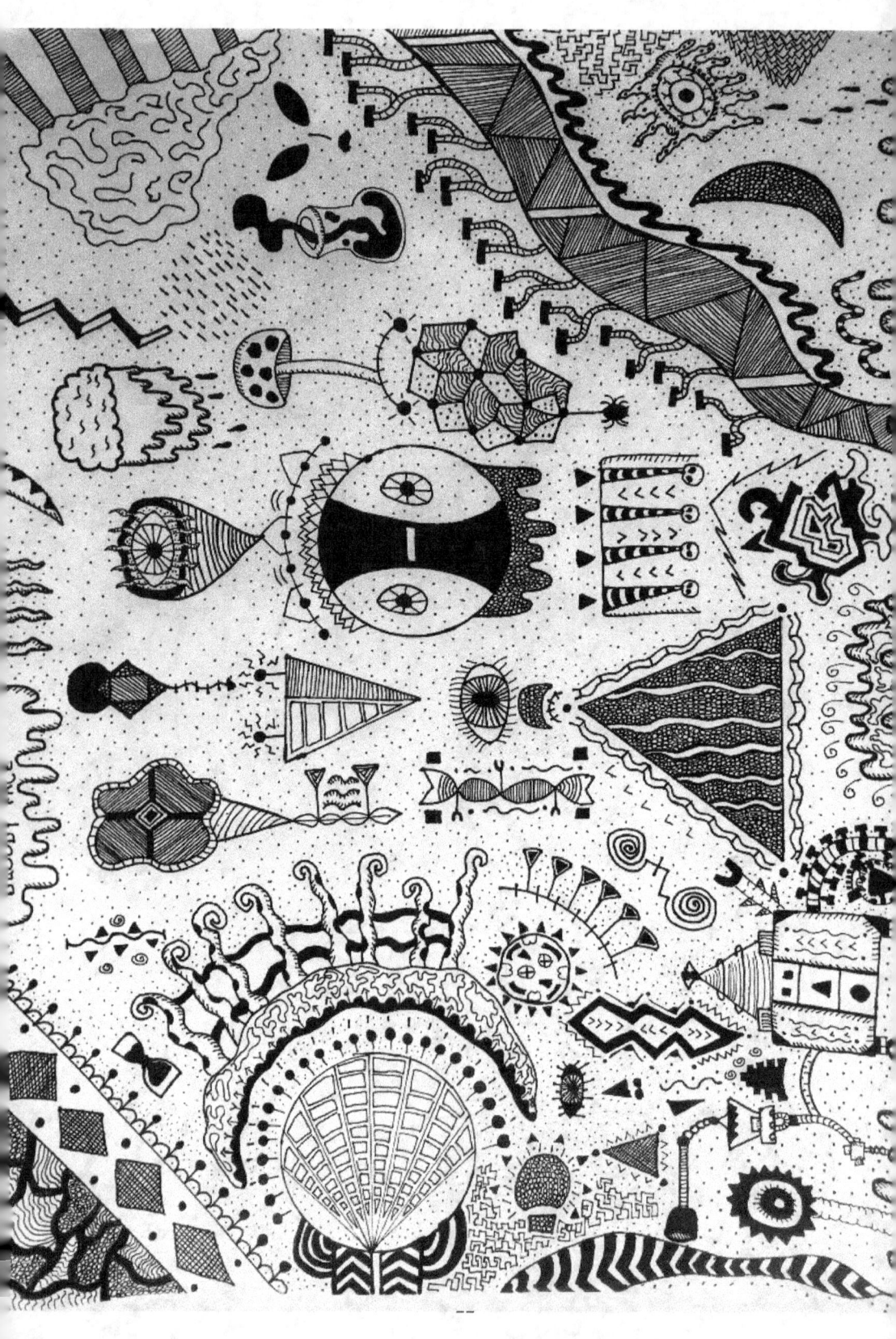

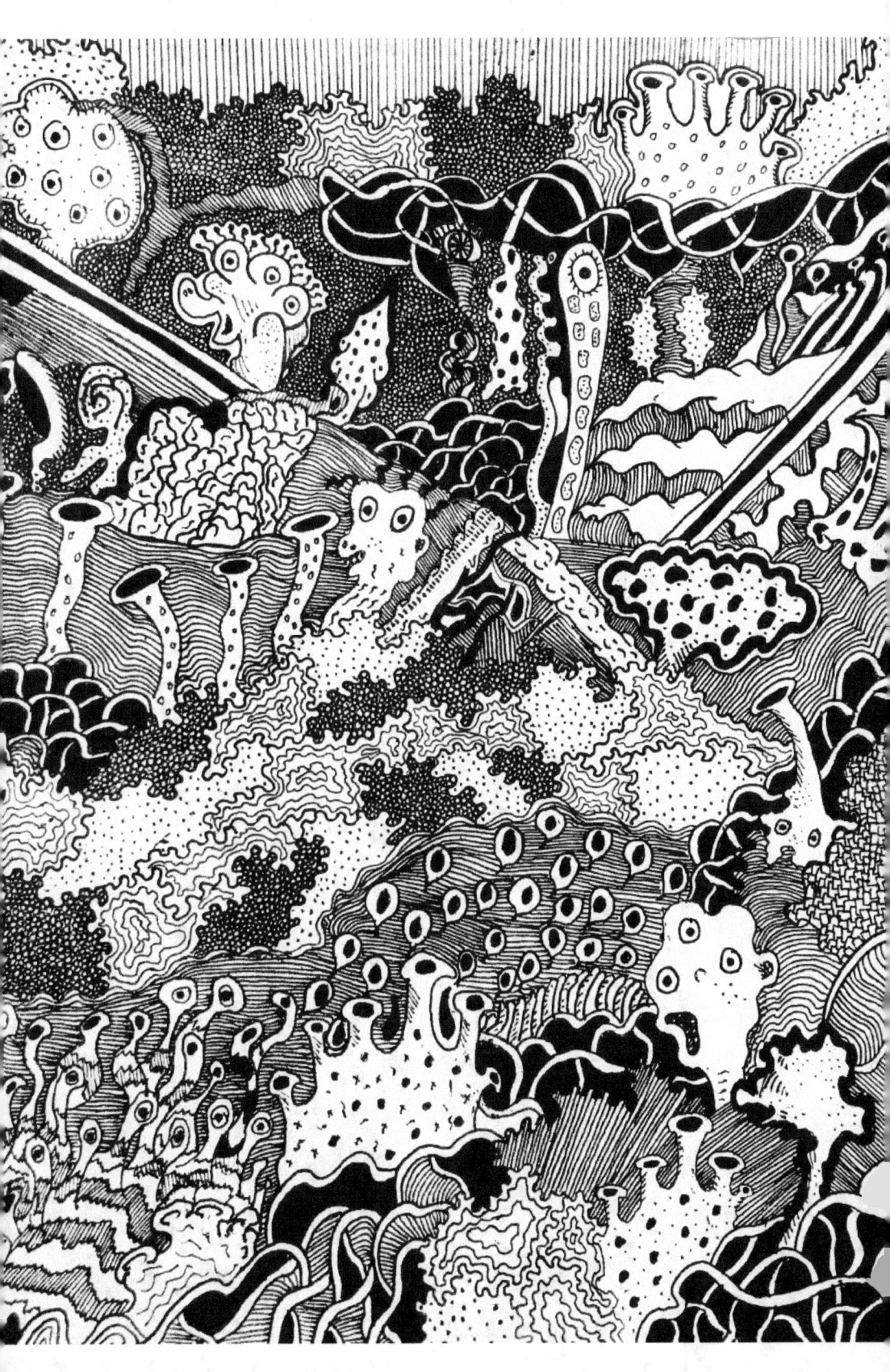

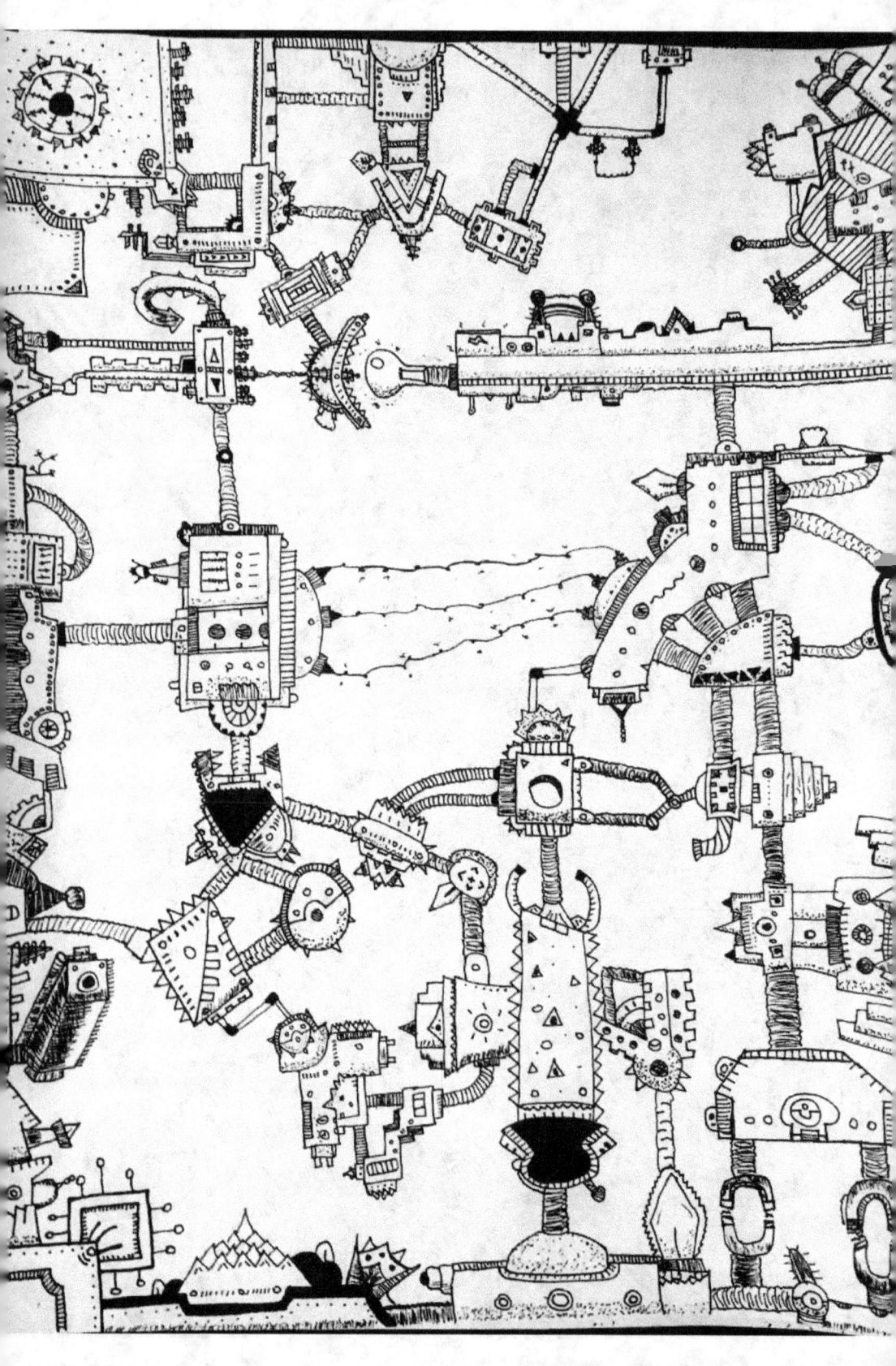

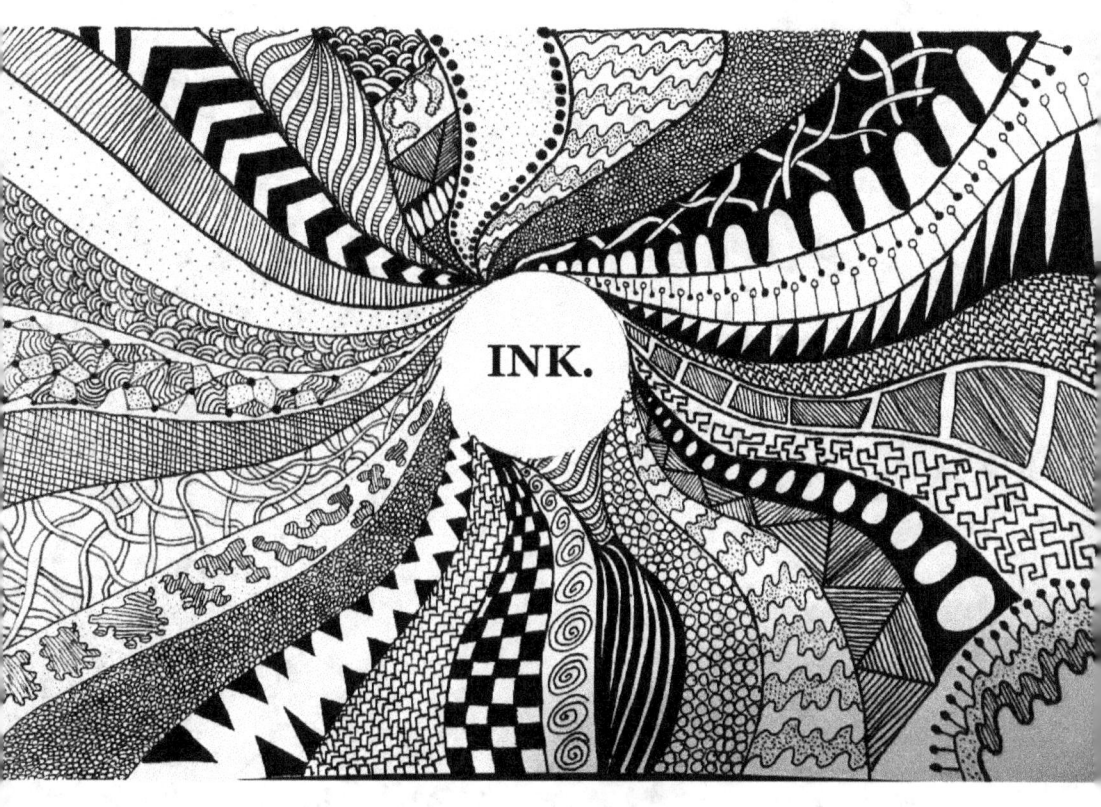

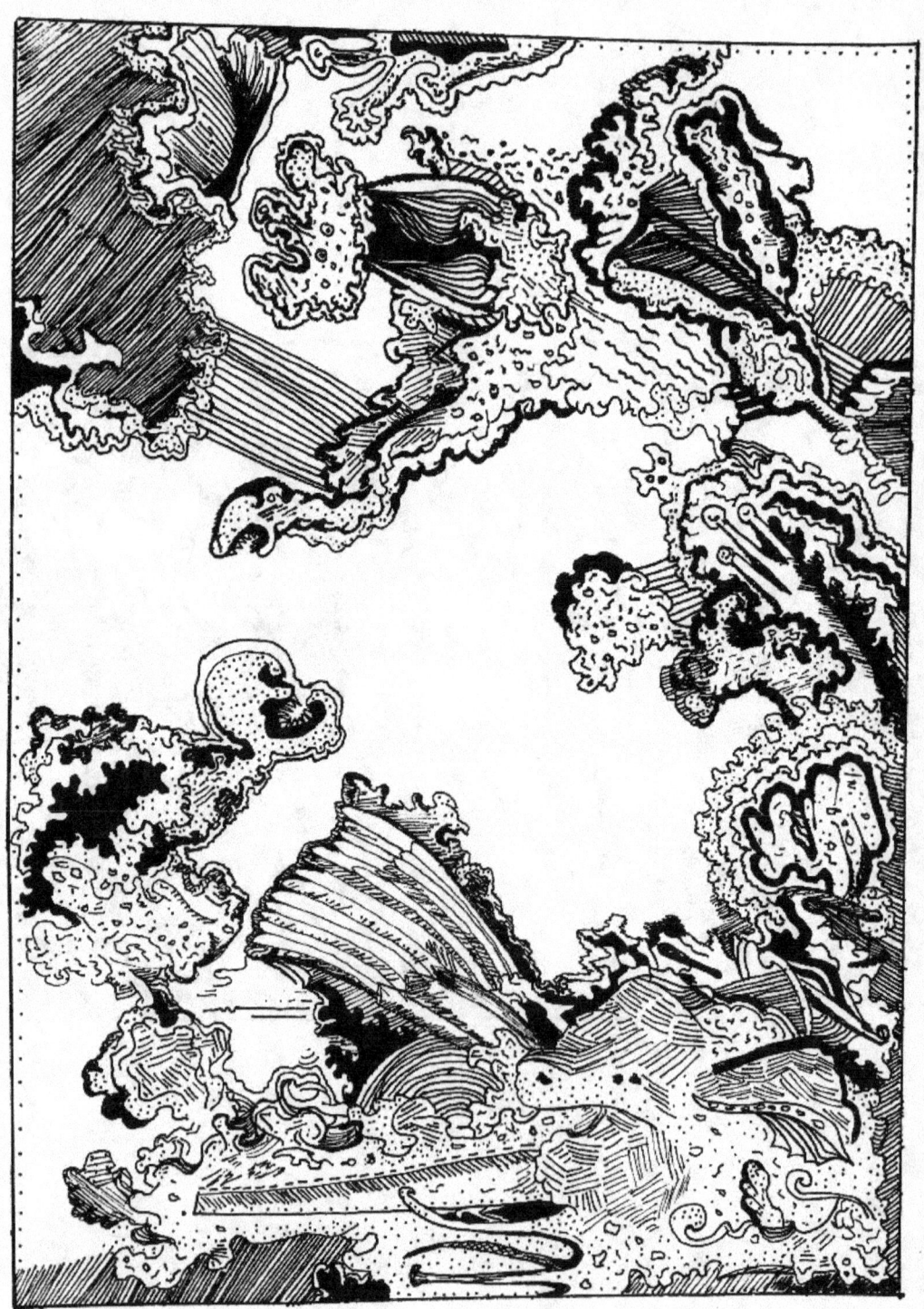

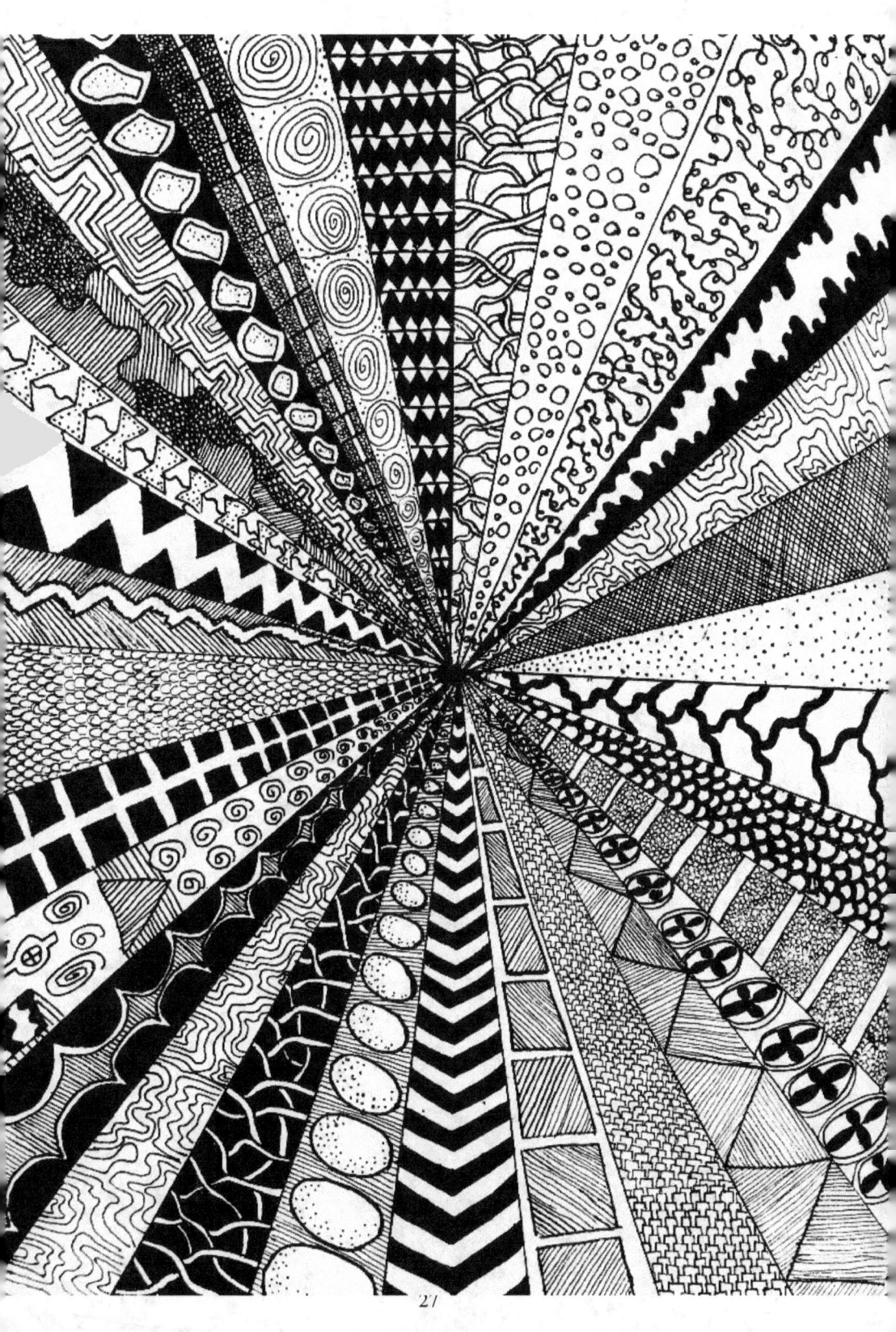

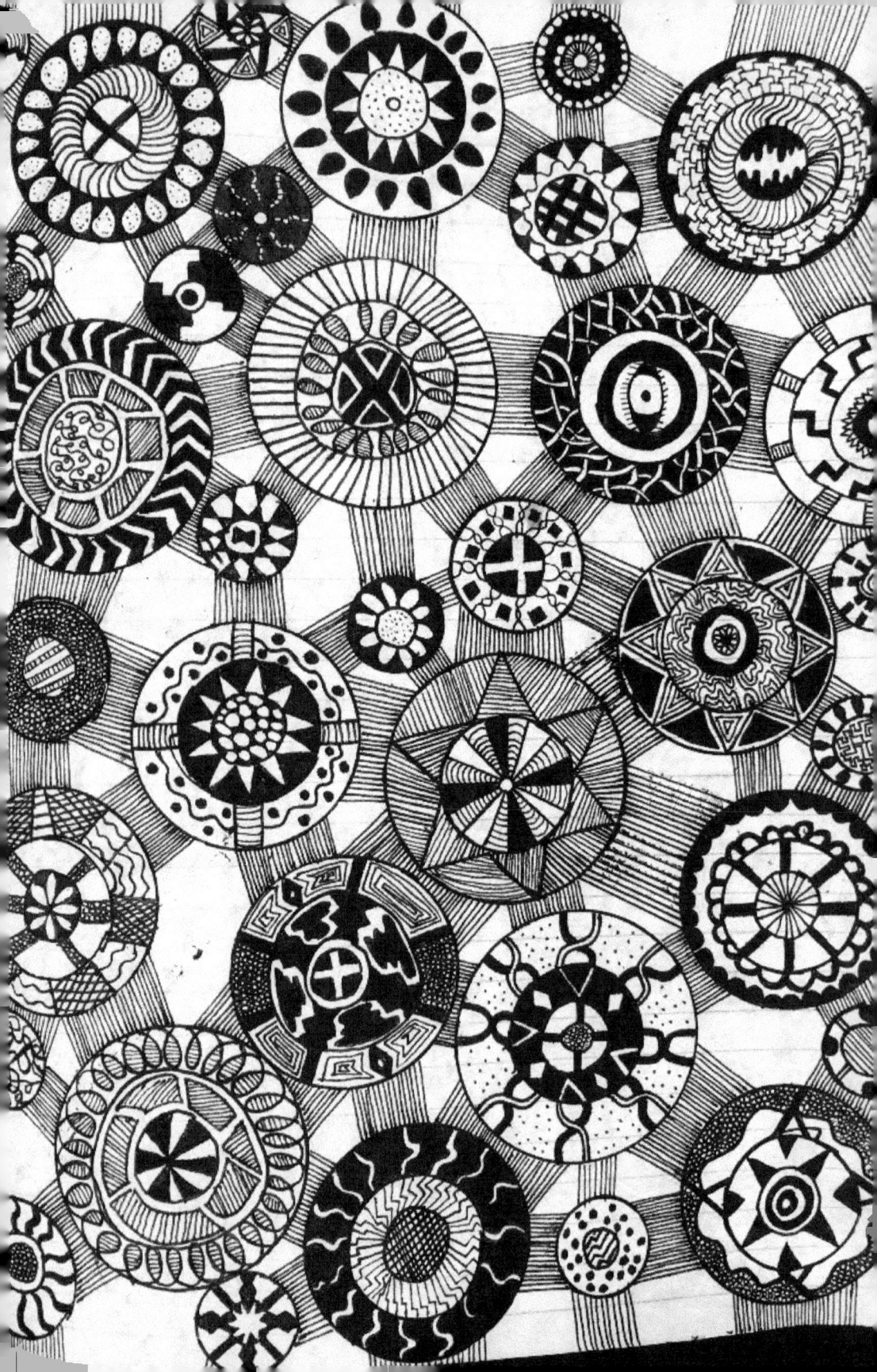

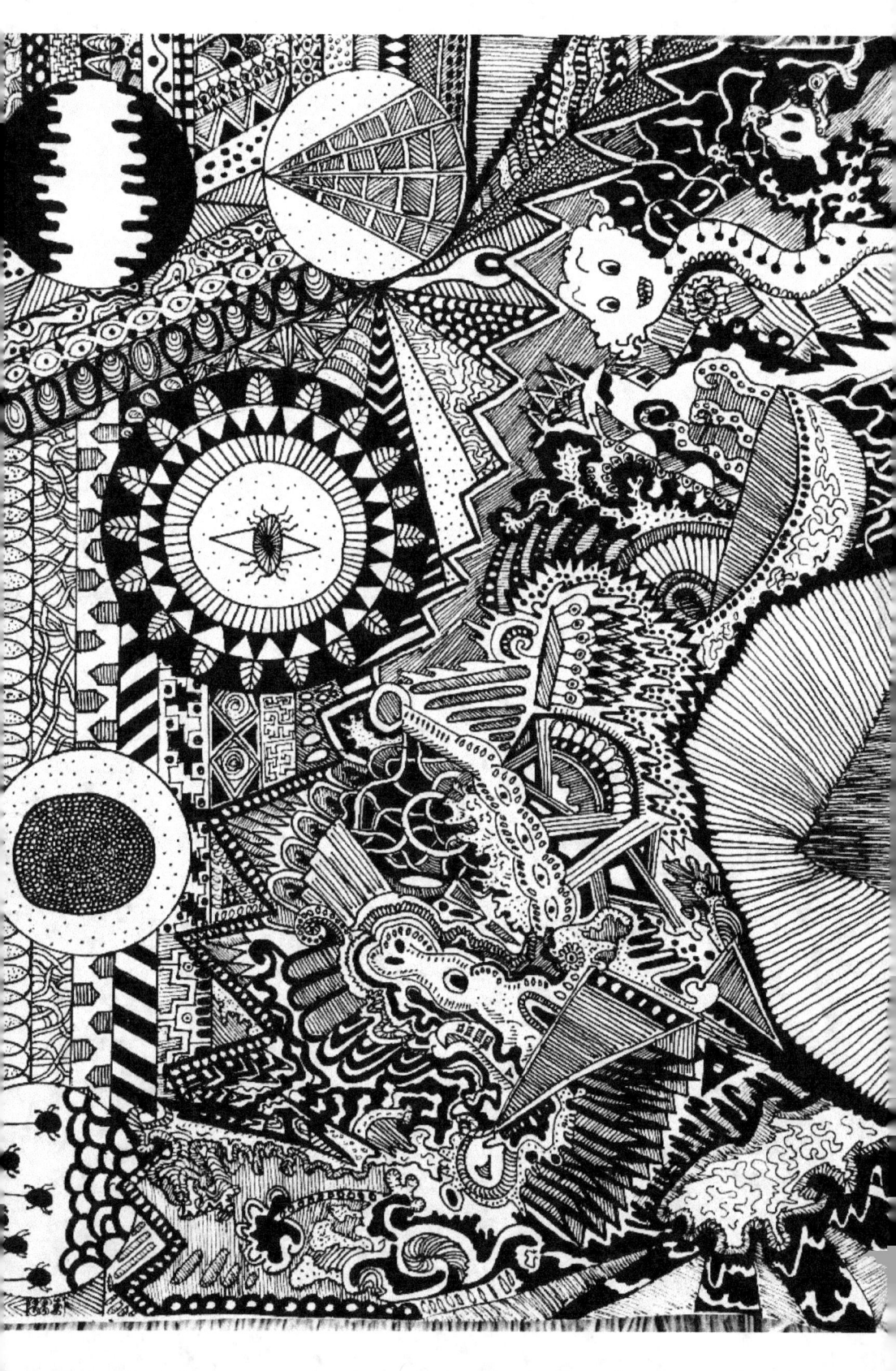

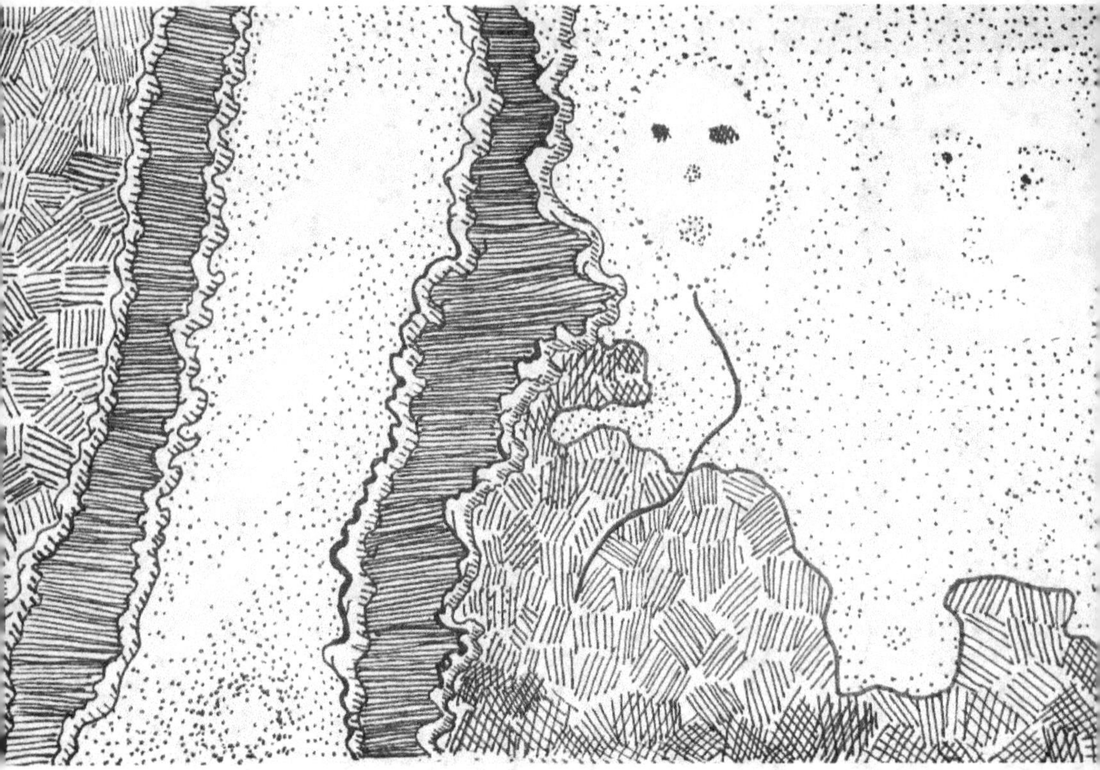

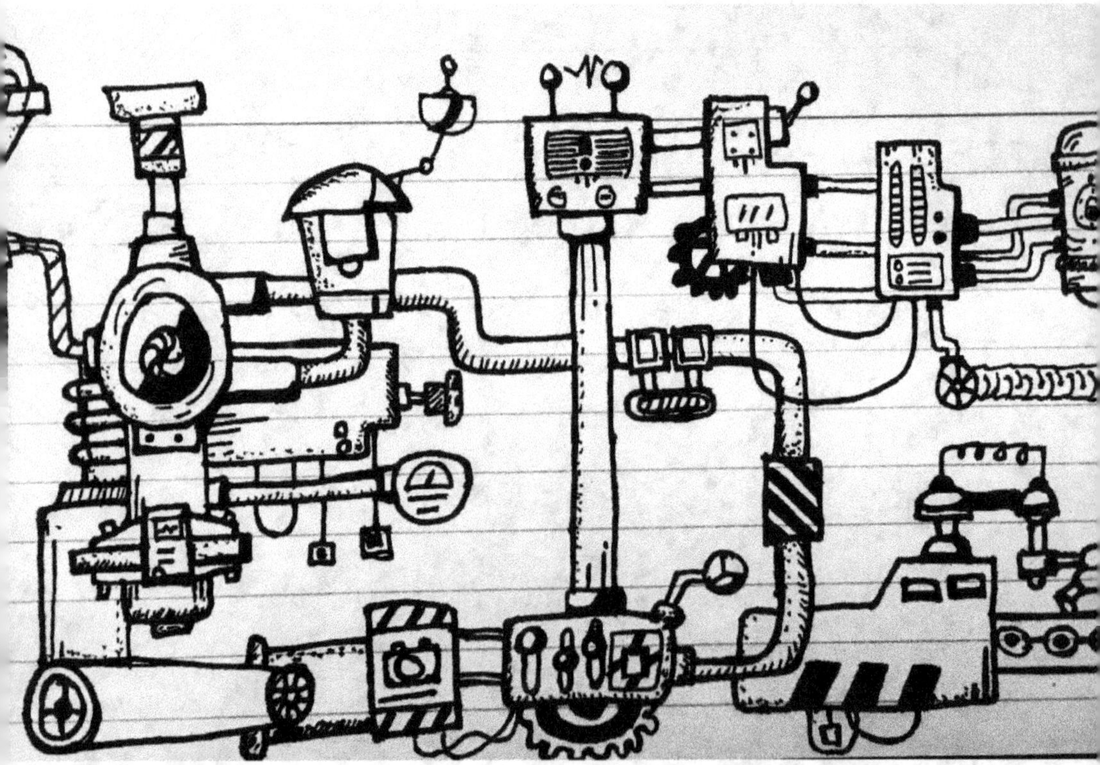

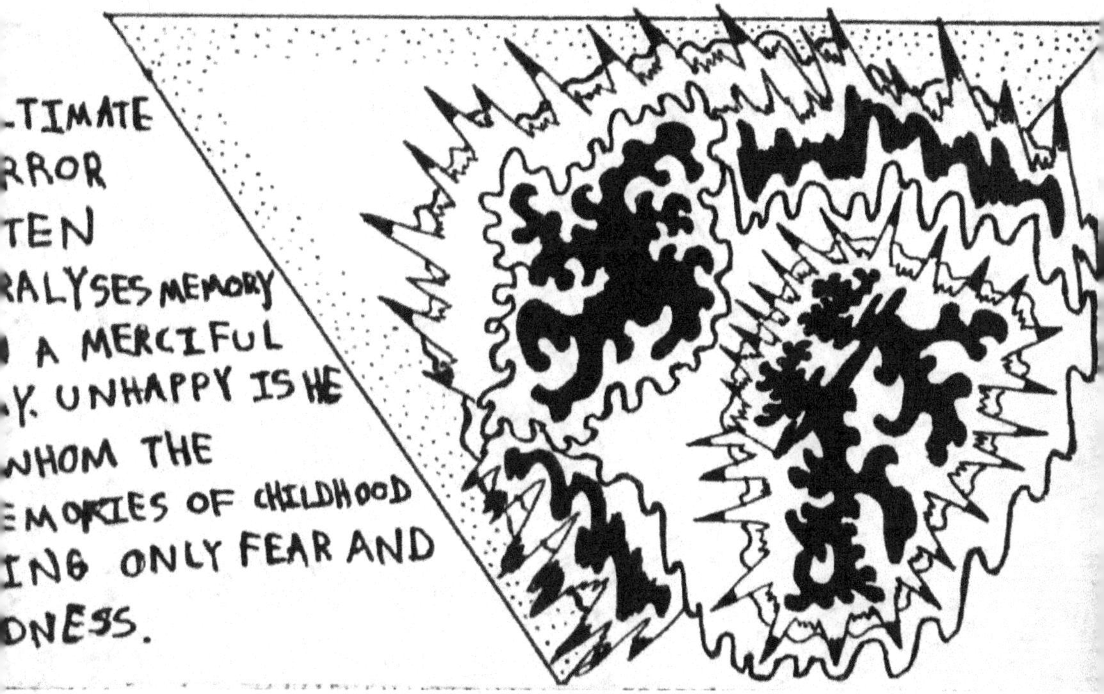

[U]LTIMATE
[TE]RROR
[OF]TEN
[PA]RALYSES MEMORY
[IN] A MERCIFUL
[WA]Y. UNHAPPY IS HE
[TO] WHOM THE
[M]EMORIES OF CHILDHOOD
[BR]ING ONLY FEAR AND
[S]ADNESS.

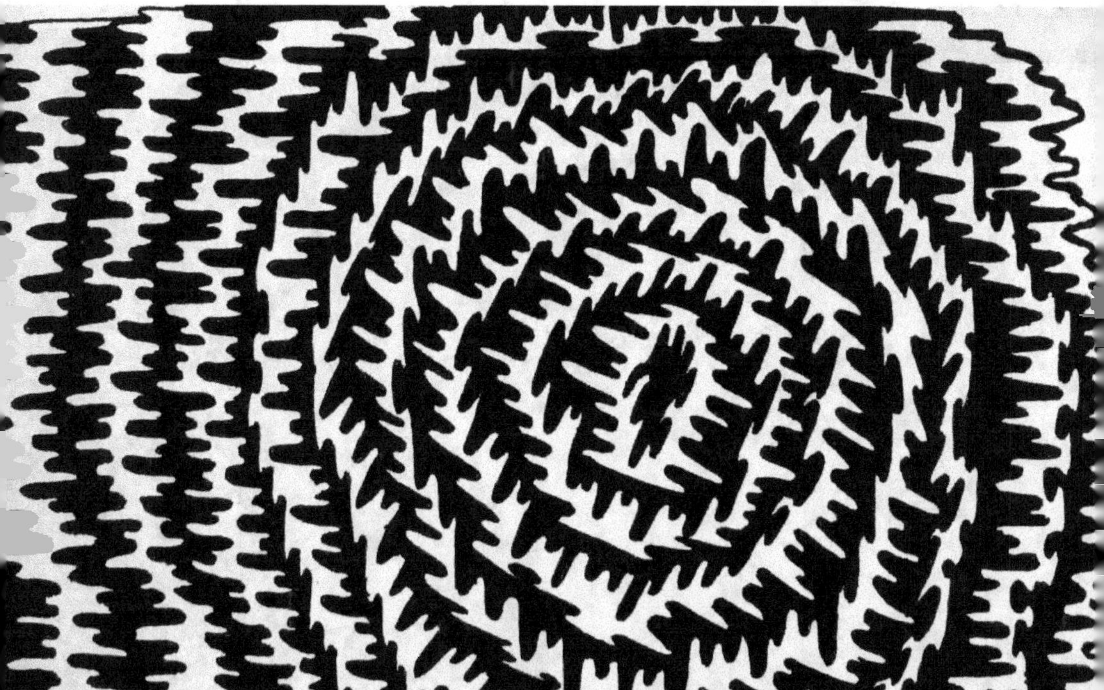

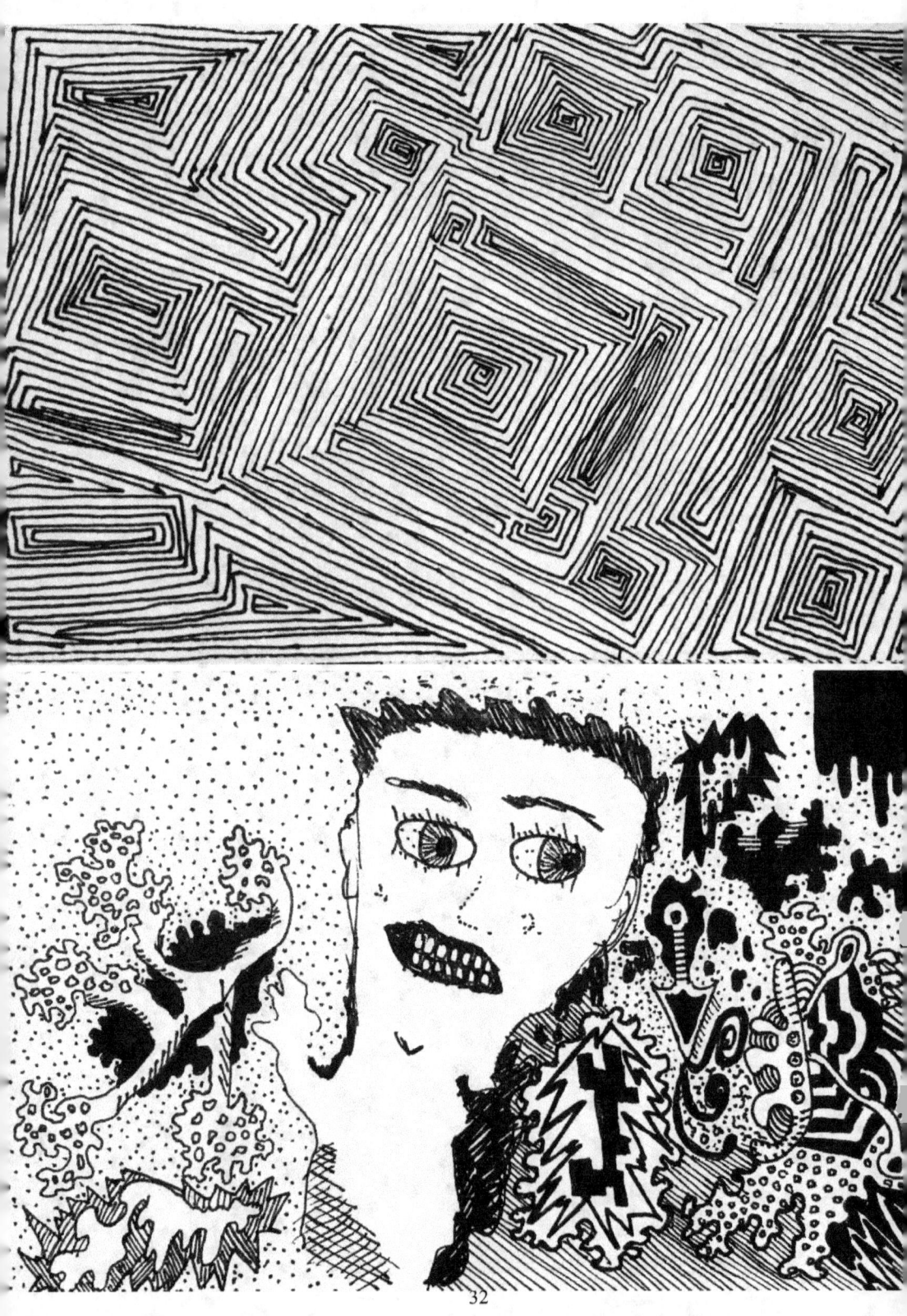

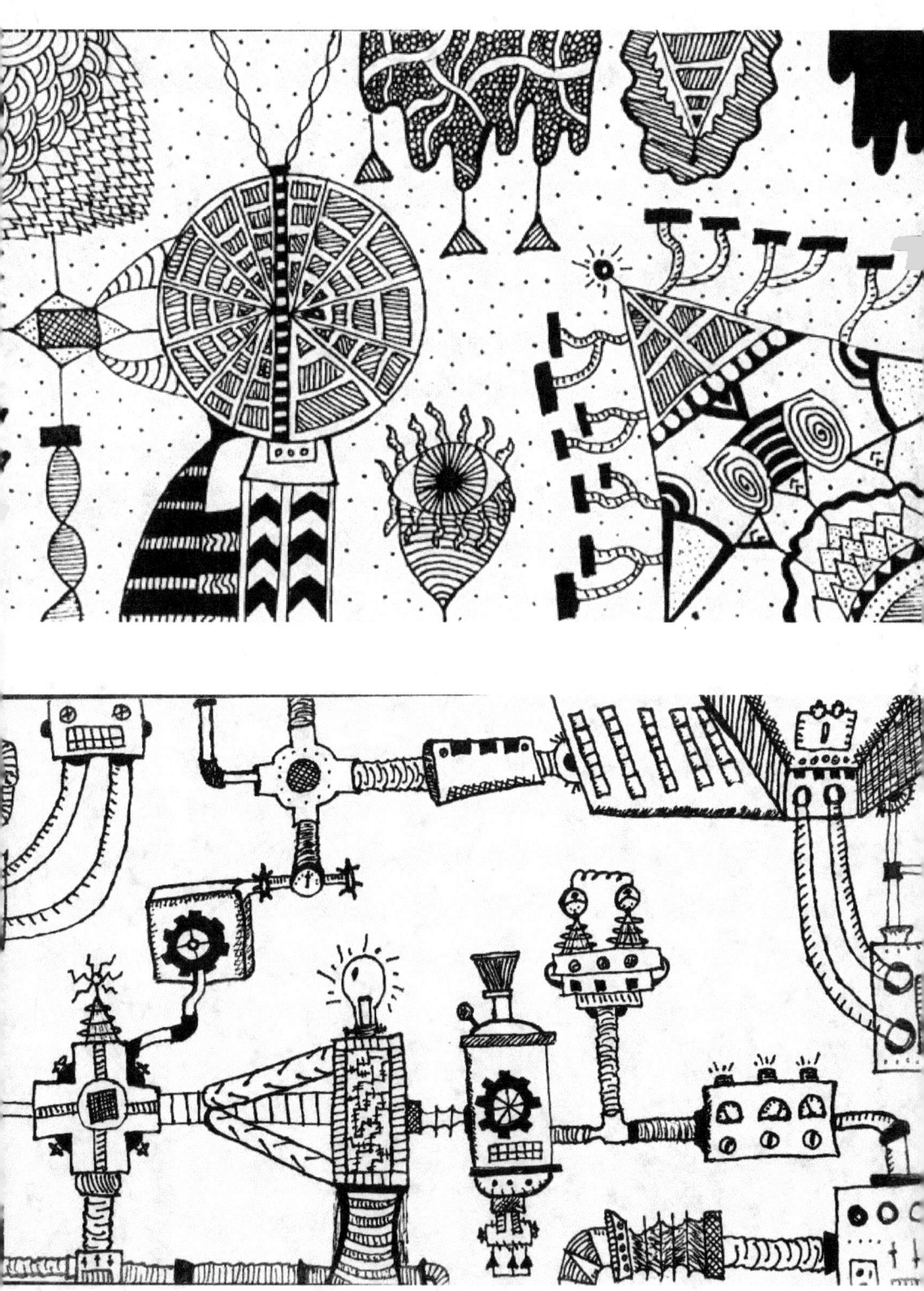

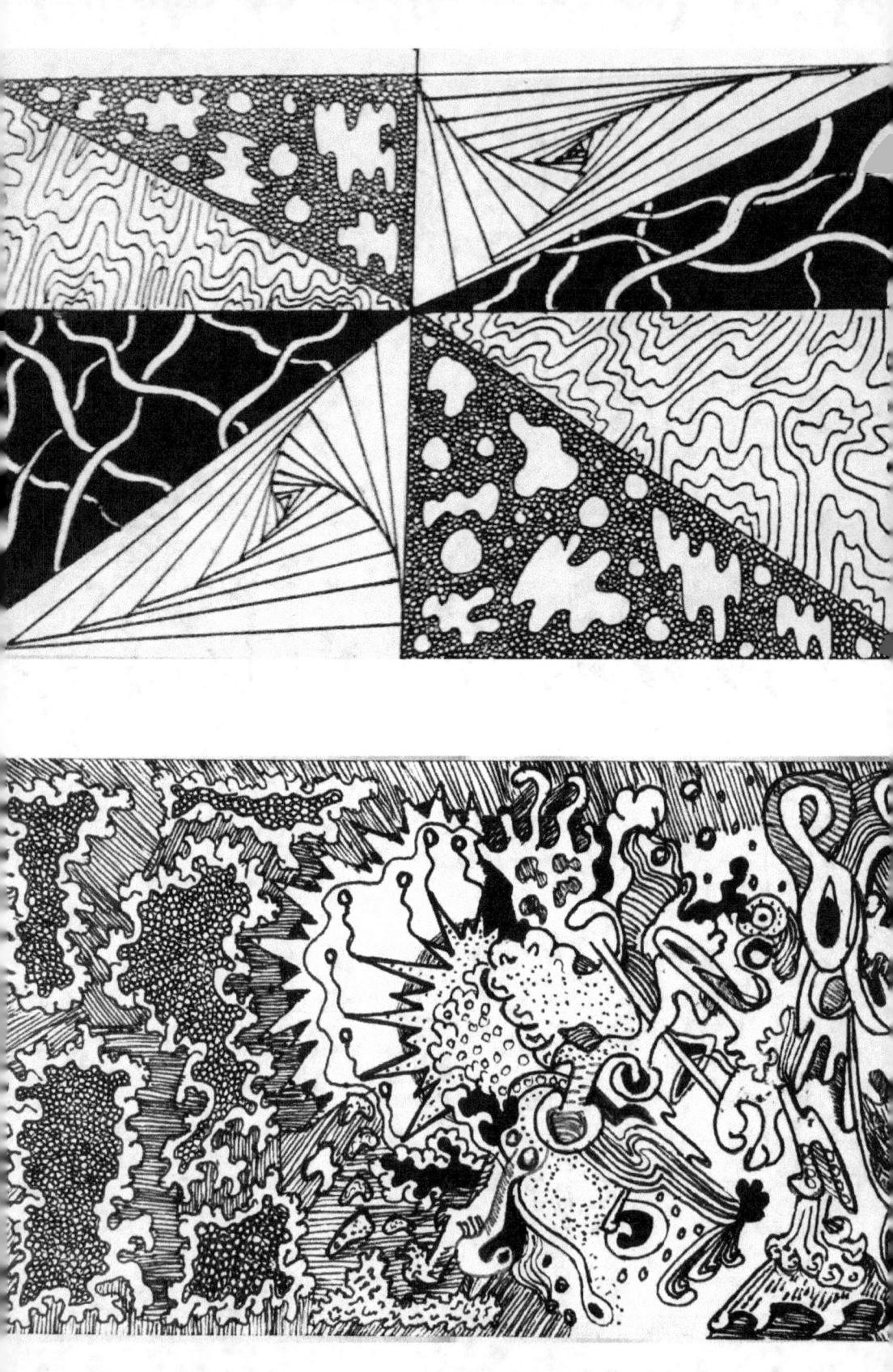

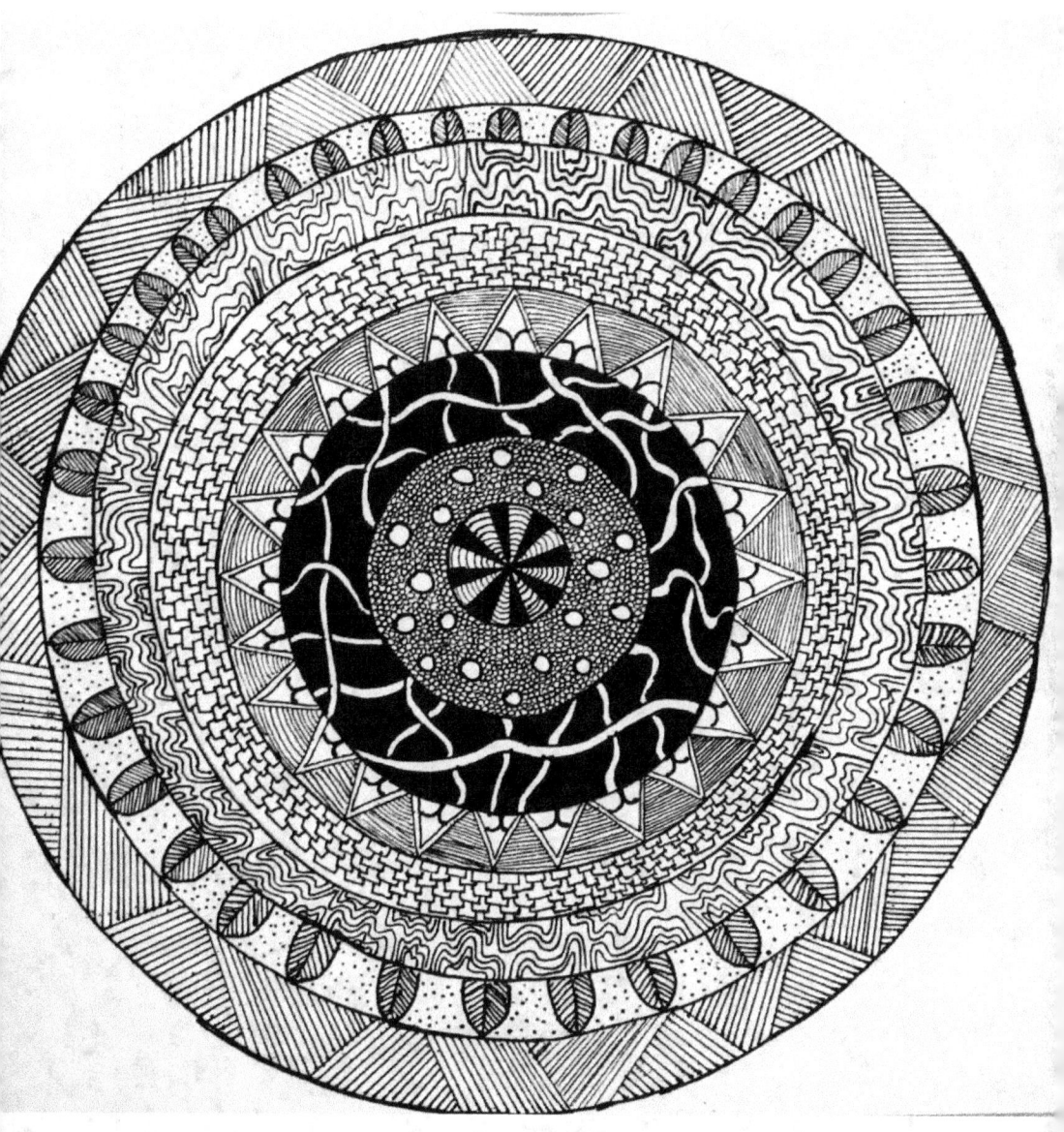

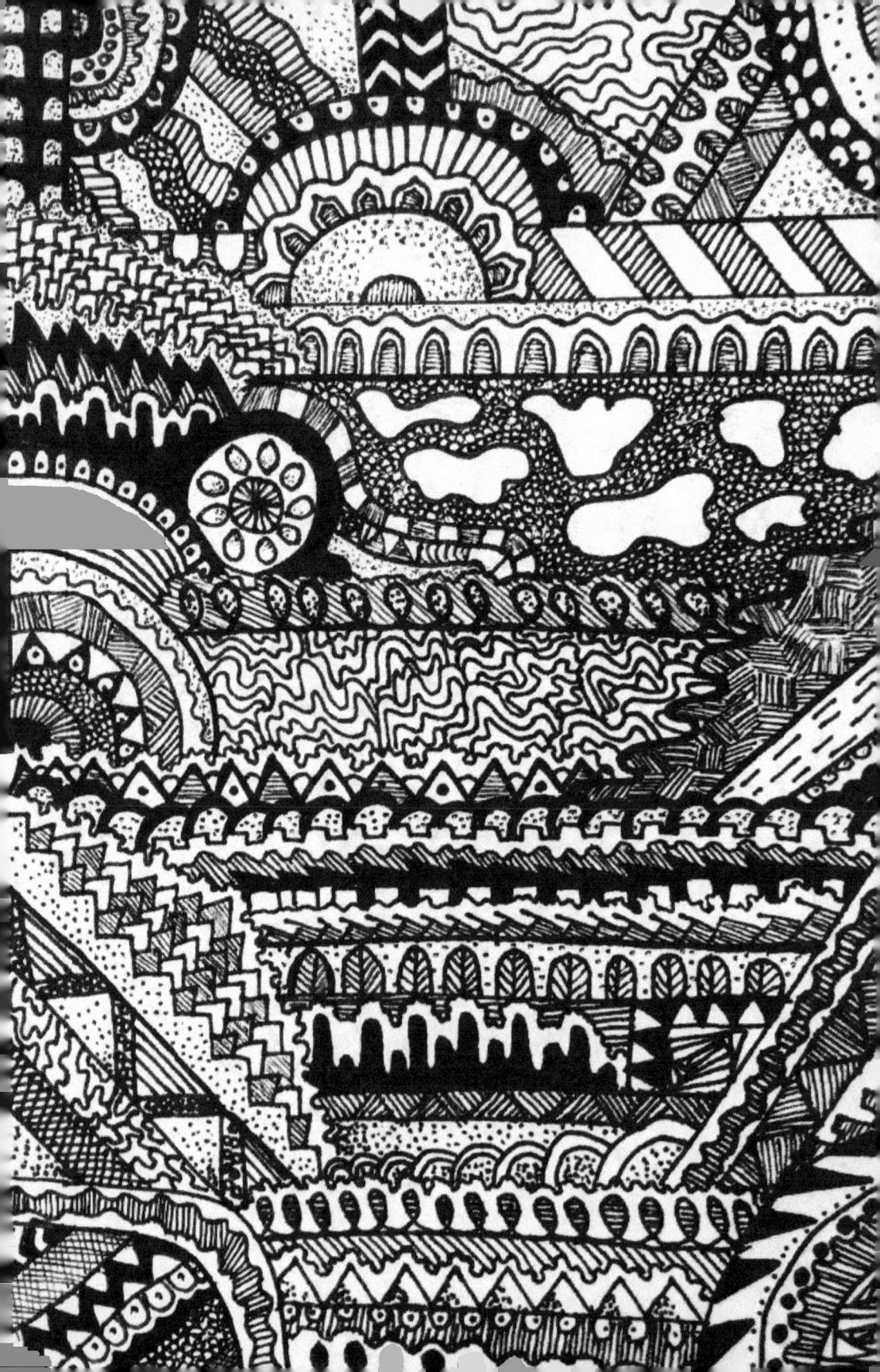

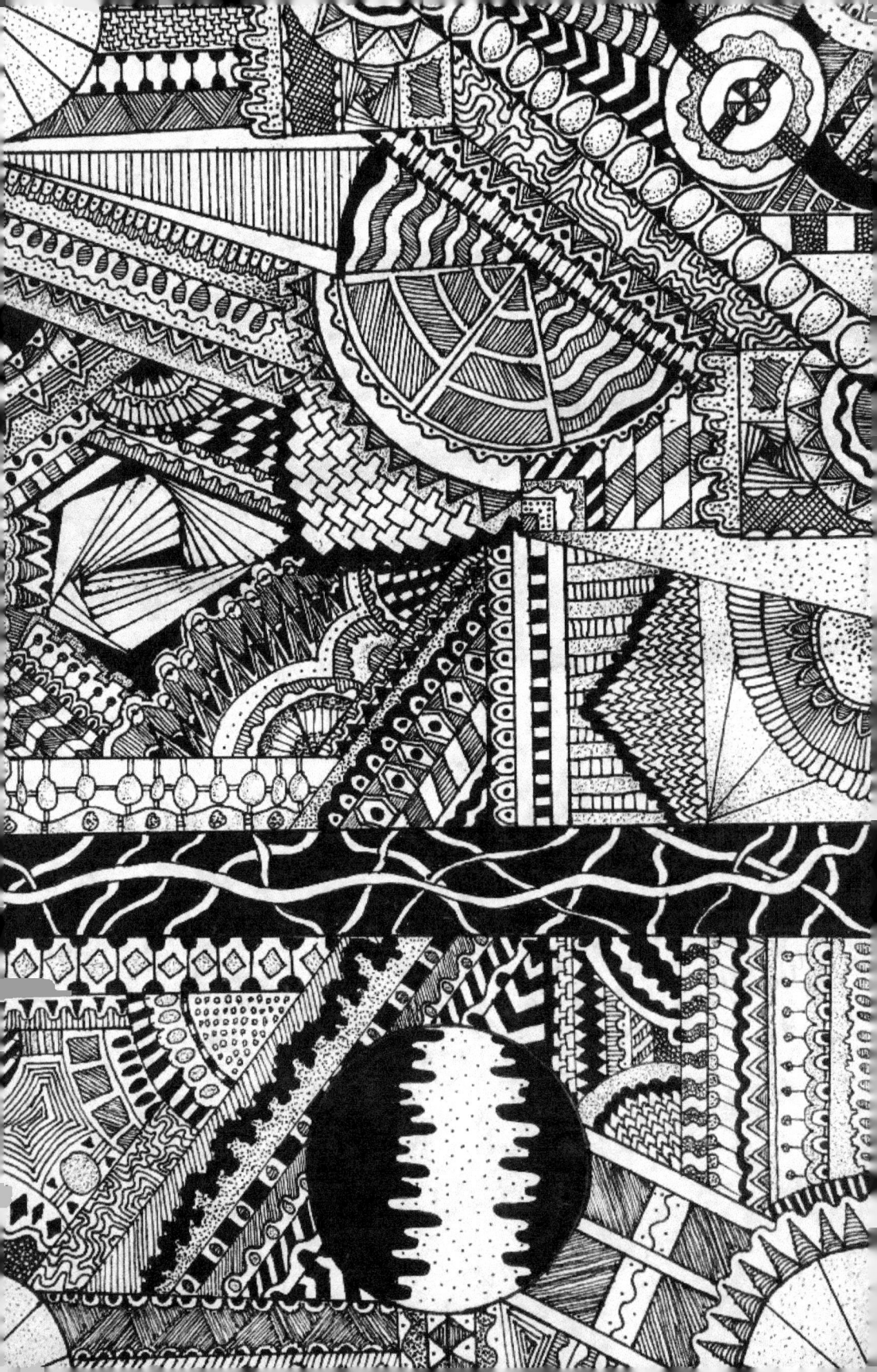

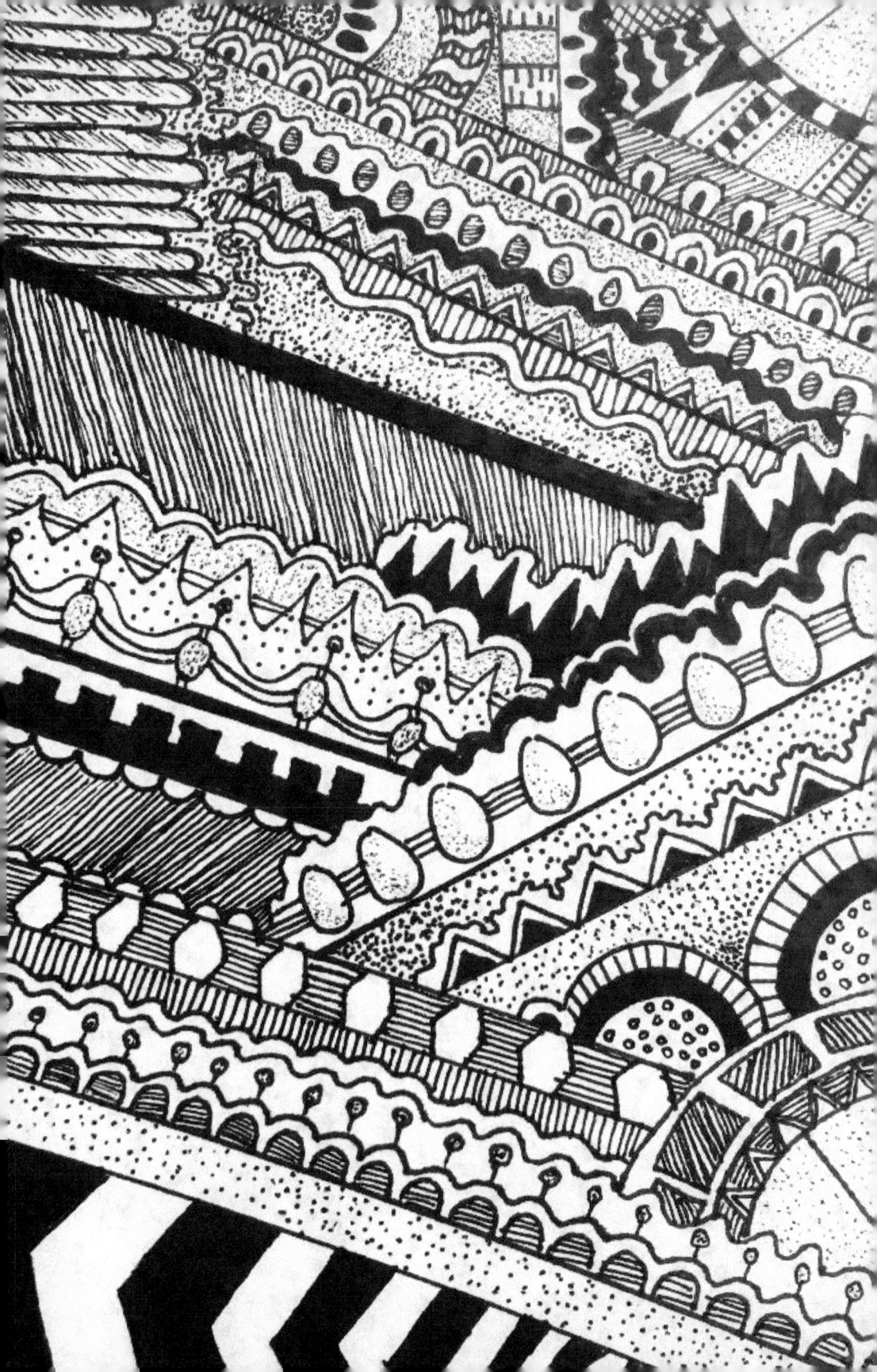

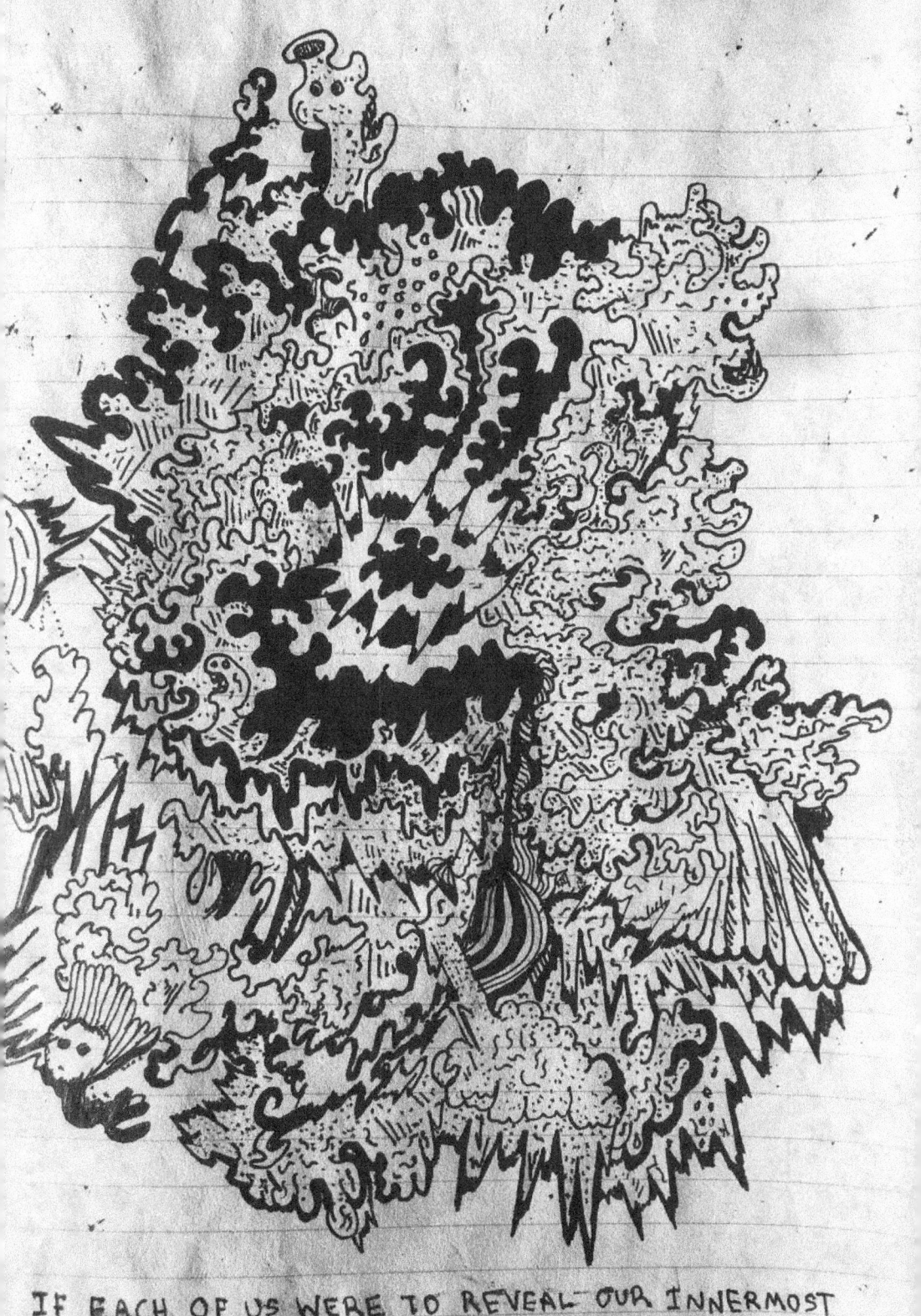

IF EACH OF US WERE TO REVEAL OUR INNERMOST SECRETS - THE WORLD WOULD BE FILLED WITH UCH A STENCH THAT EACH ONE OF US WOULD

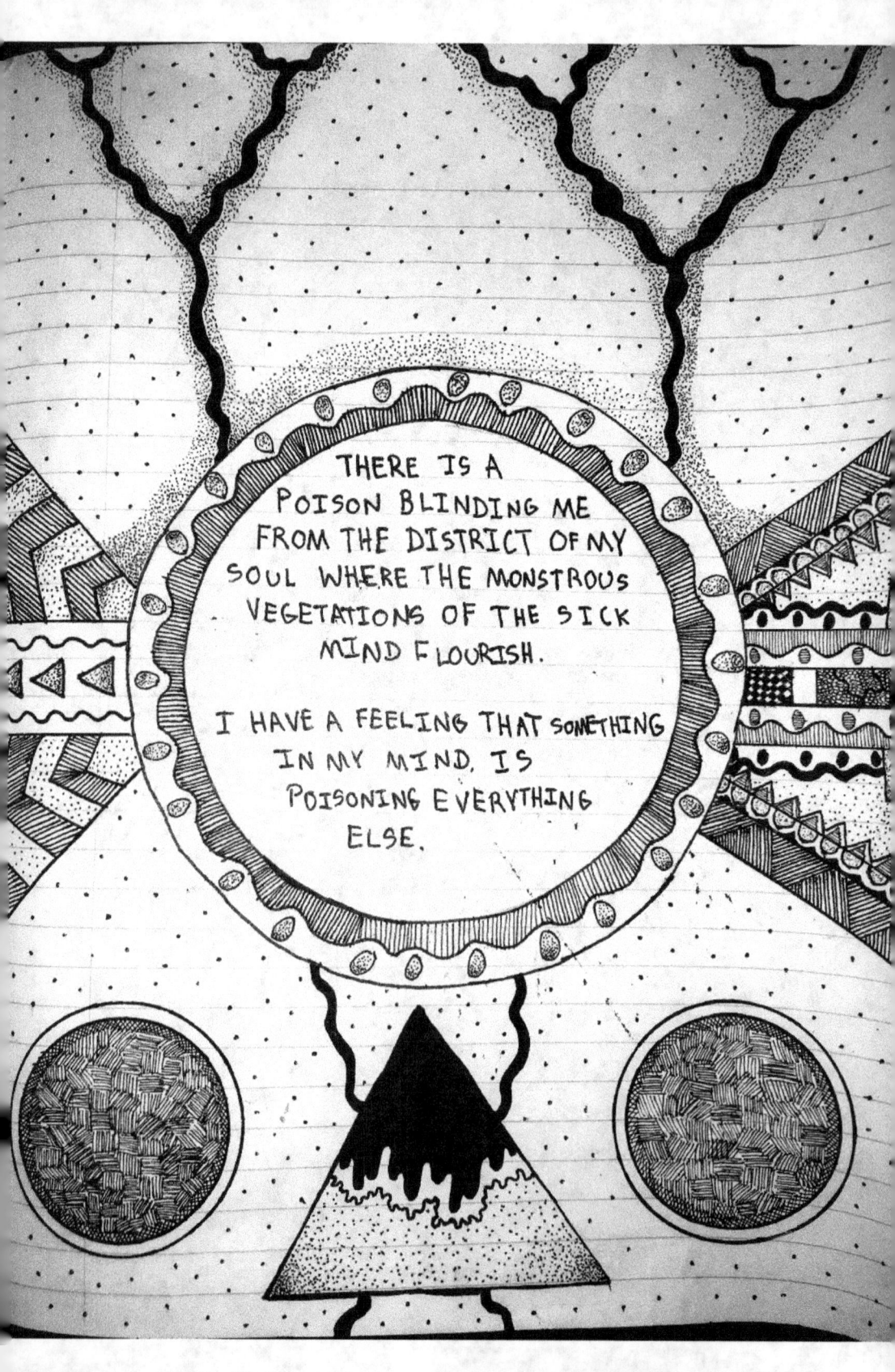

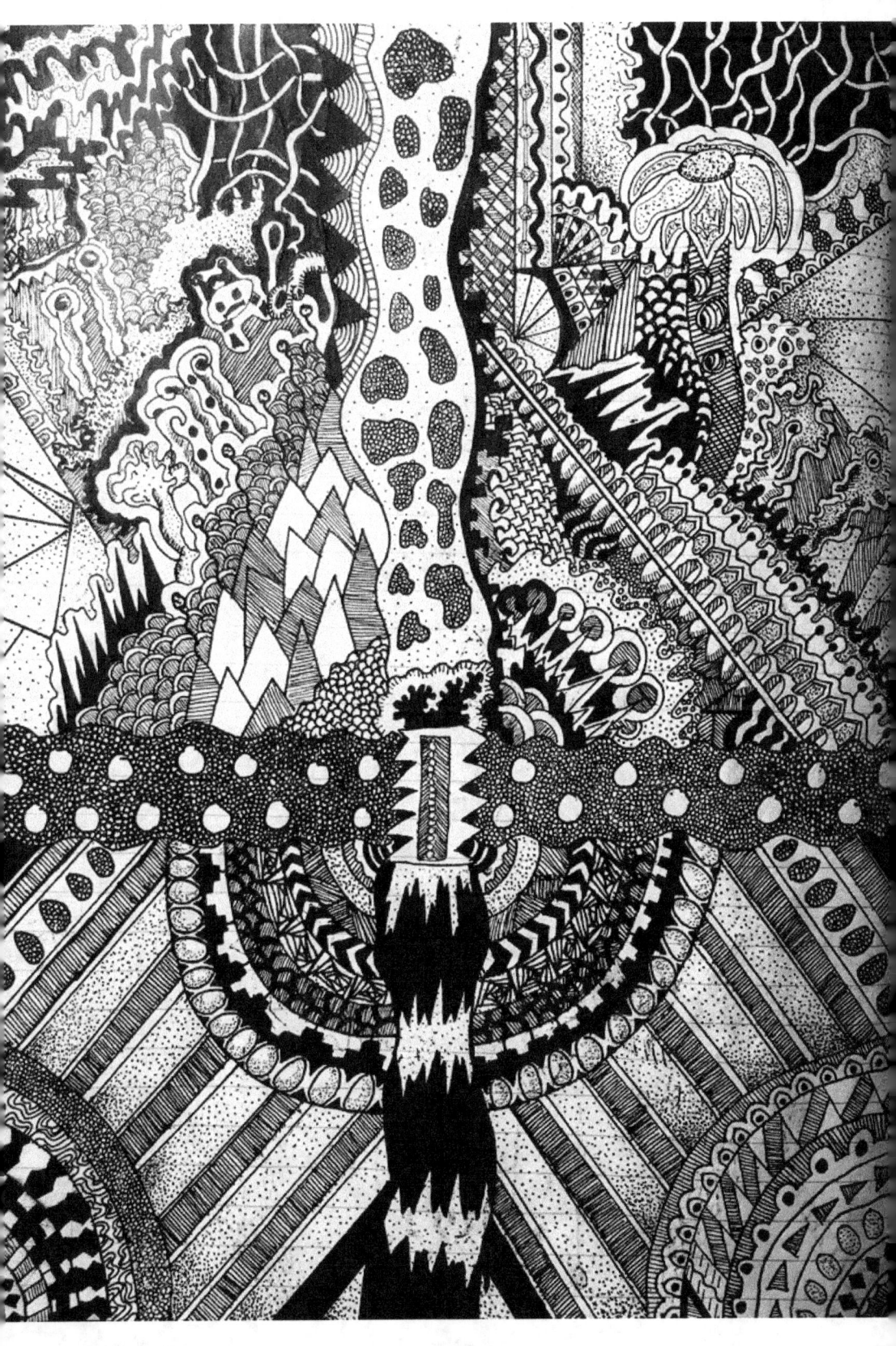

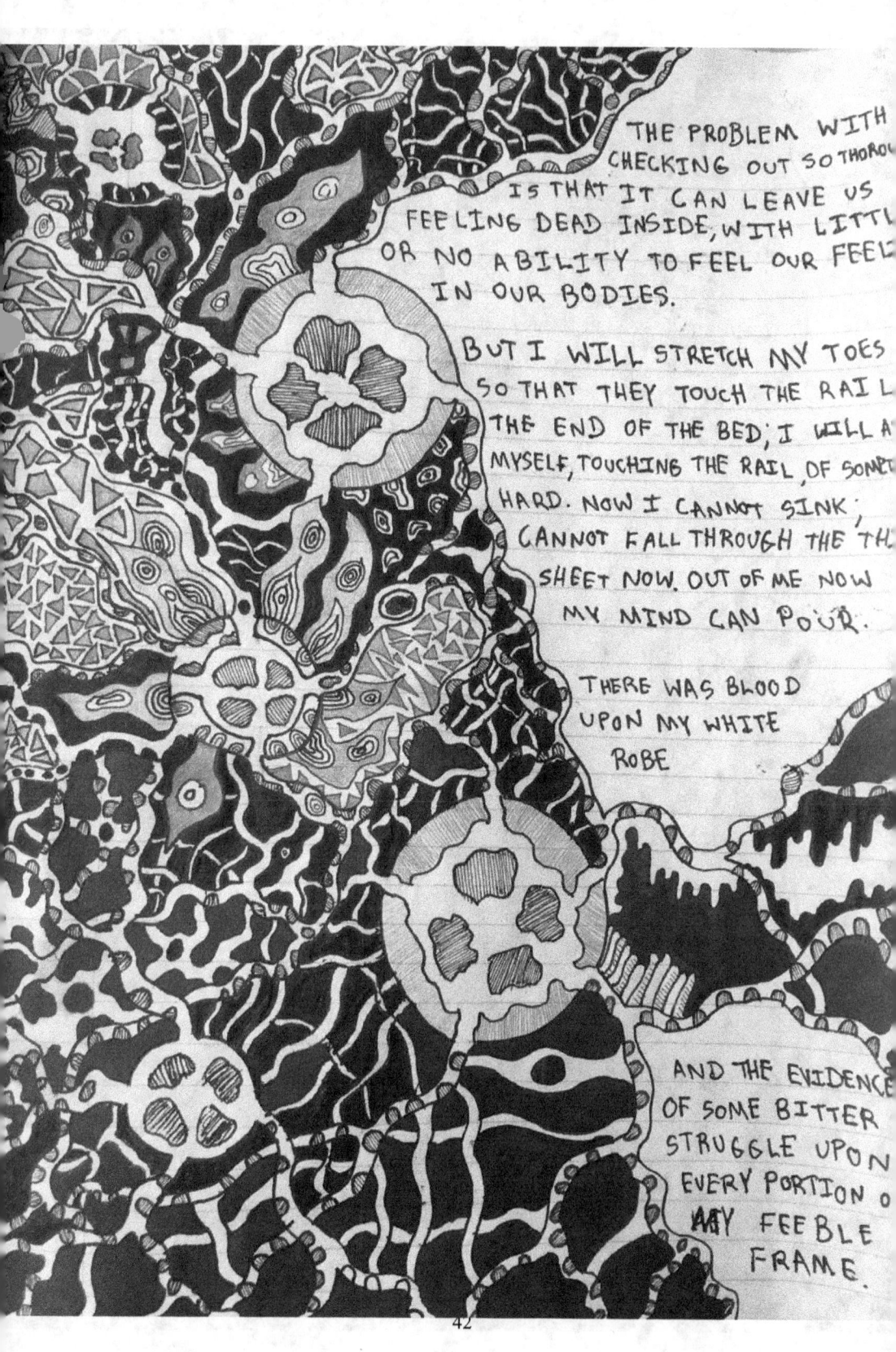

THE PROBLEM WITH CHECKING OUT SO THOROU[GHLY] IS THAT IT CAN LEAVE US FEELING DEAD INSIDE, WITH LITTL[E] OR NO ABILITY TO FEEL OUR FEEL[INGS] IN OUR BODIES.

BUT I WILL STRETCH MY TOES SO THAT THEY TOUCH THE RAIL [AT] THE END OF THE BED; I WILL A[NCHOR] MYSELF, TOUCHING THE RAIL, OF SOME[THING] HARD. NOW I CANNOT SINK, CANNOT FALL THROUGH THE TH[IN] SHEET NOW. OUT OF ME NOW MY MIND CAN POUR.

THERE WAS BLOOD UPON MY WHITE ROBE

AND THE EVIDENCE OF SOME BITTER STRUGGLE UPON EVERY PORTION O[F] MY FEEBLE FRAME.

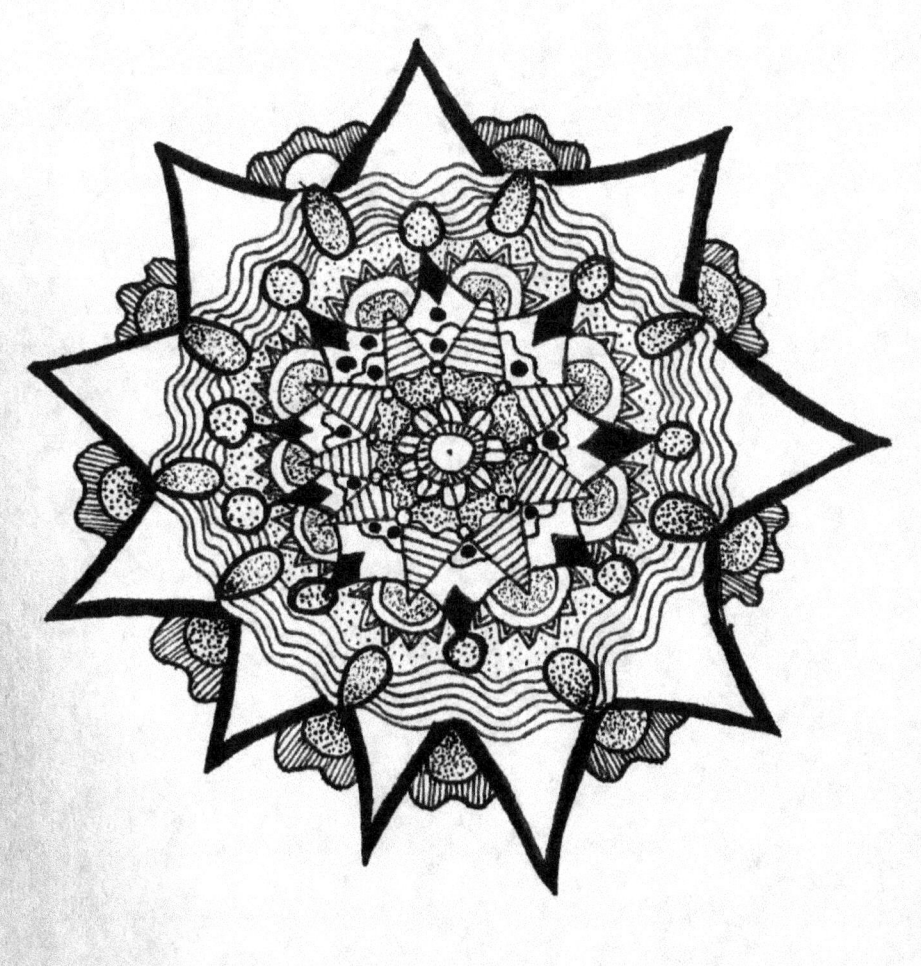

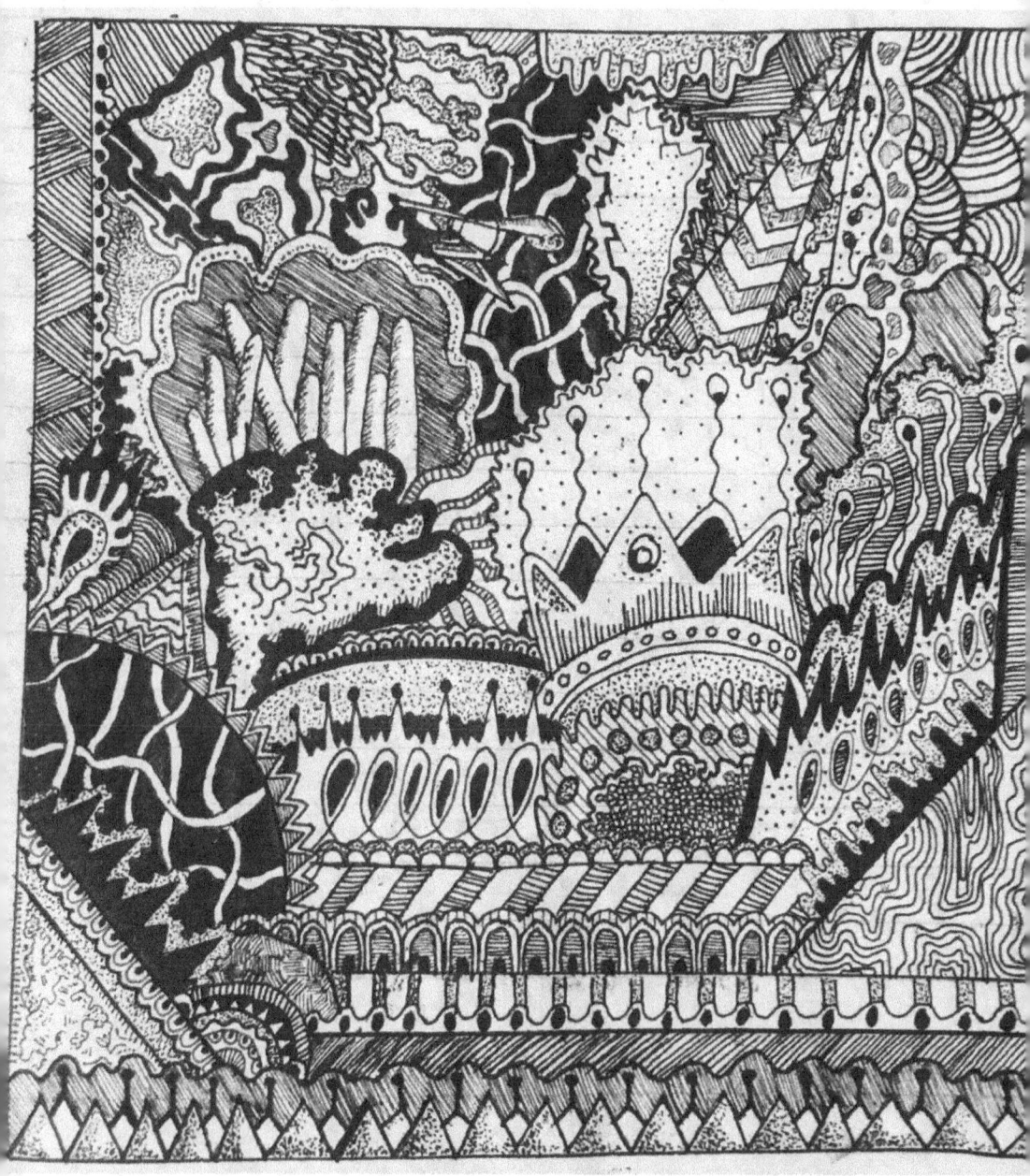

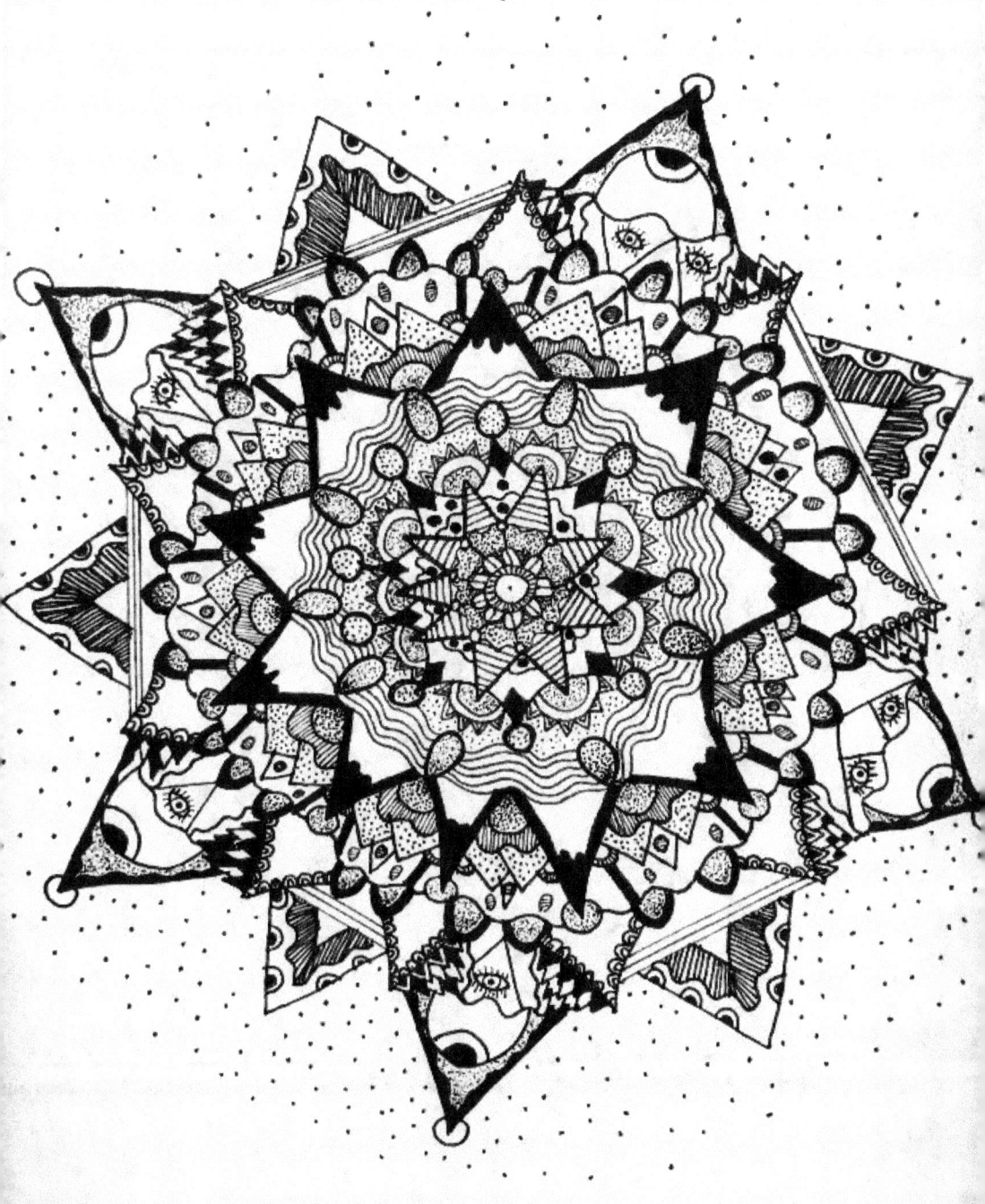

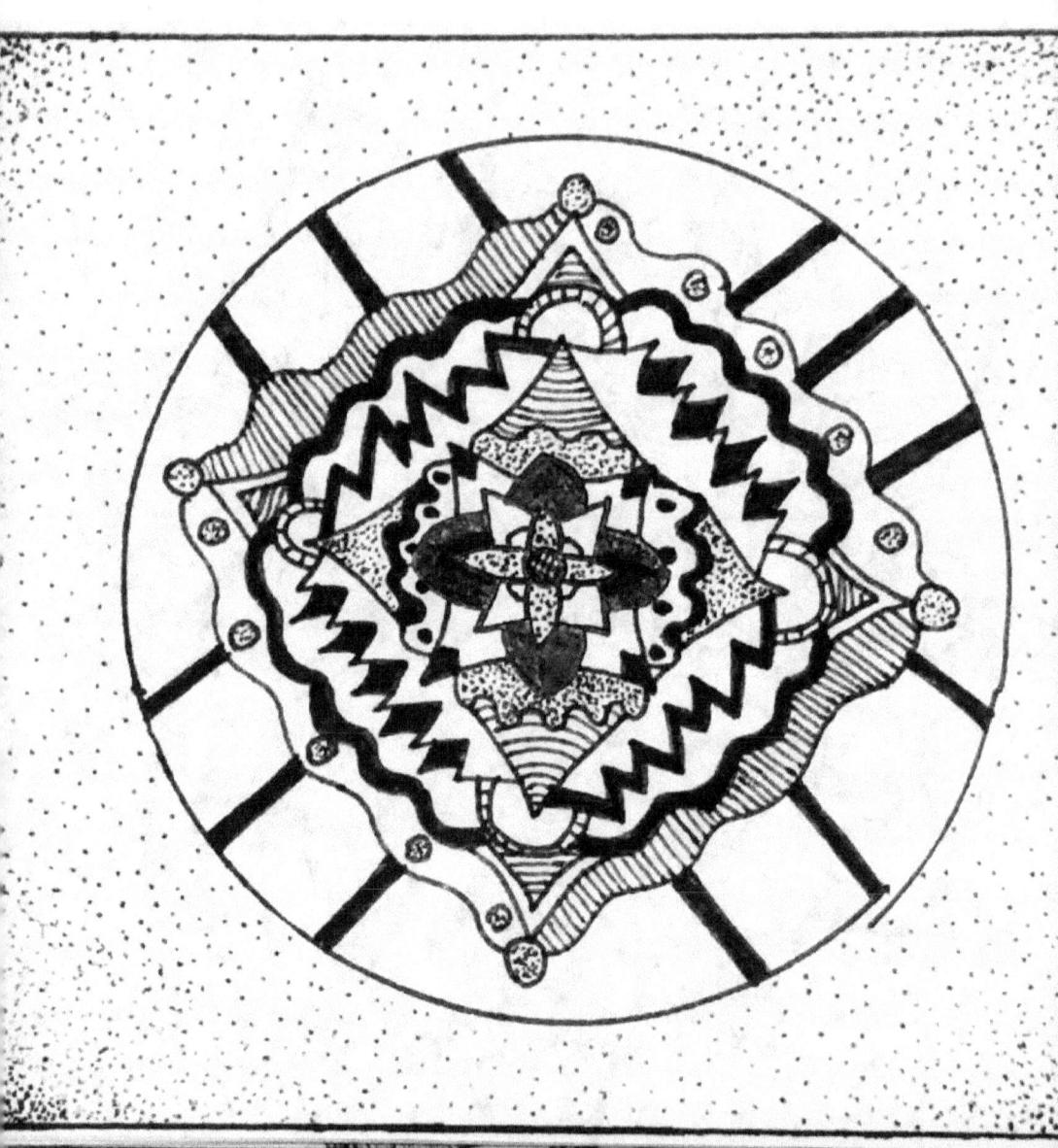

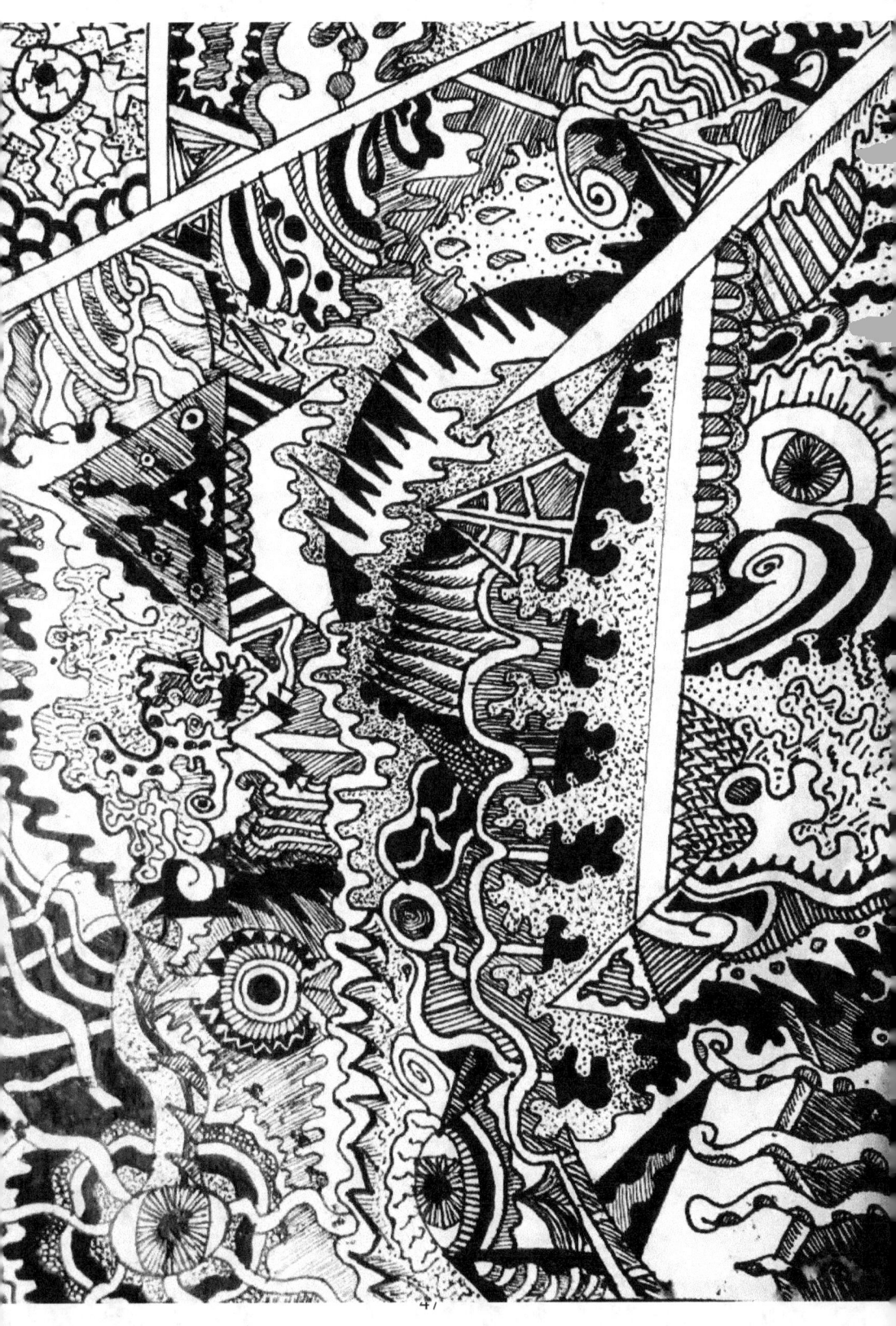

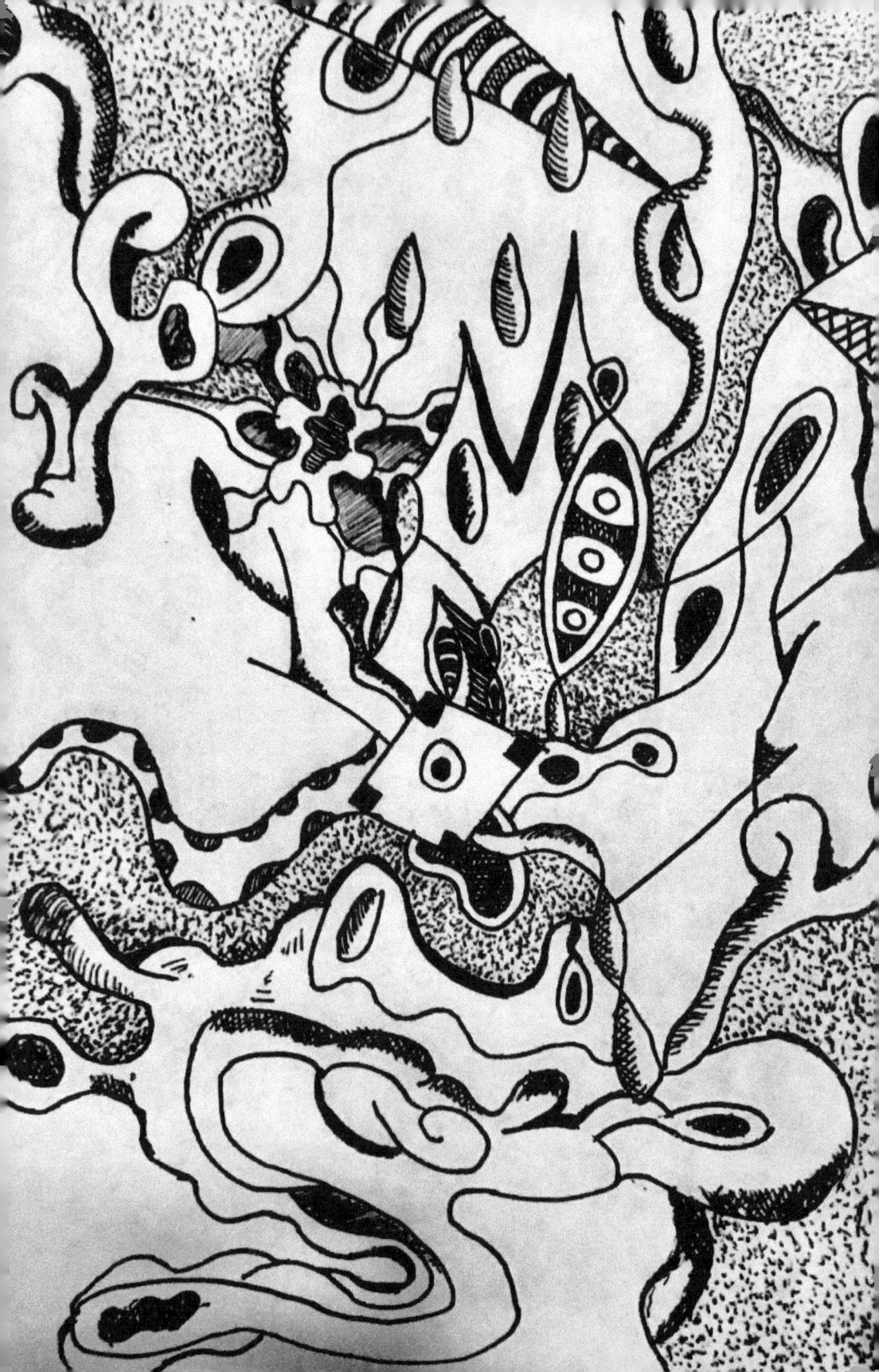

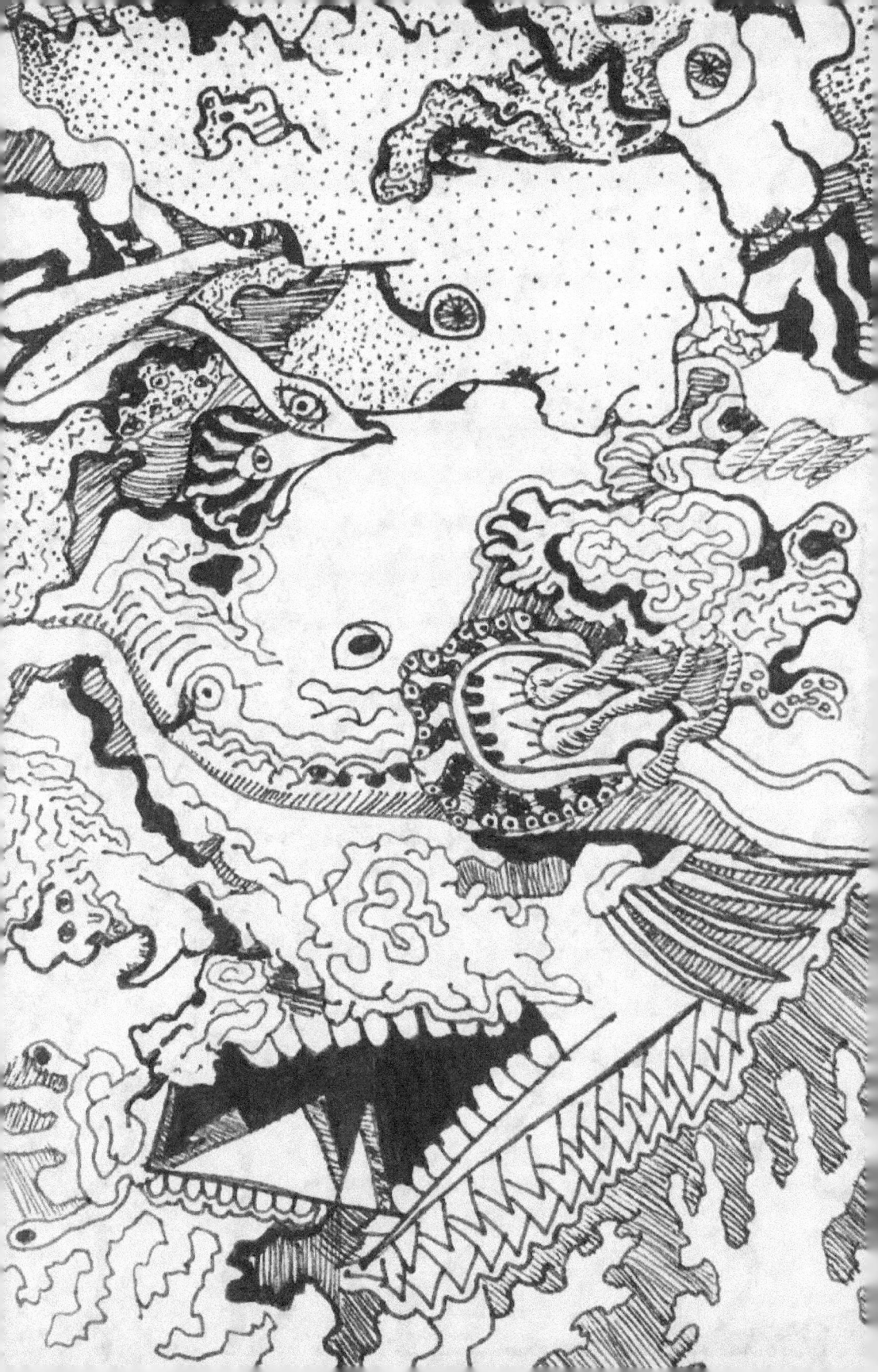

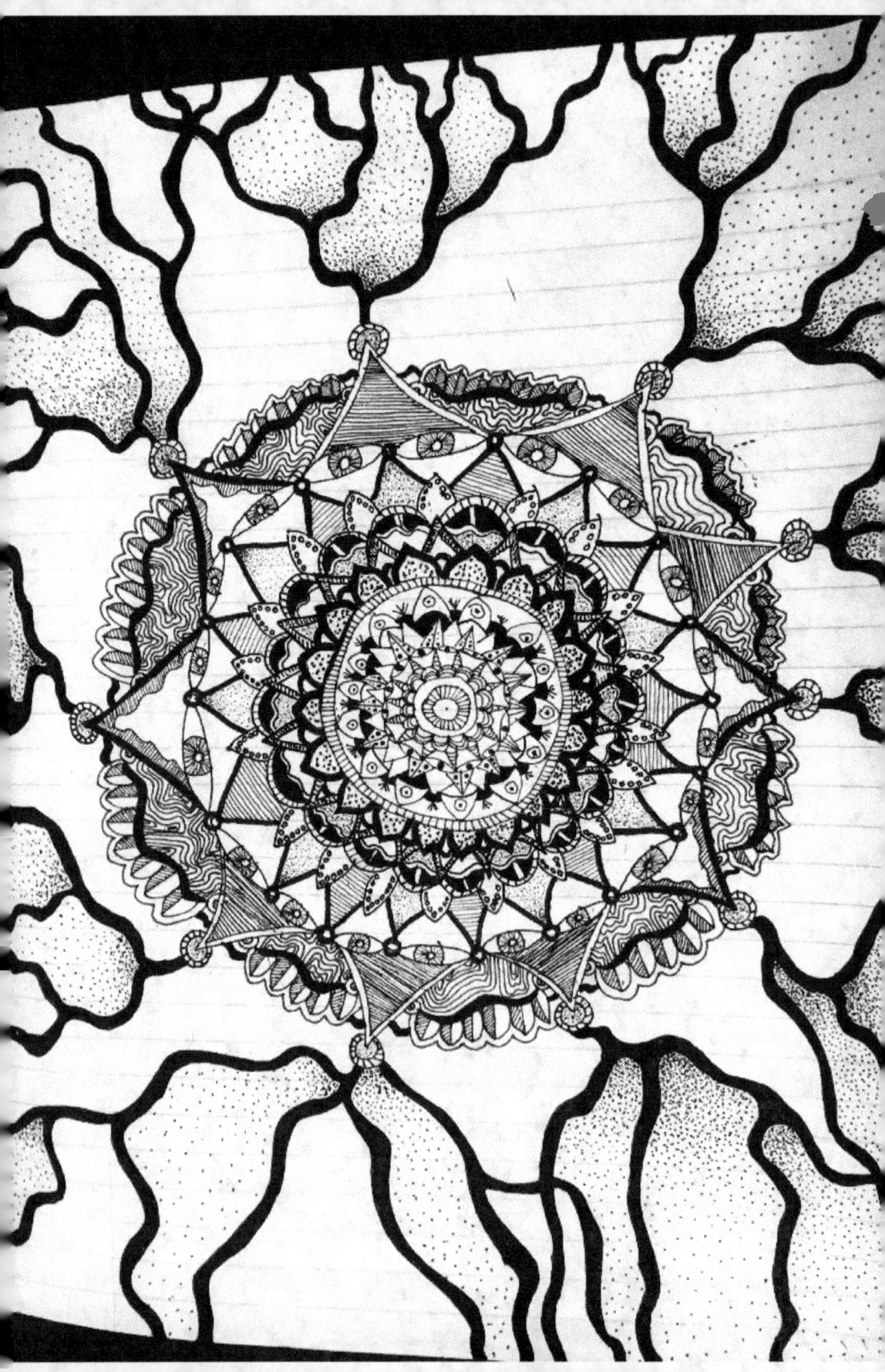

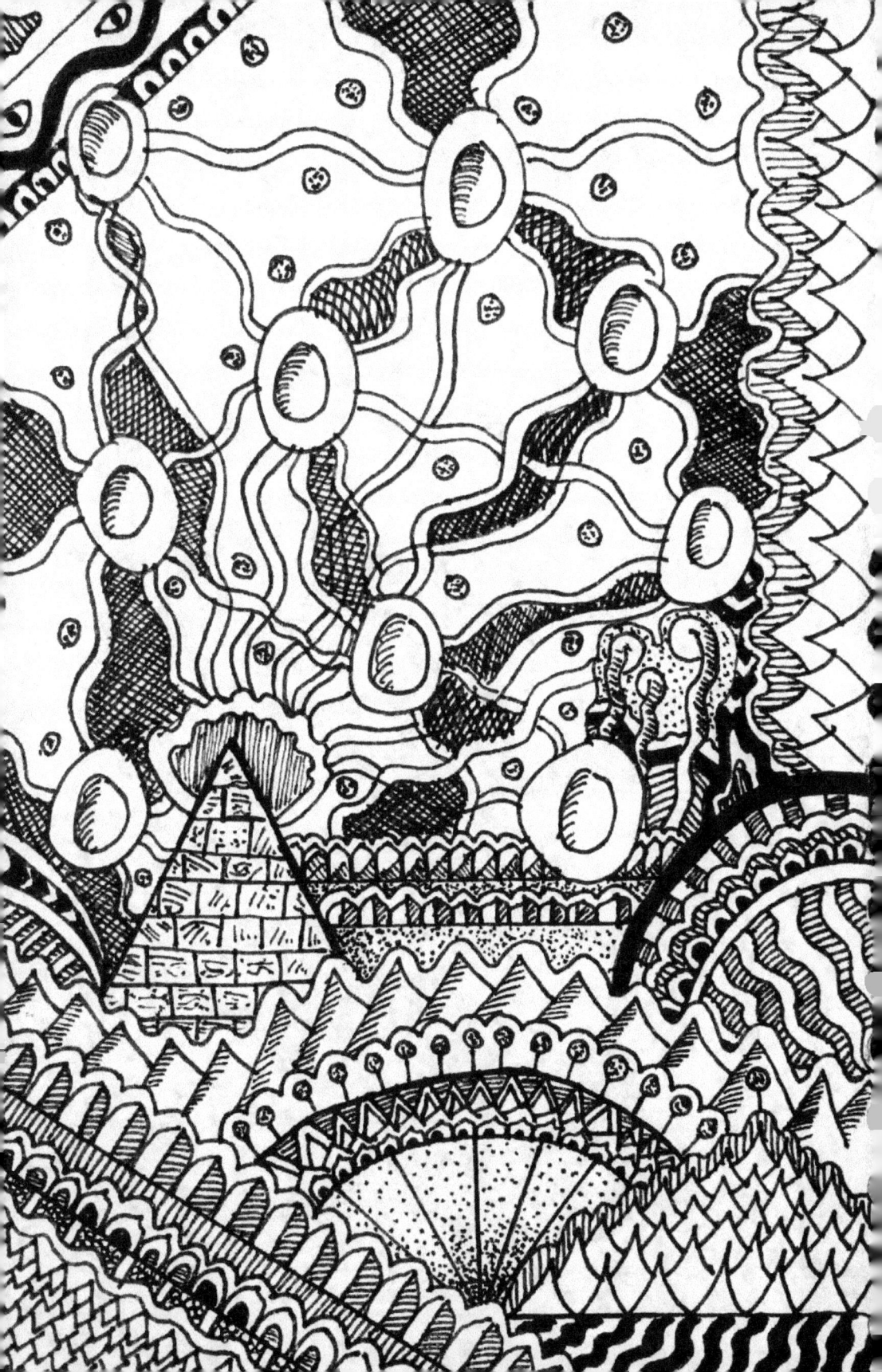

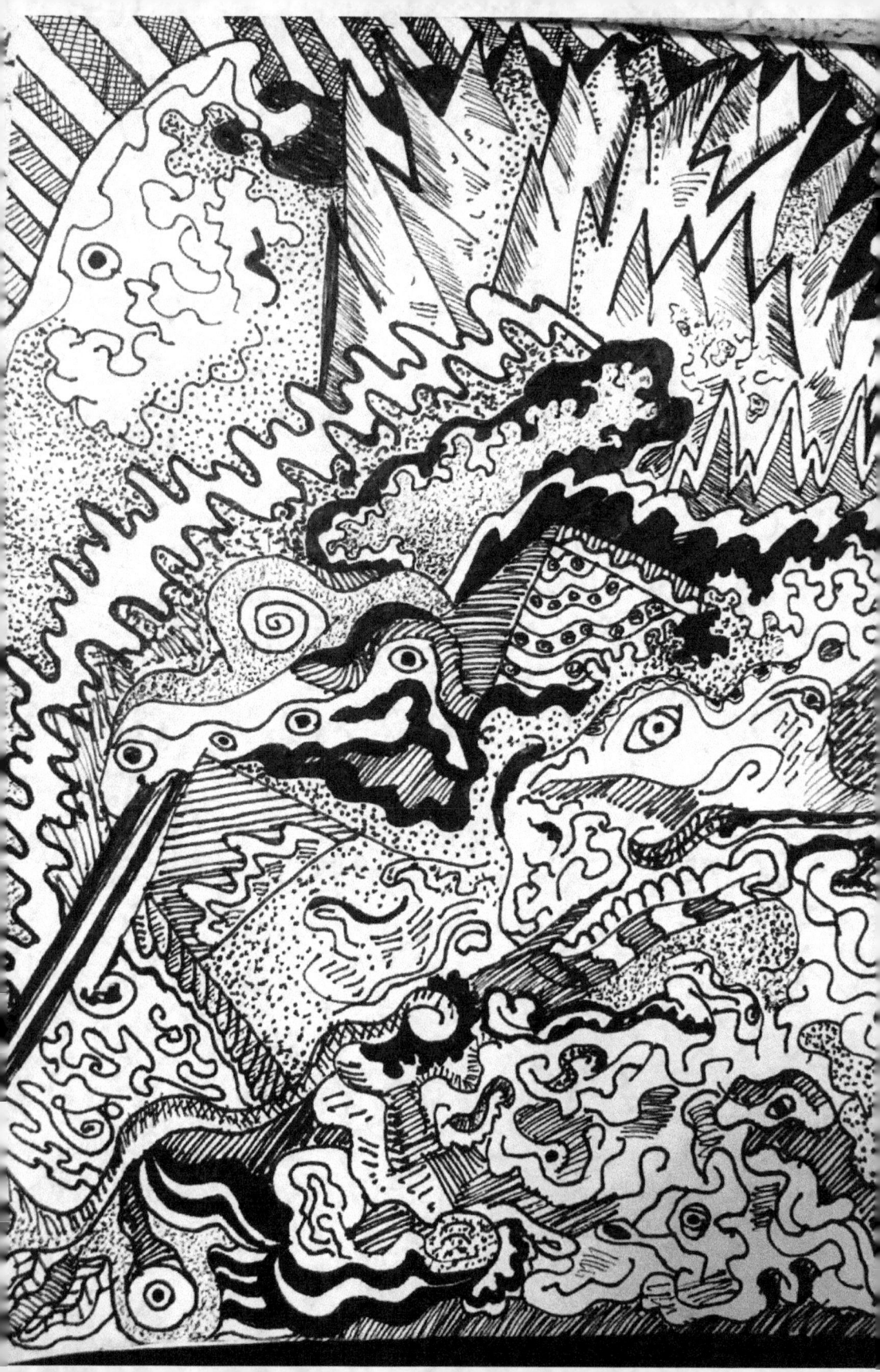

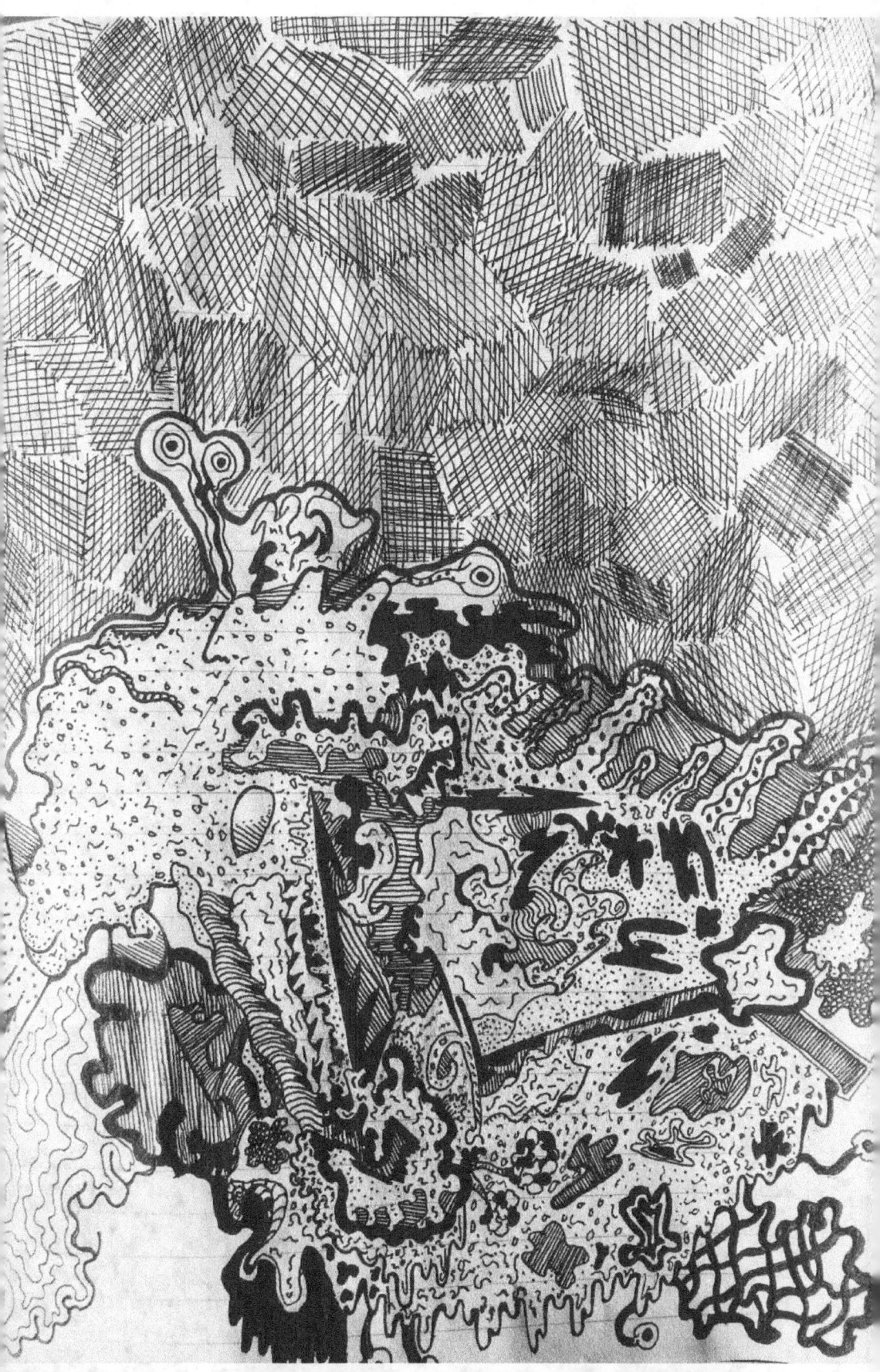

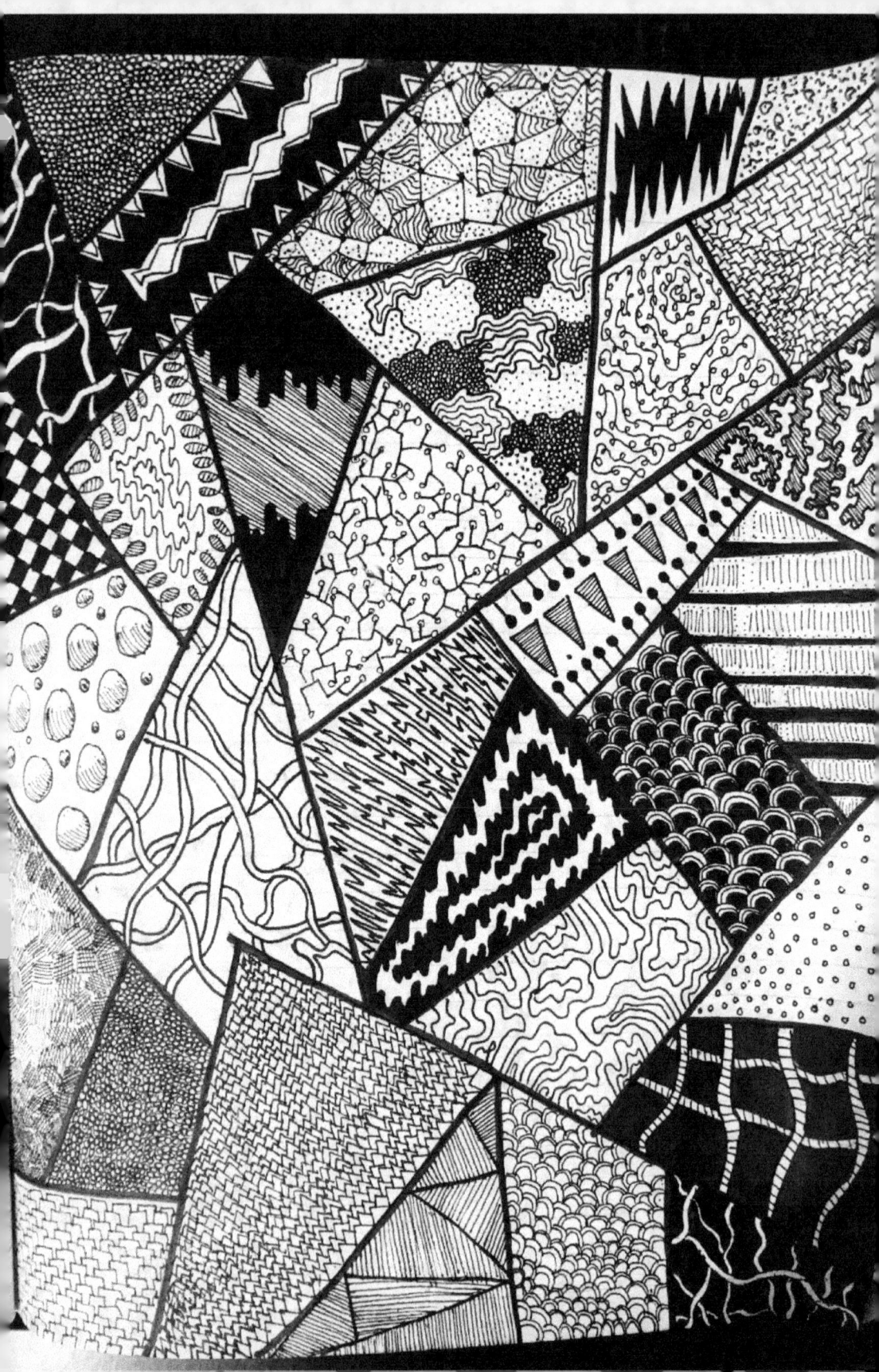

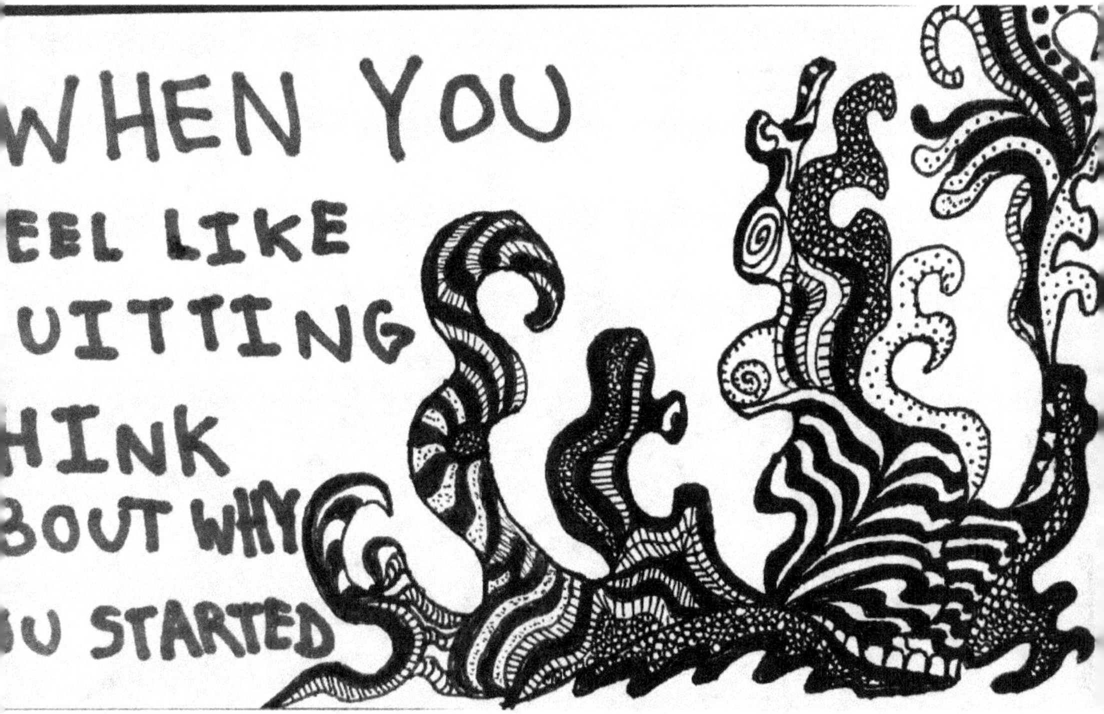

WHEN YOU
FEEL LIKE
QUITTING
THINK
ABOUT WHY
YOU STARTED

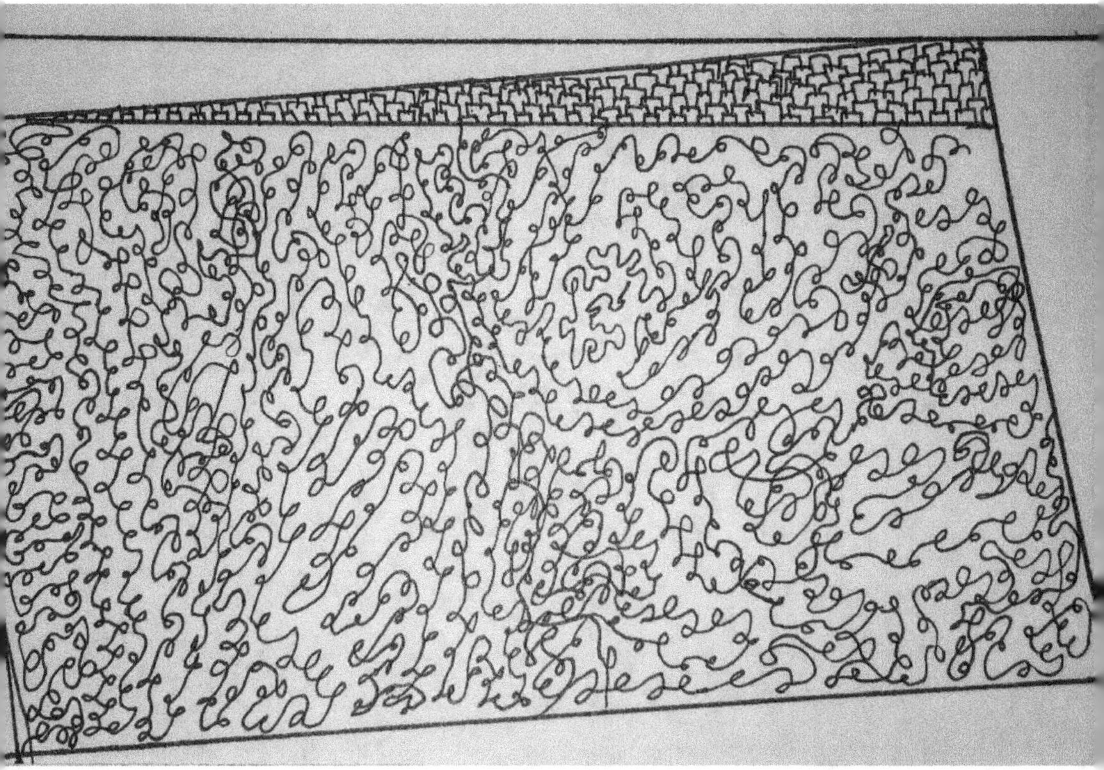

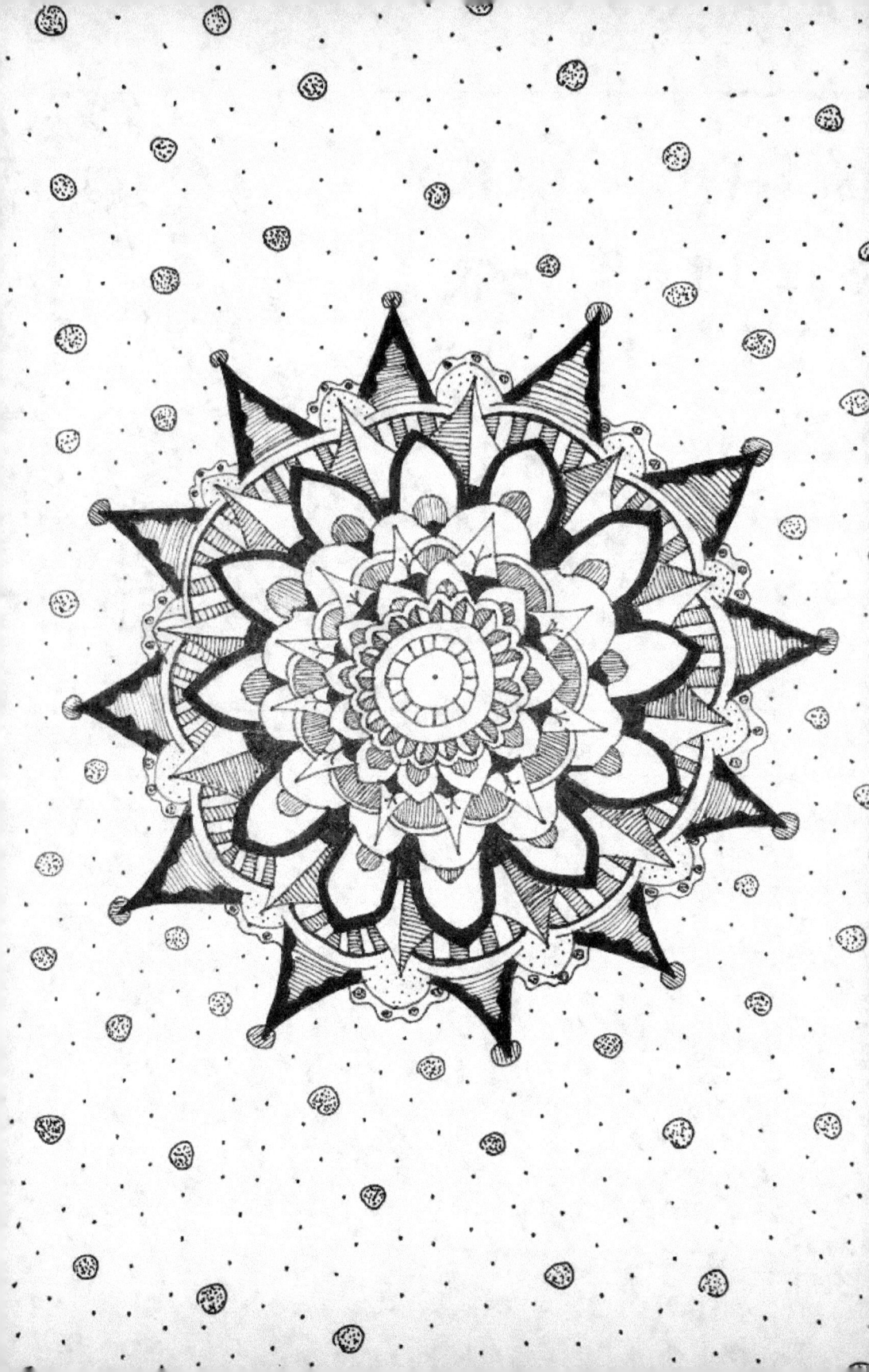

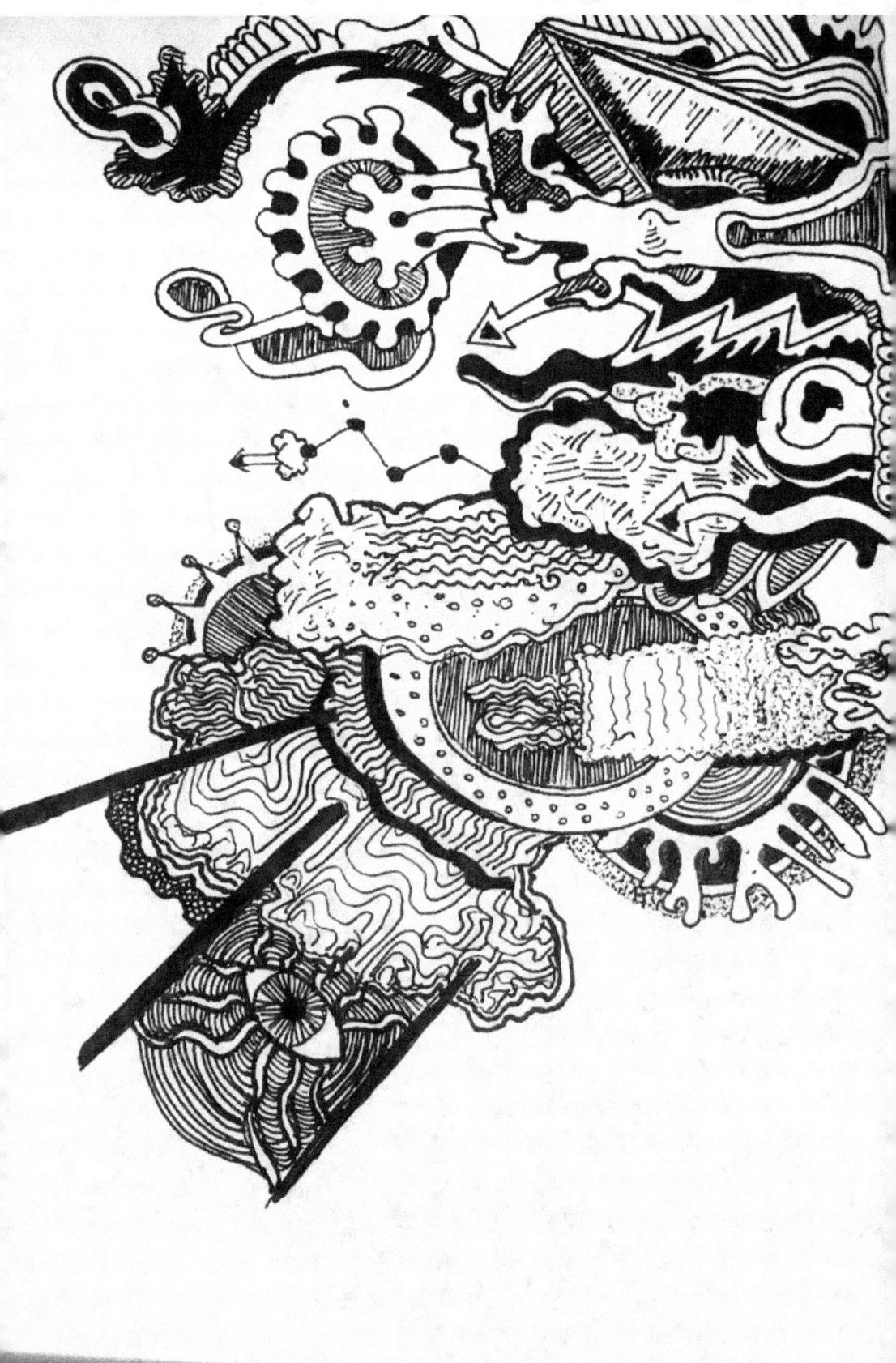

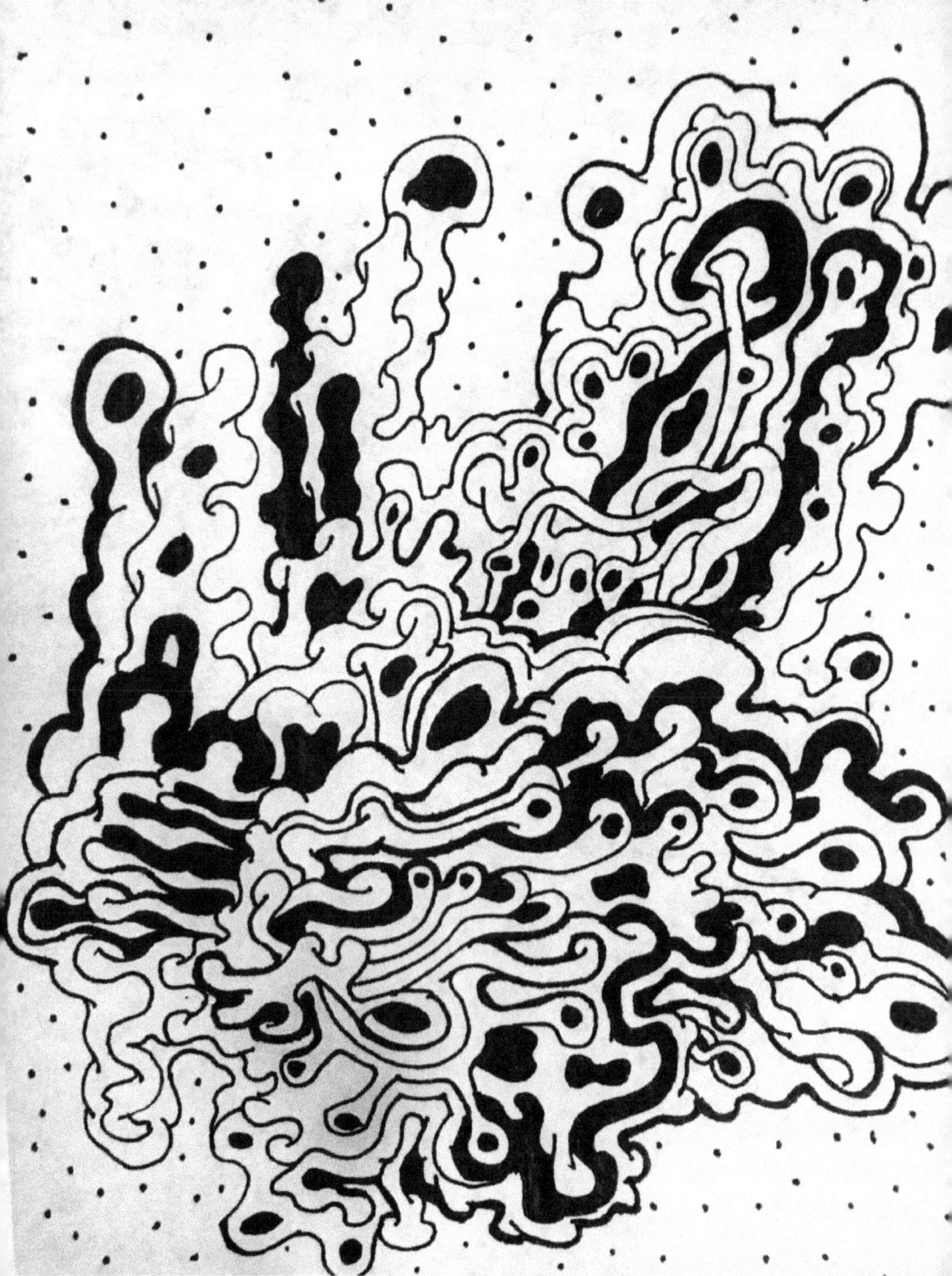

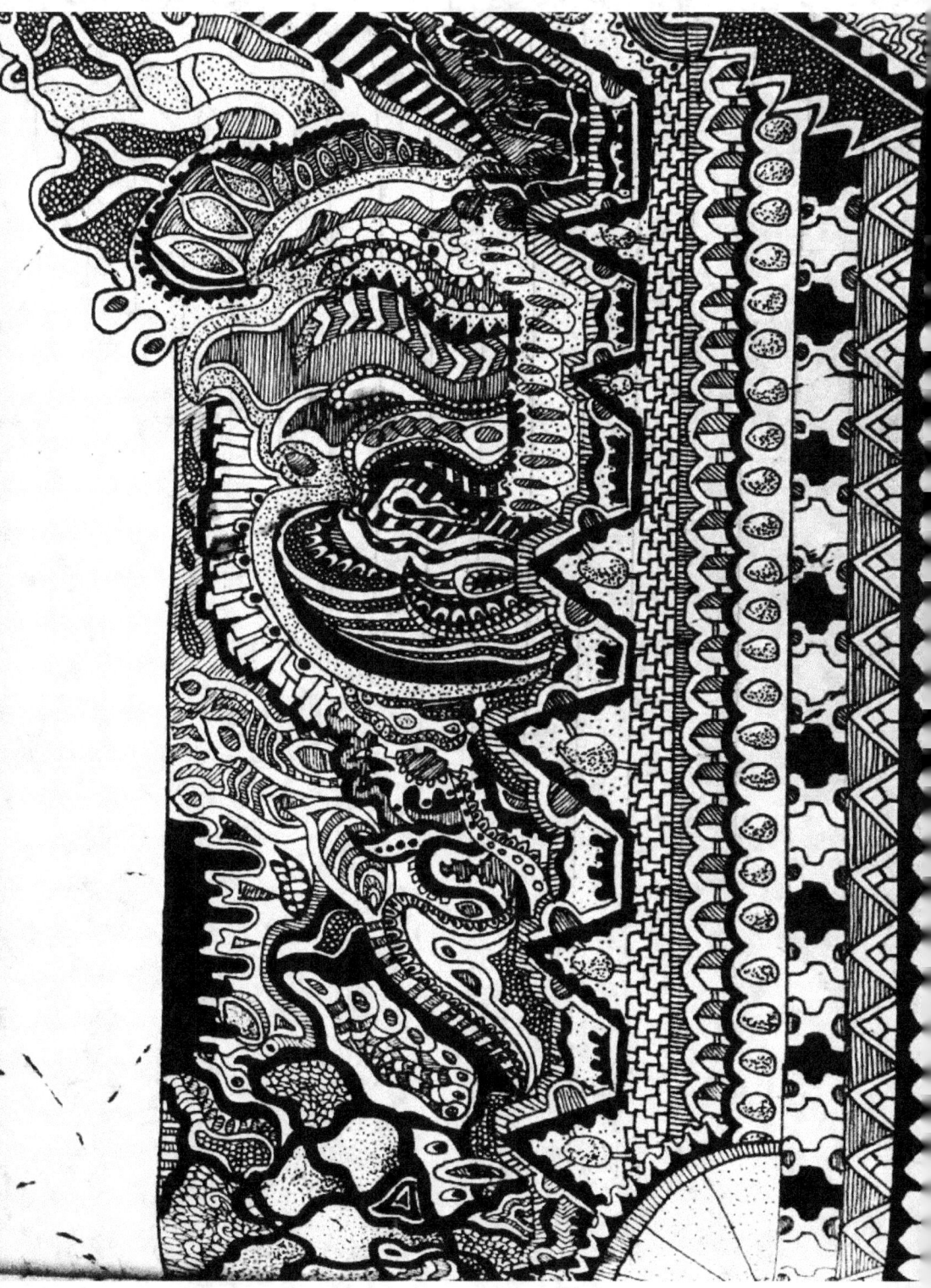

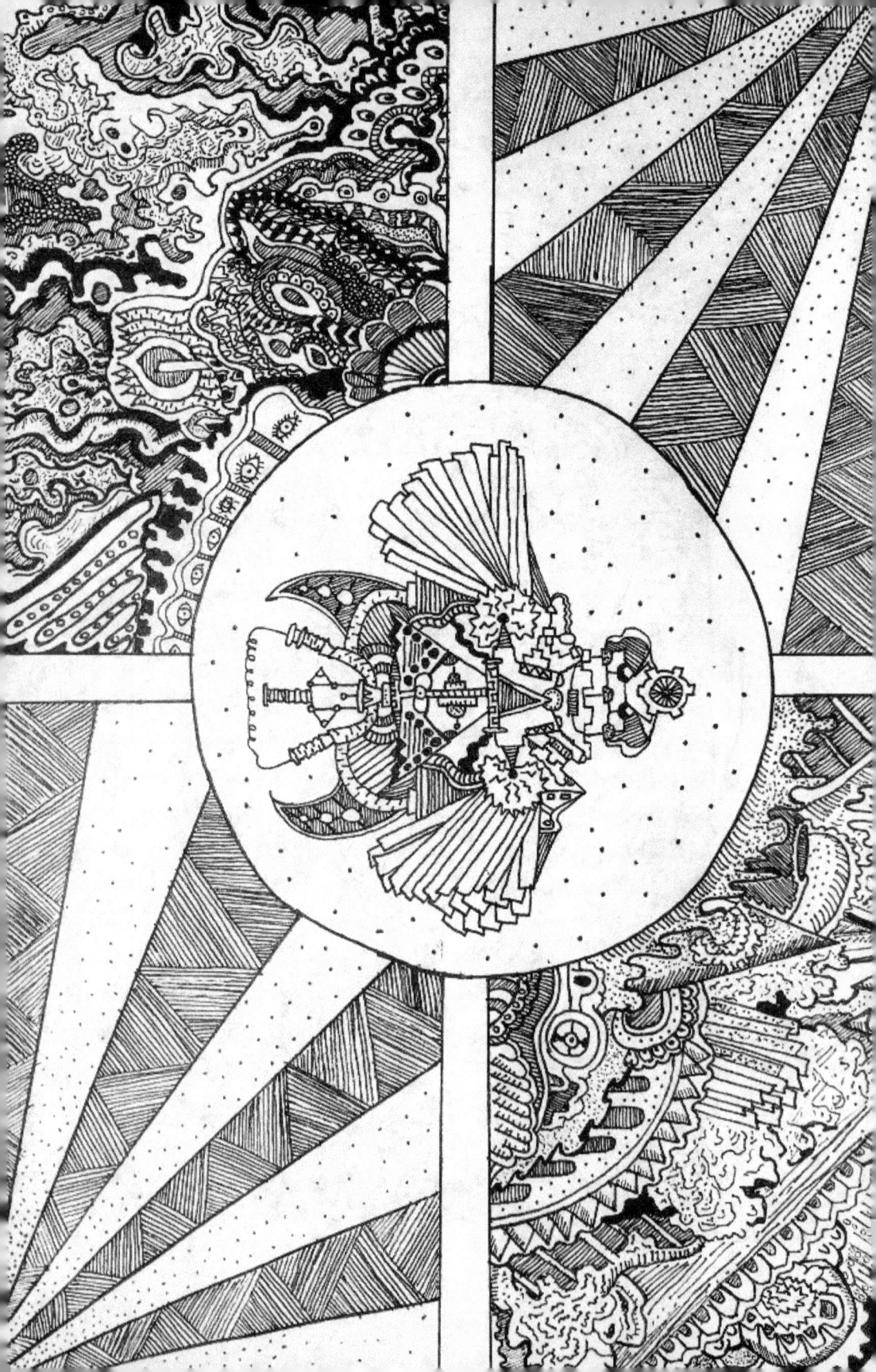

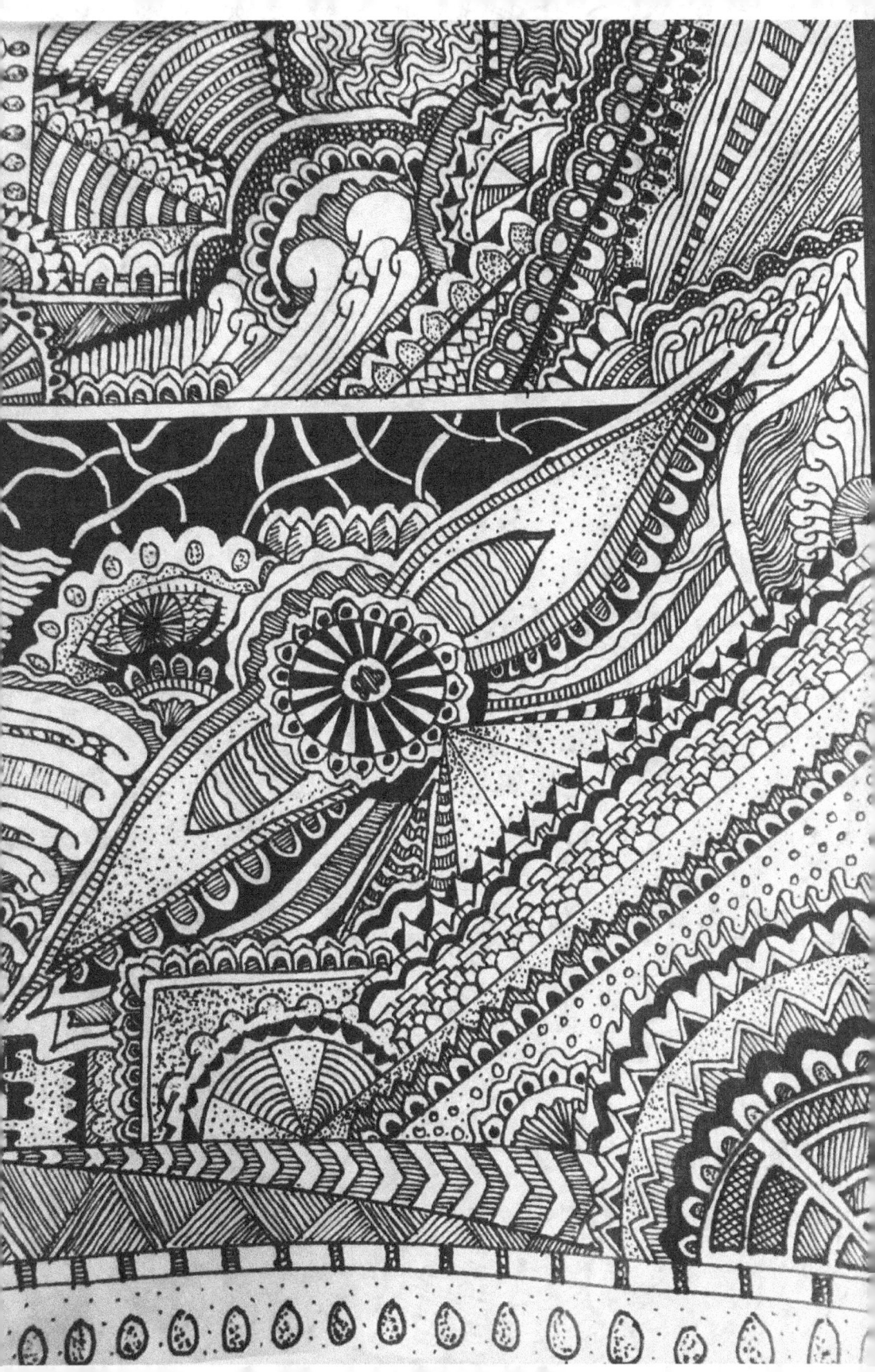

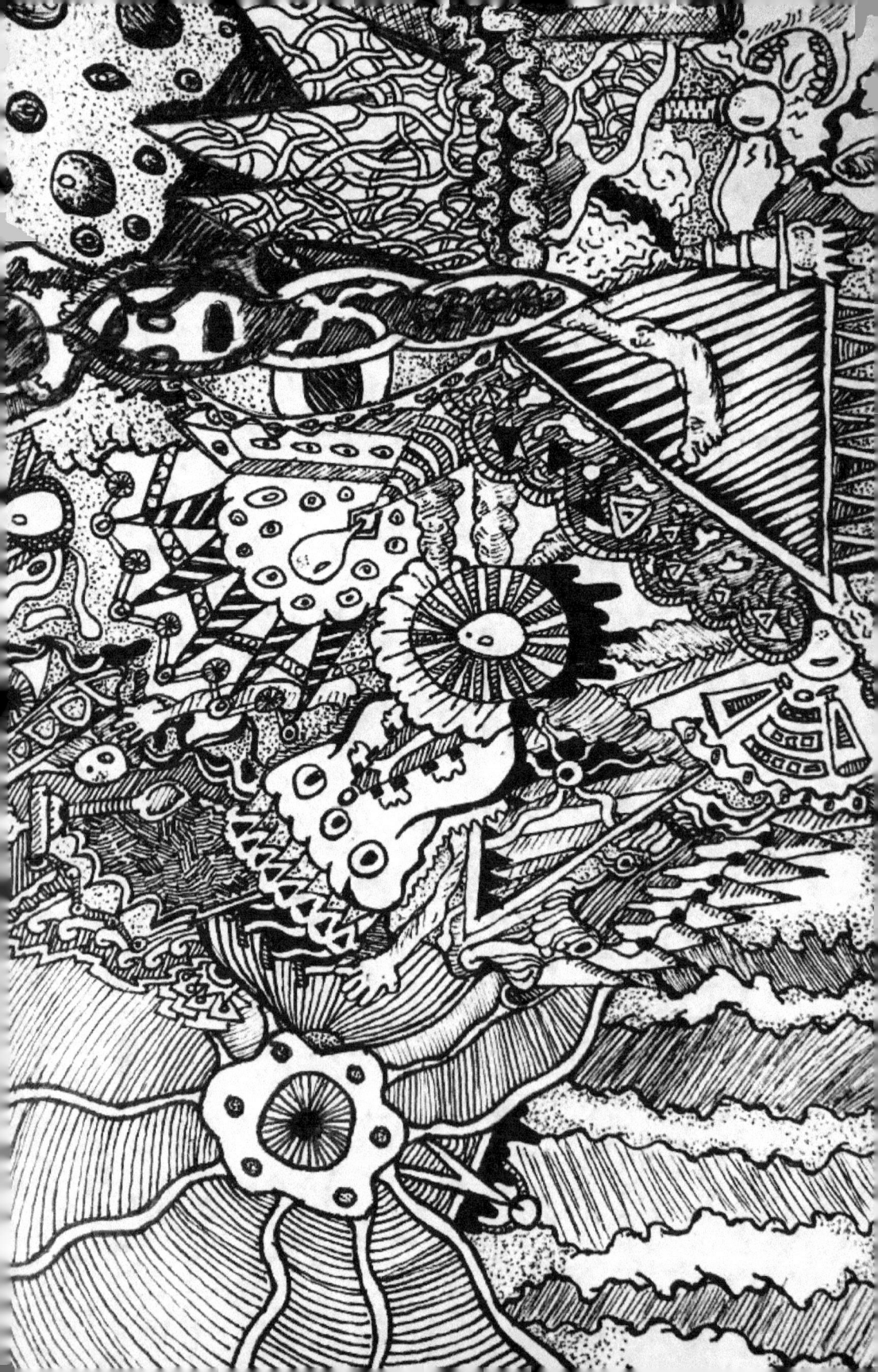

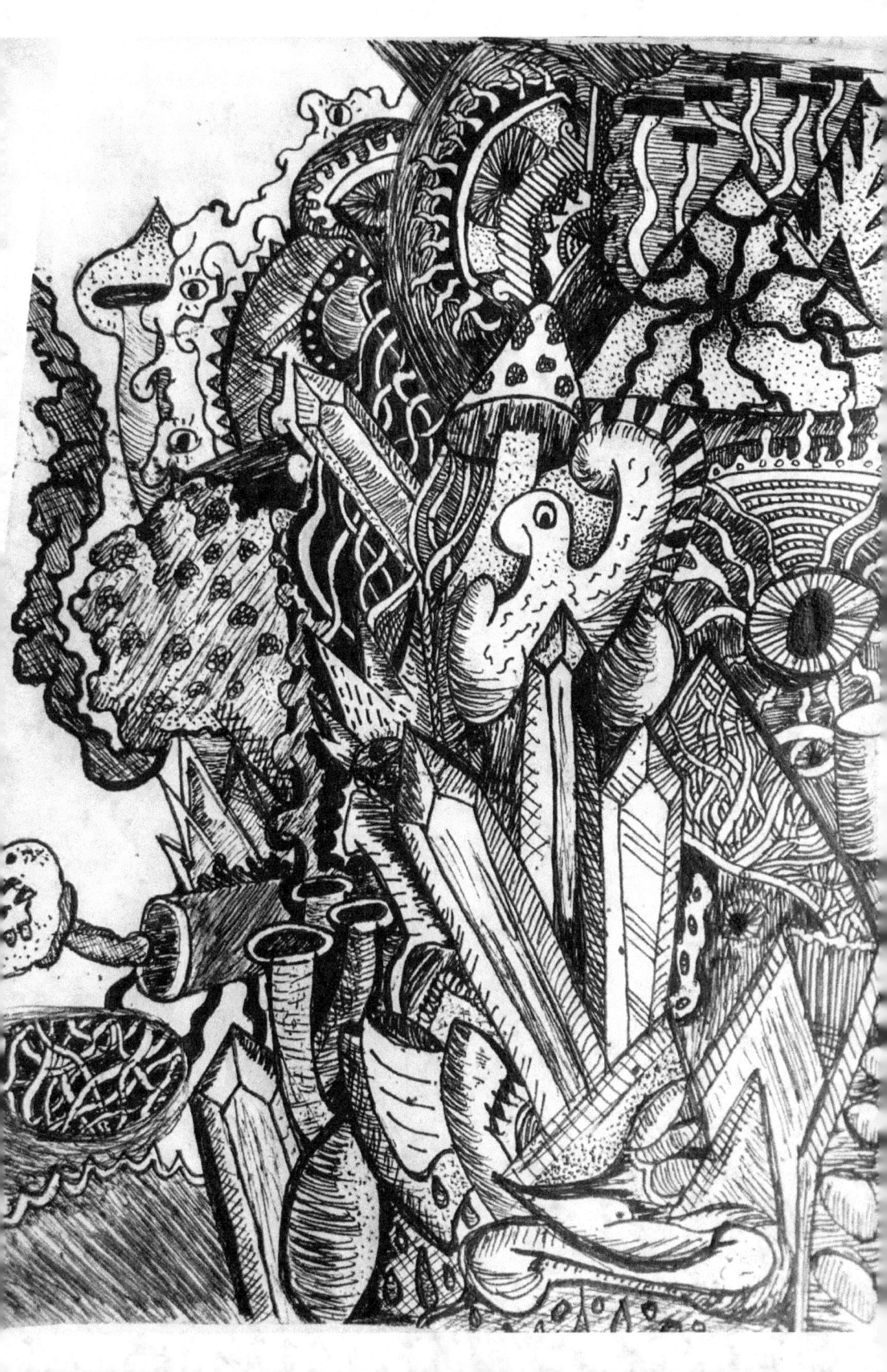

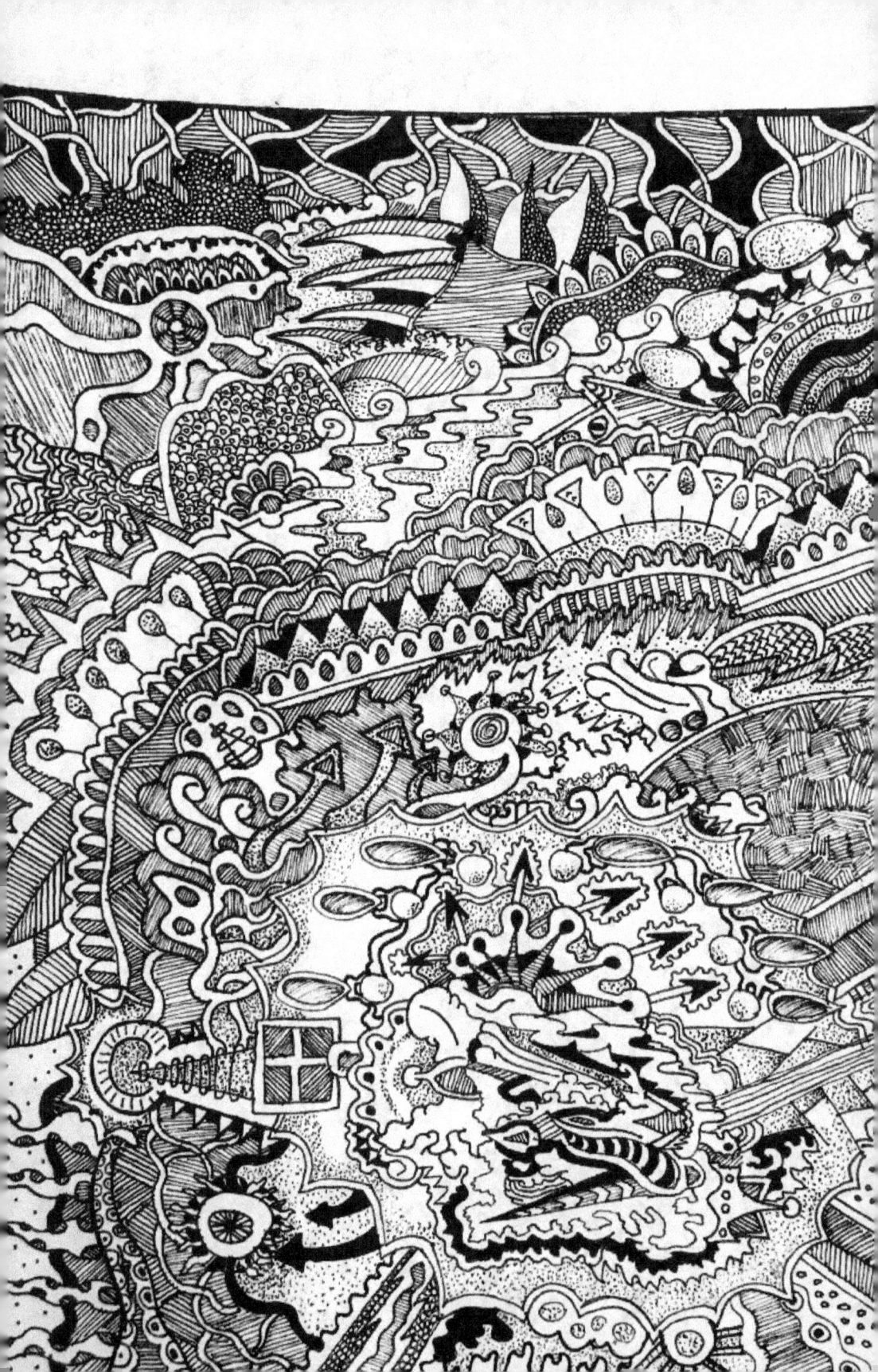

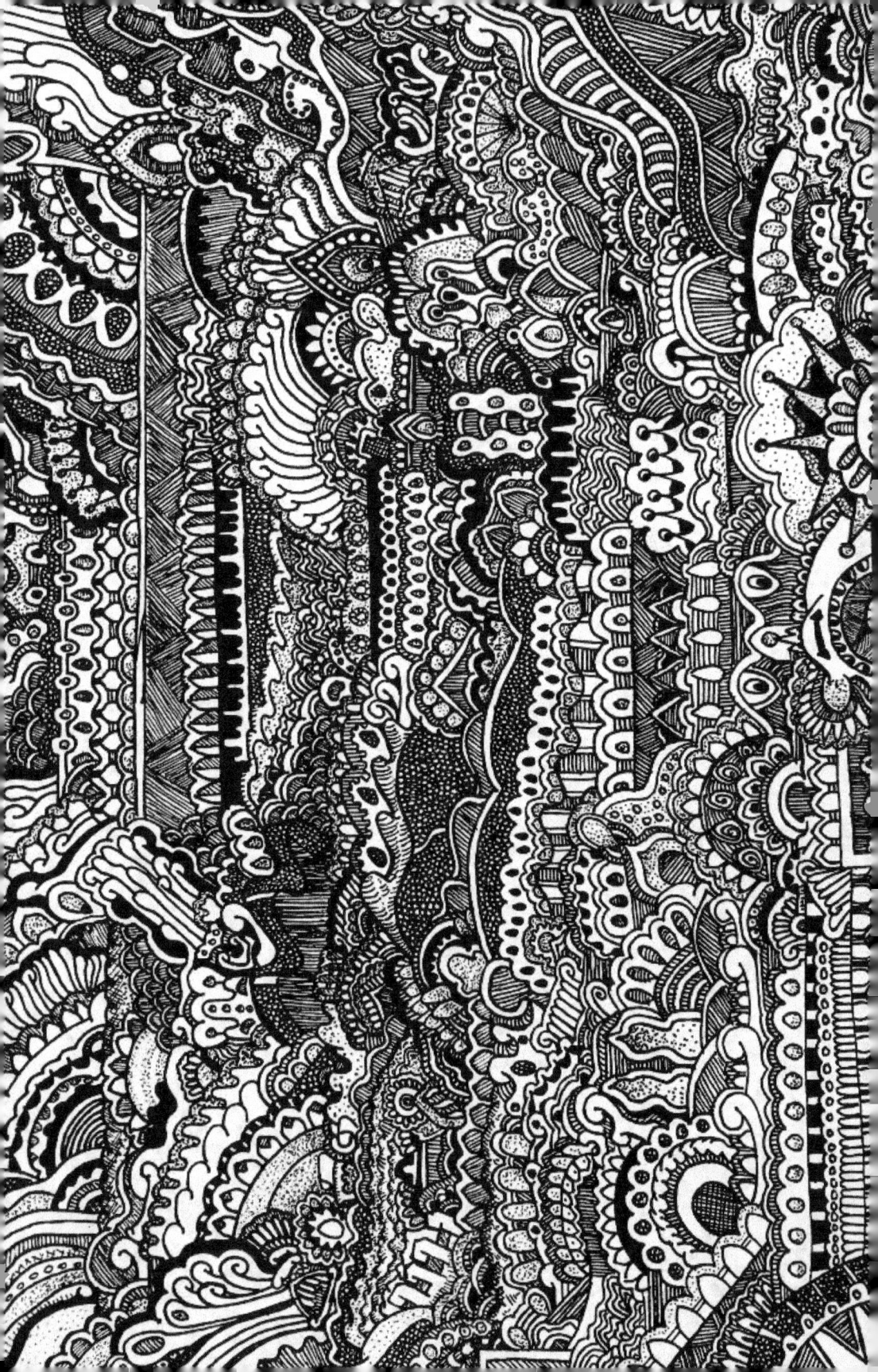

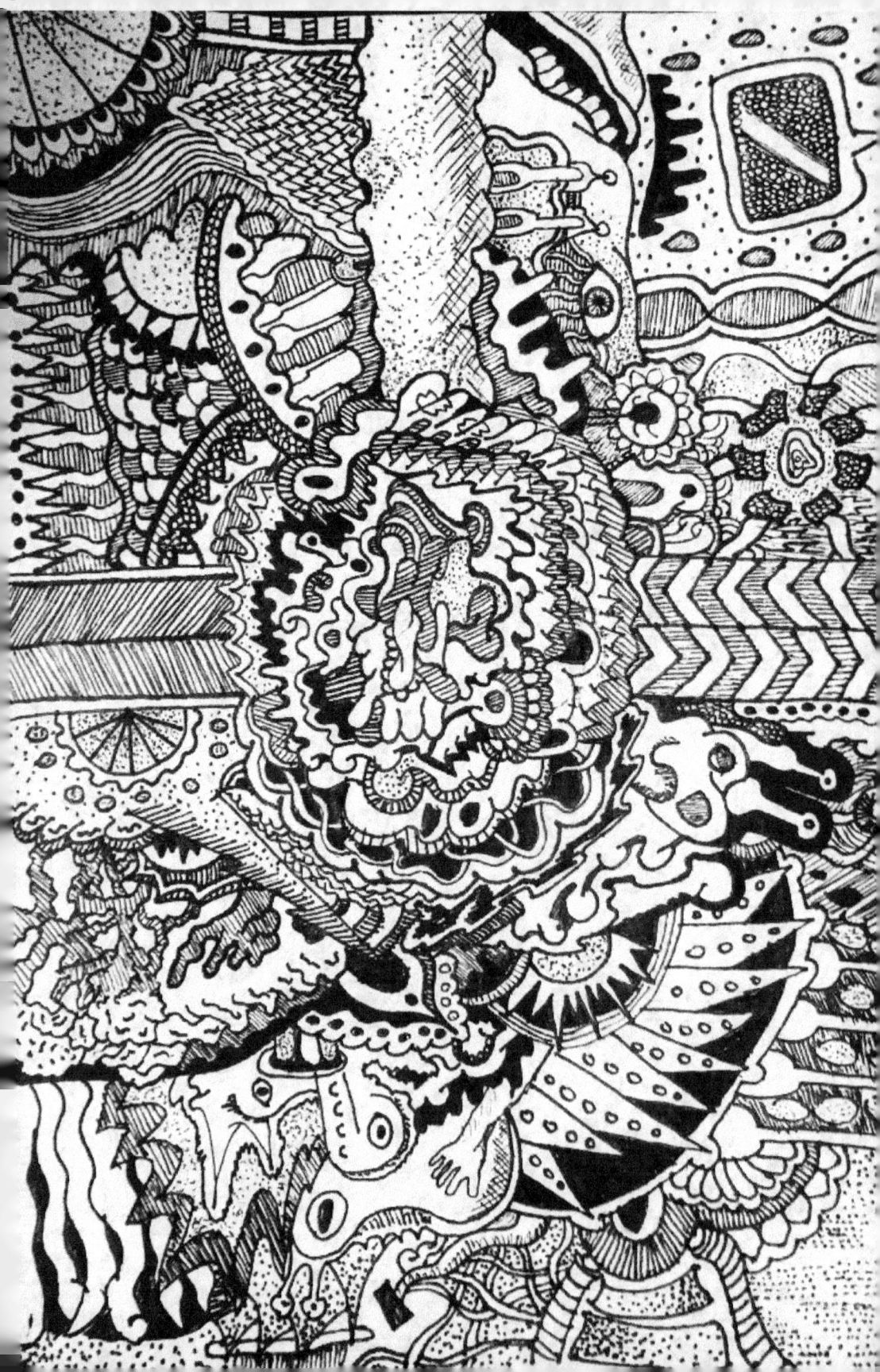

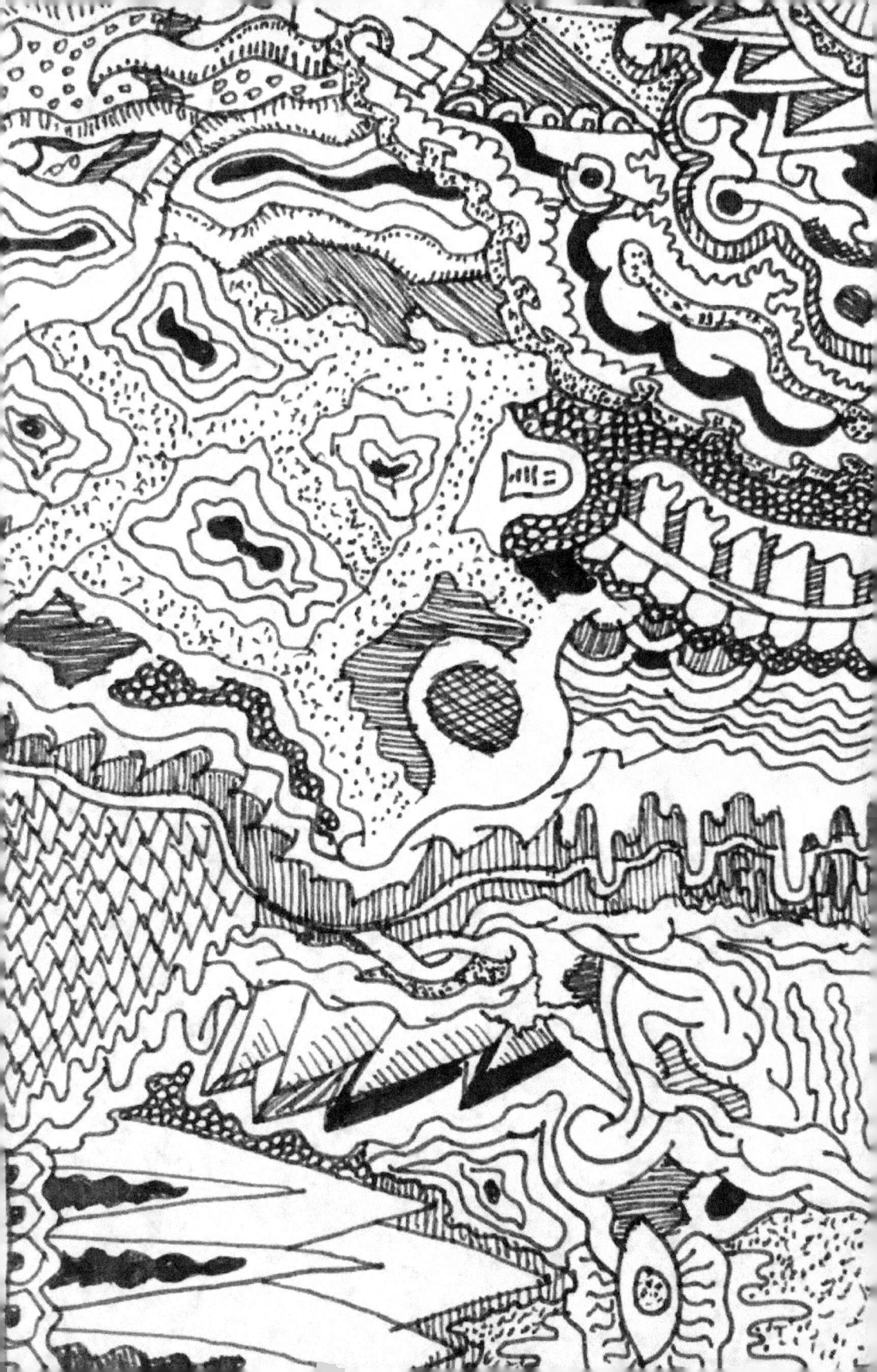

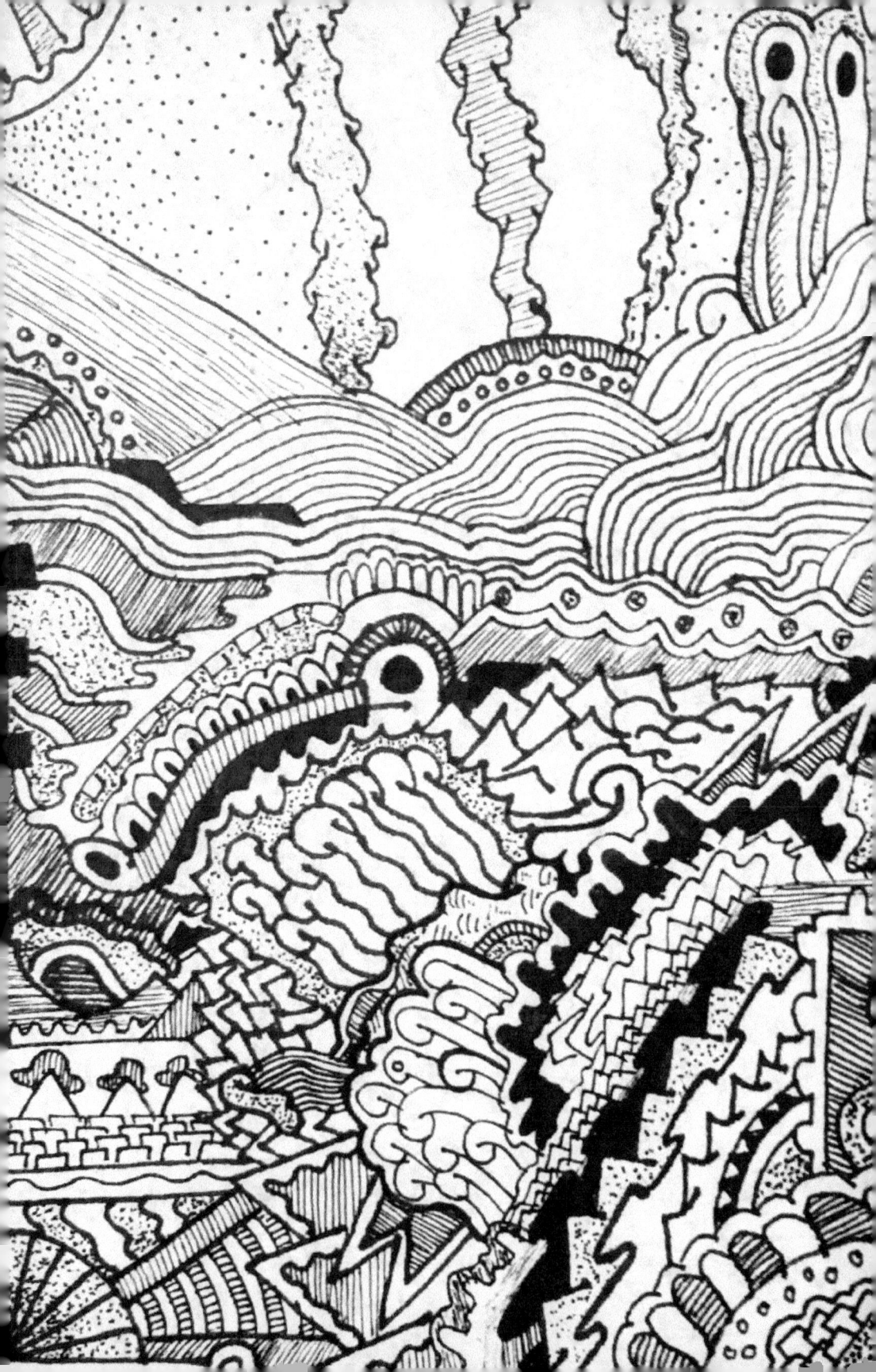

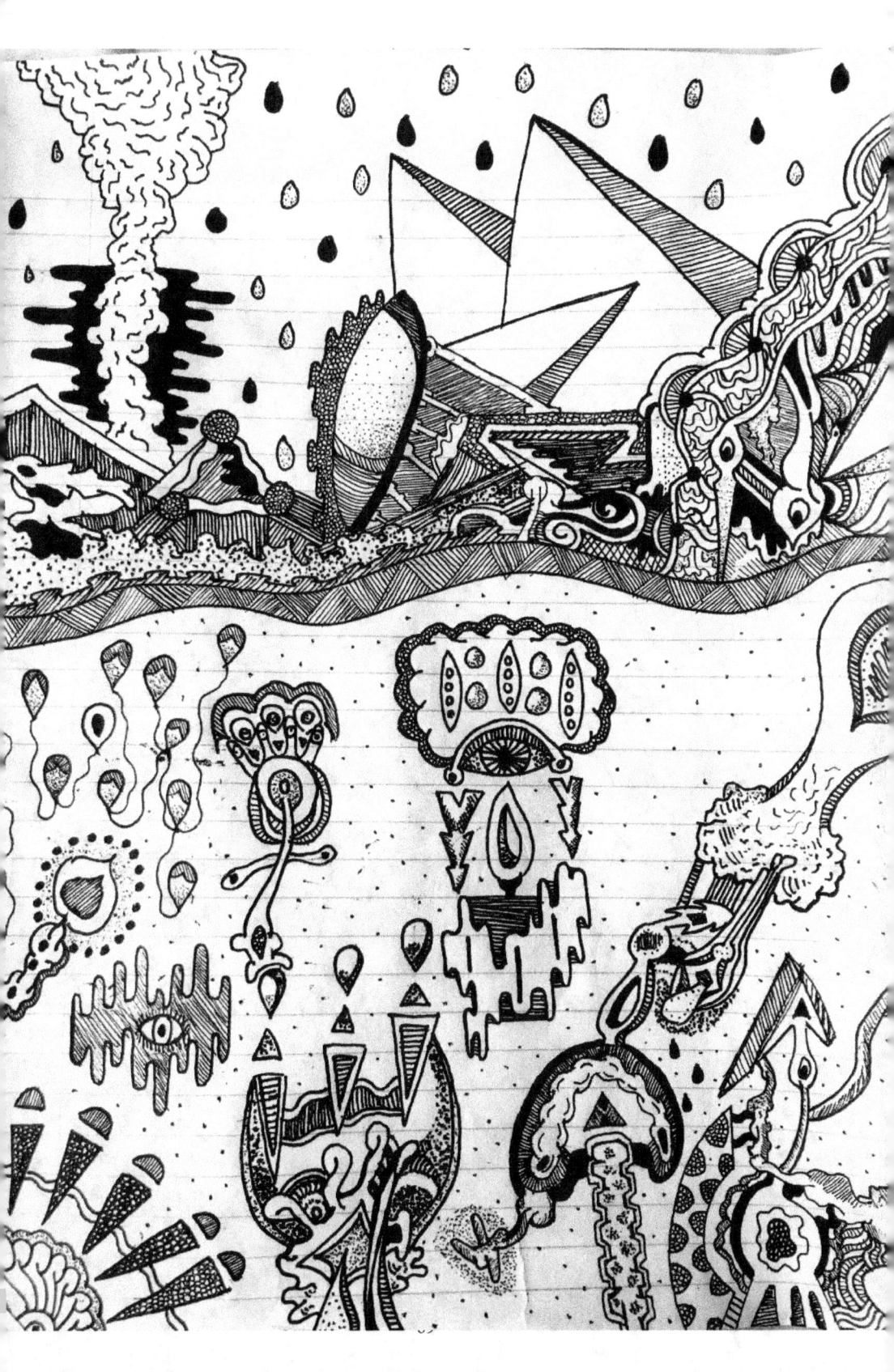

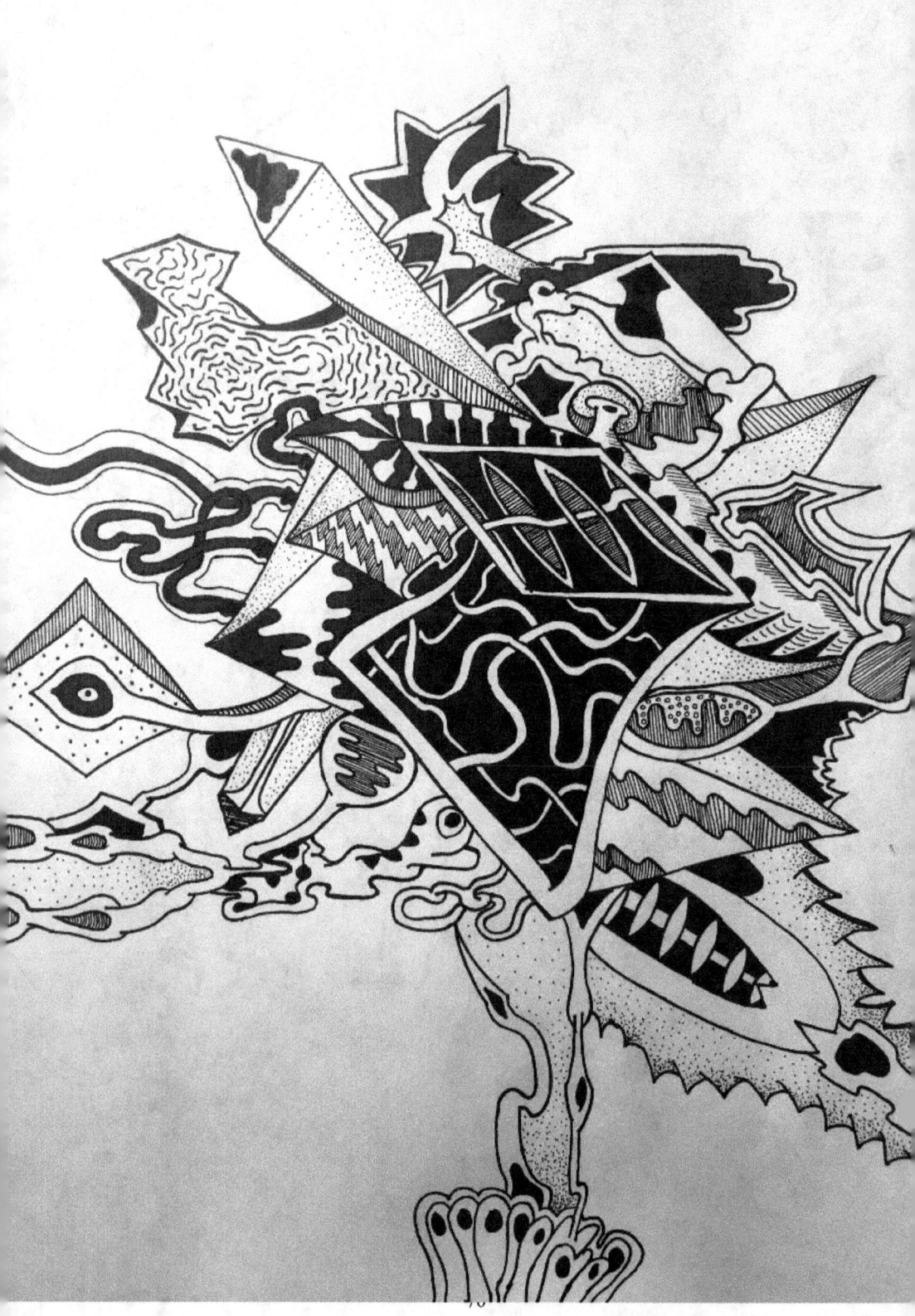

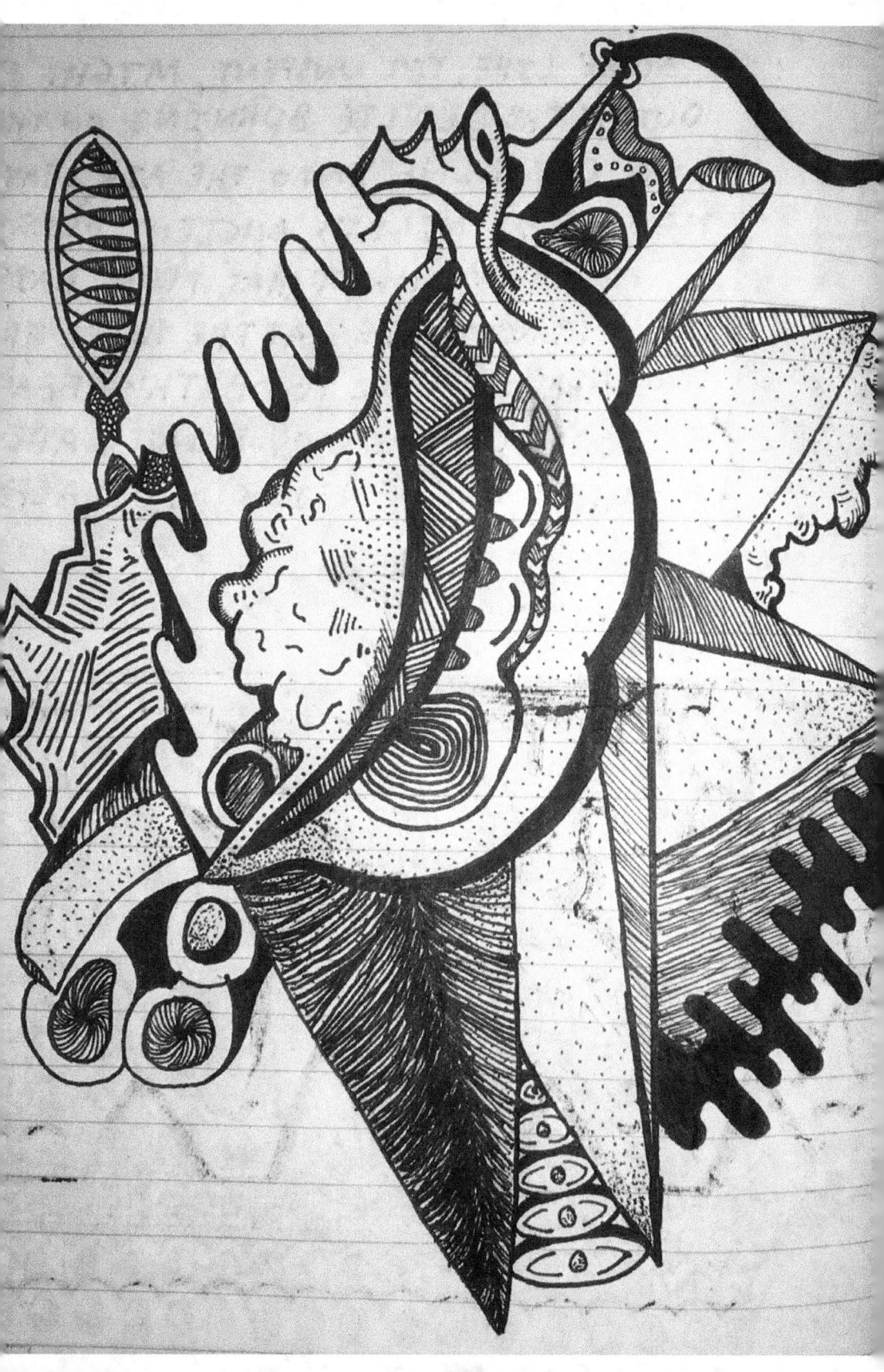

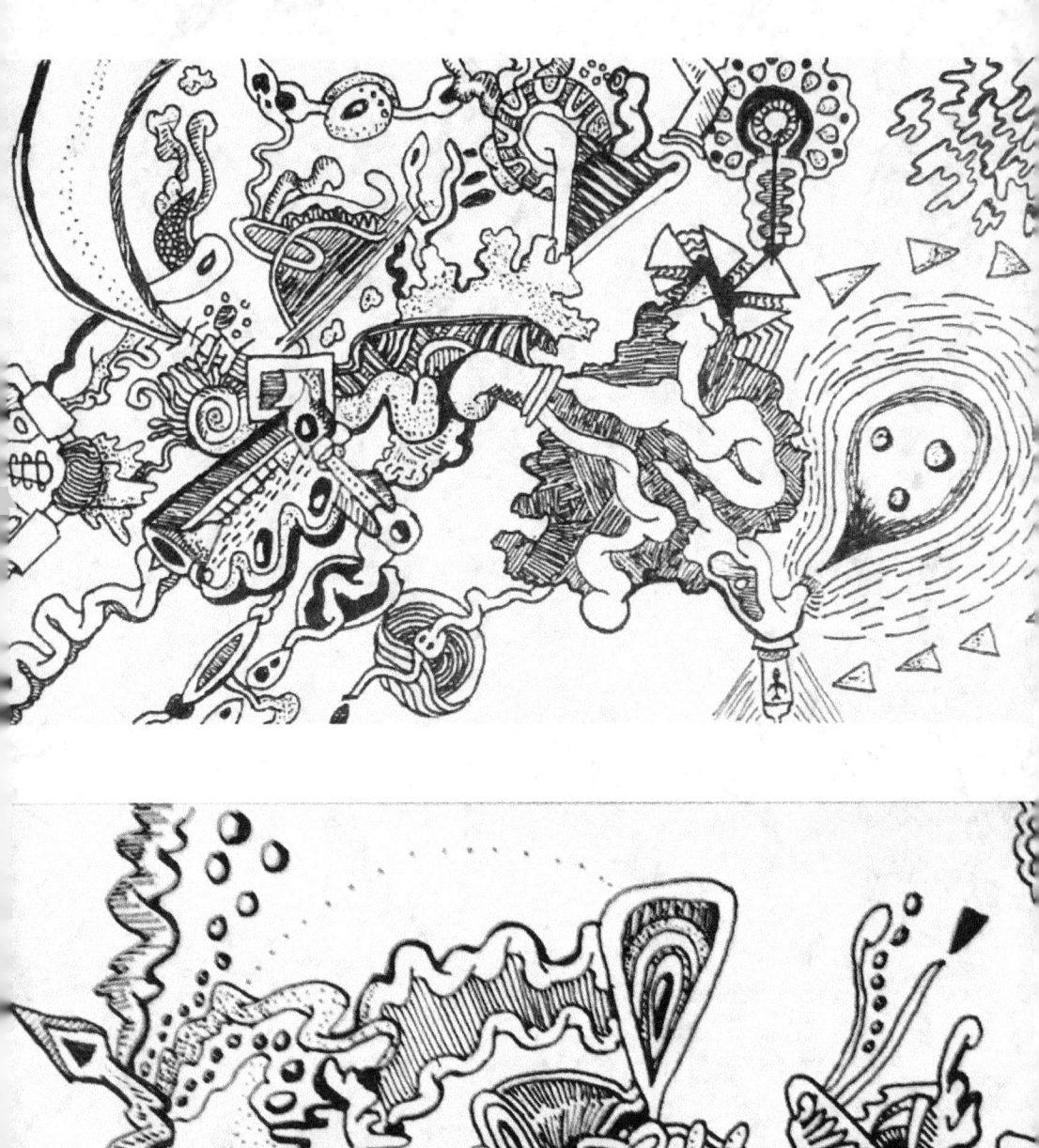

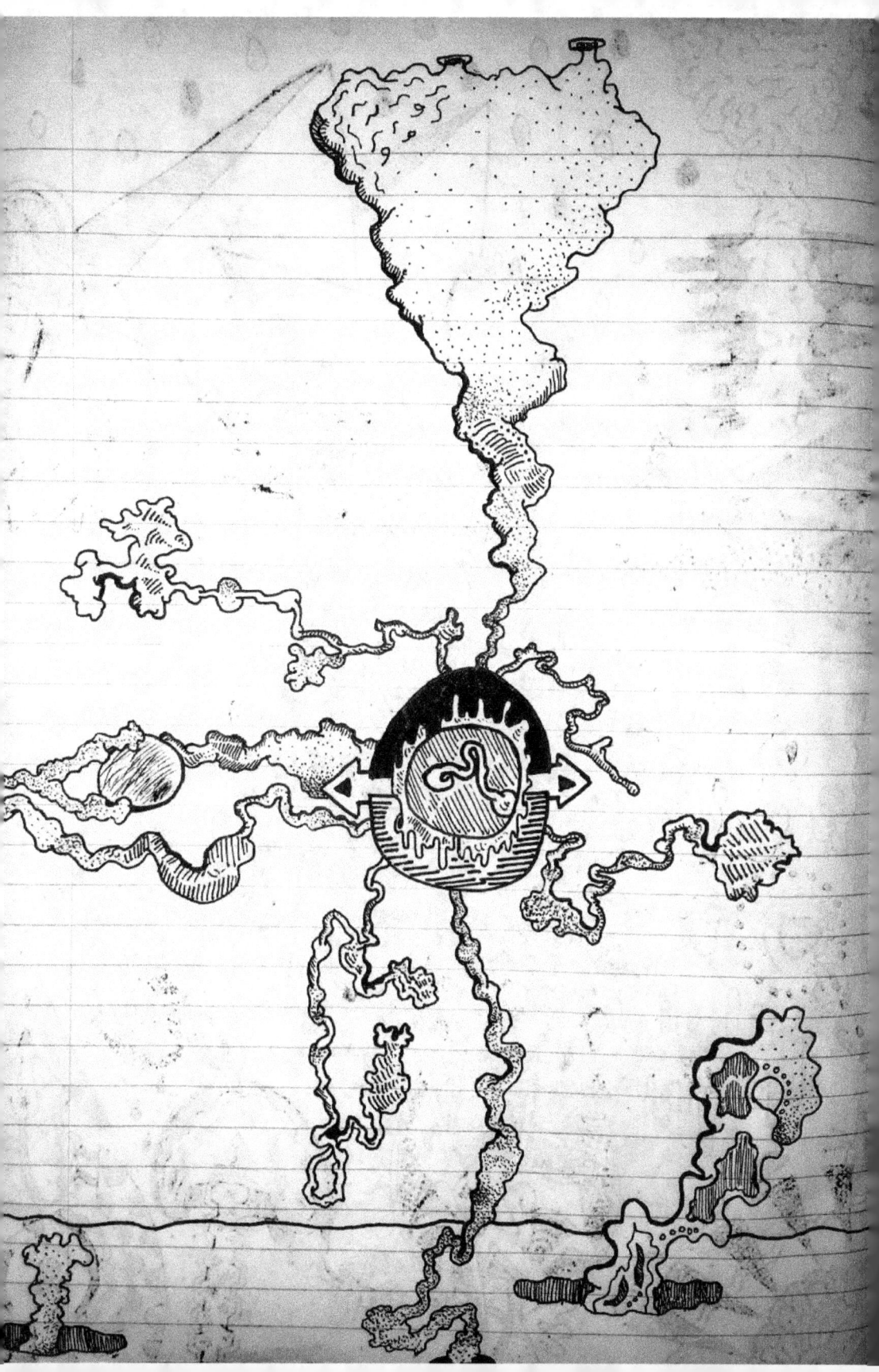

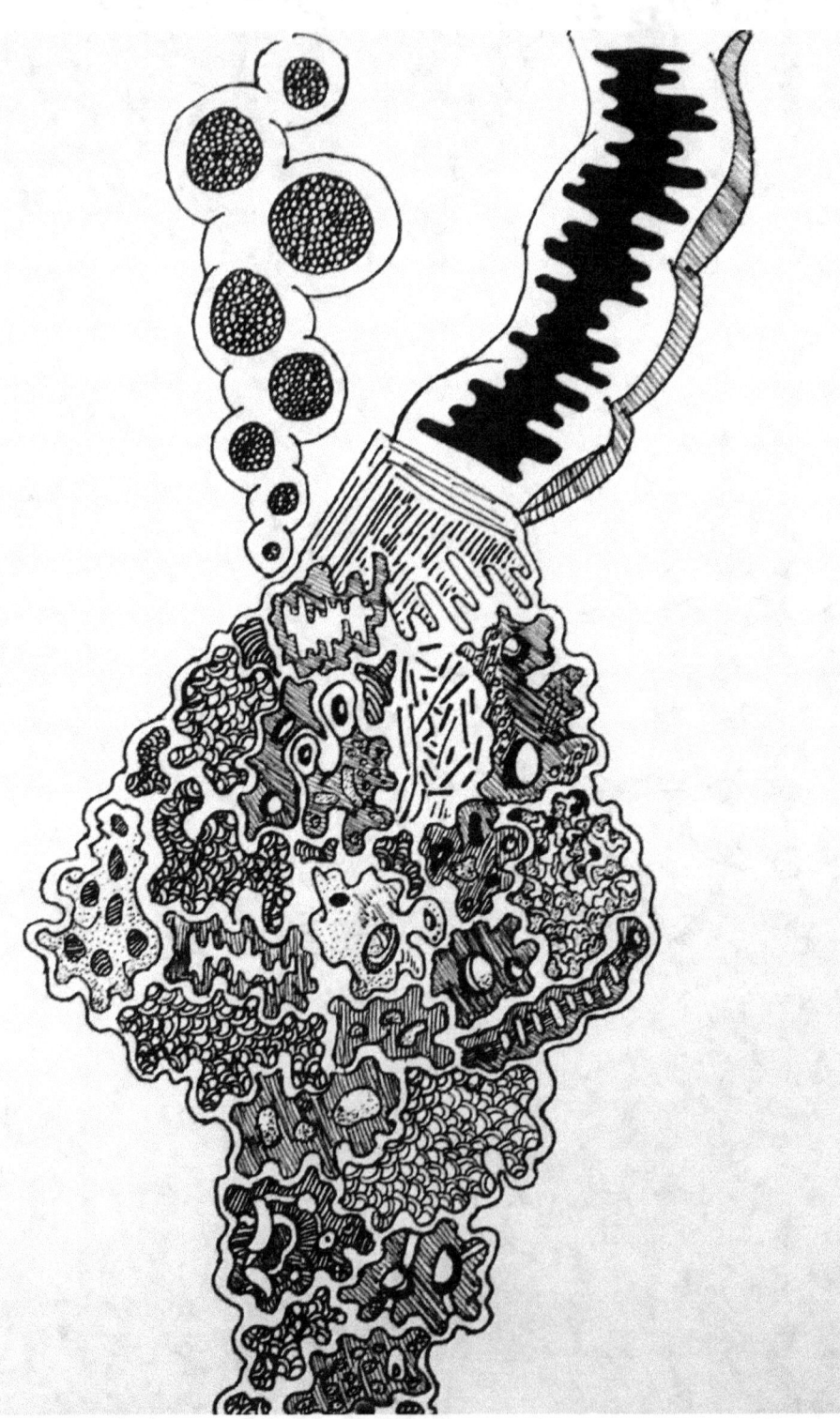

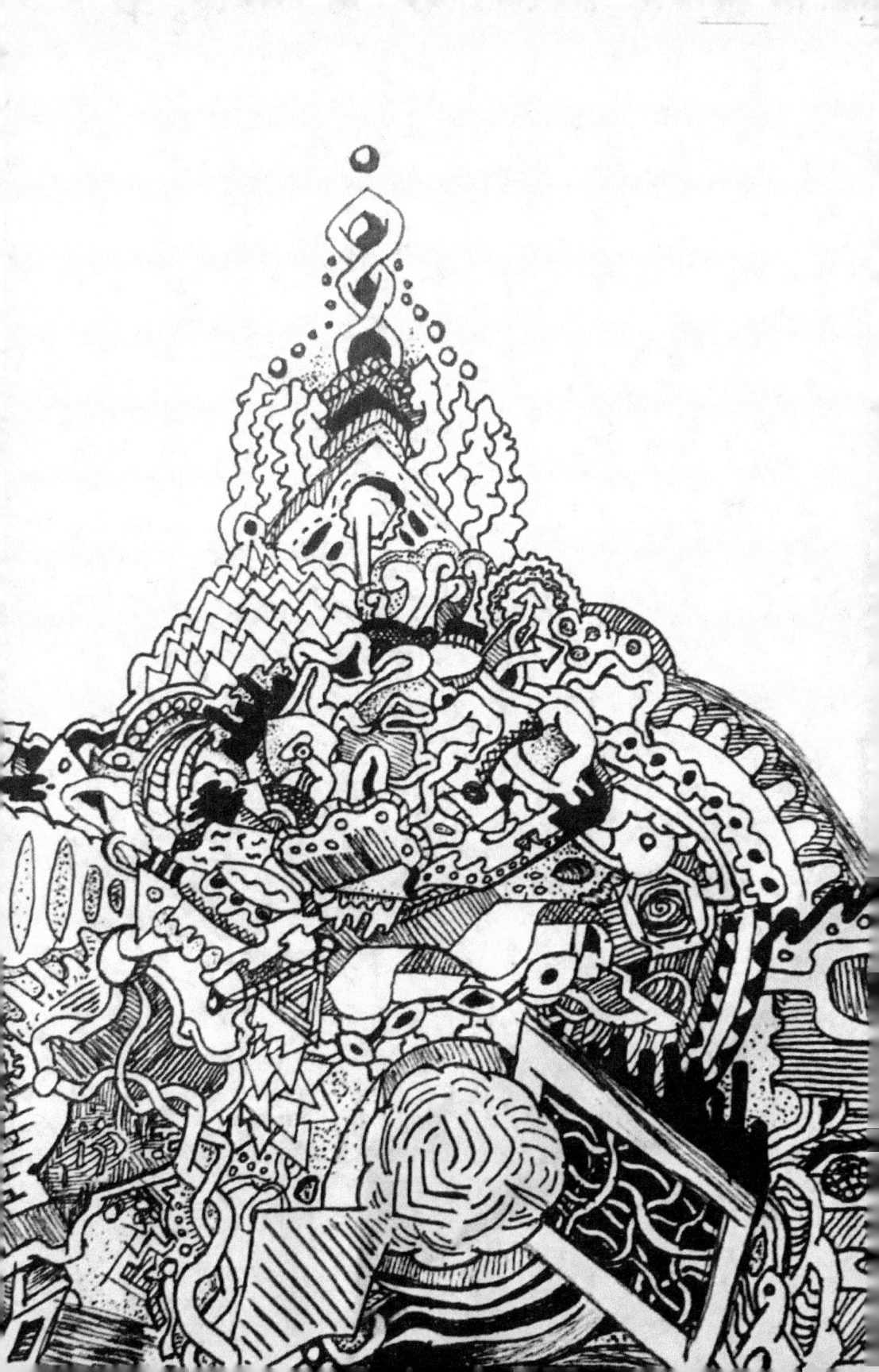

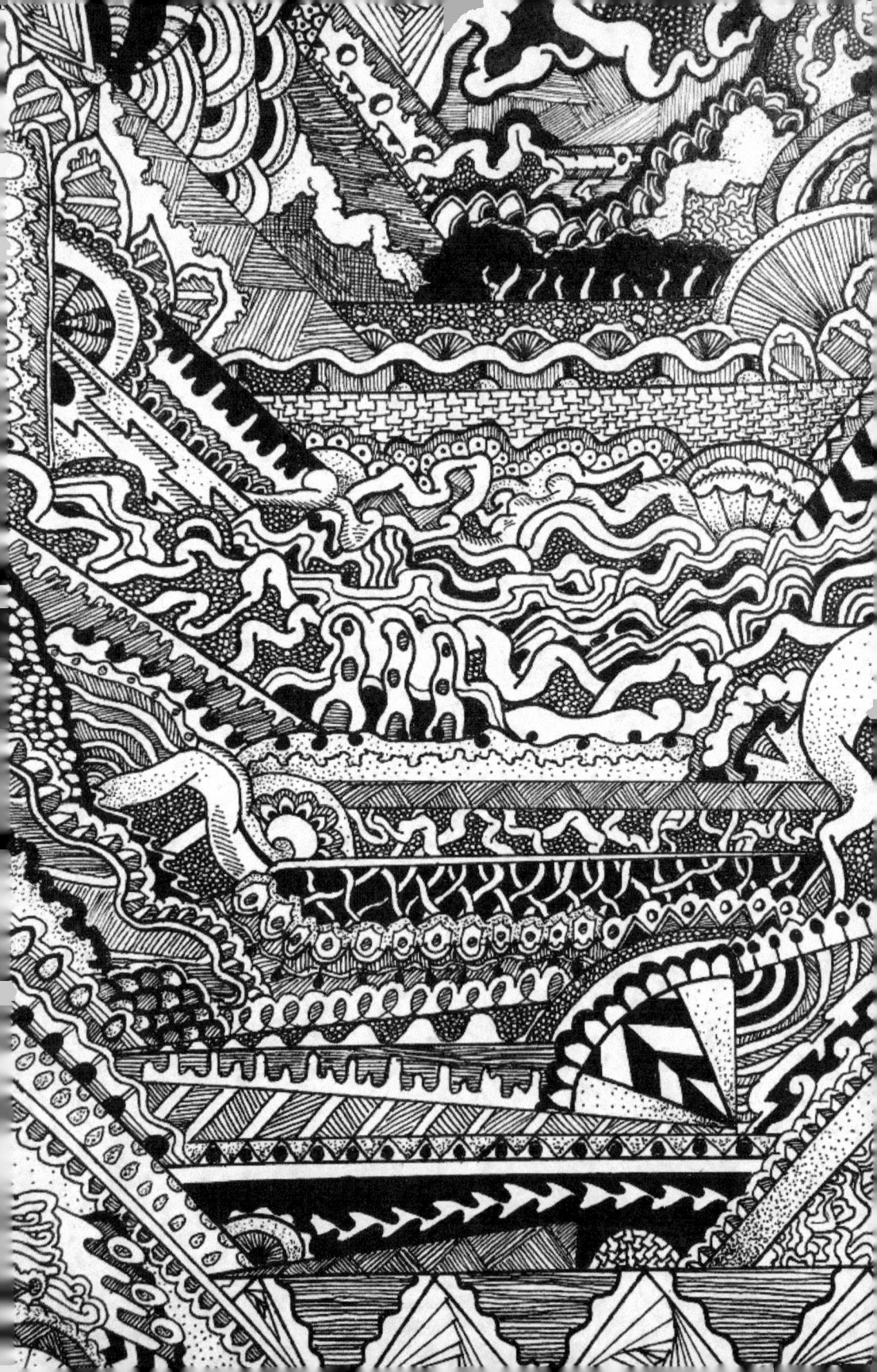

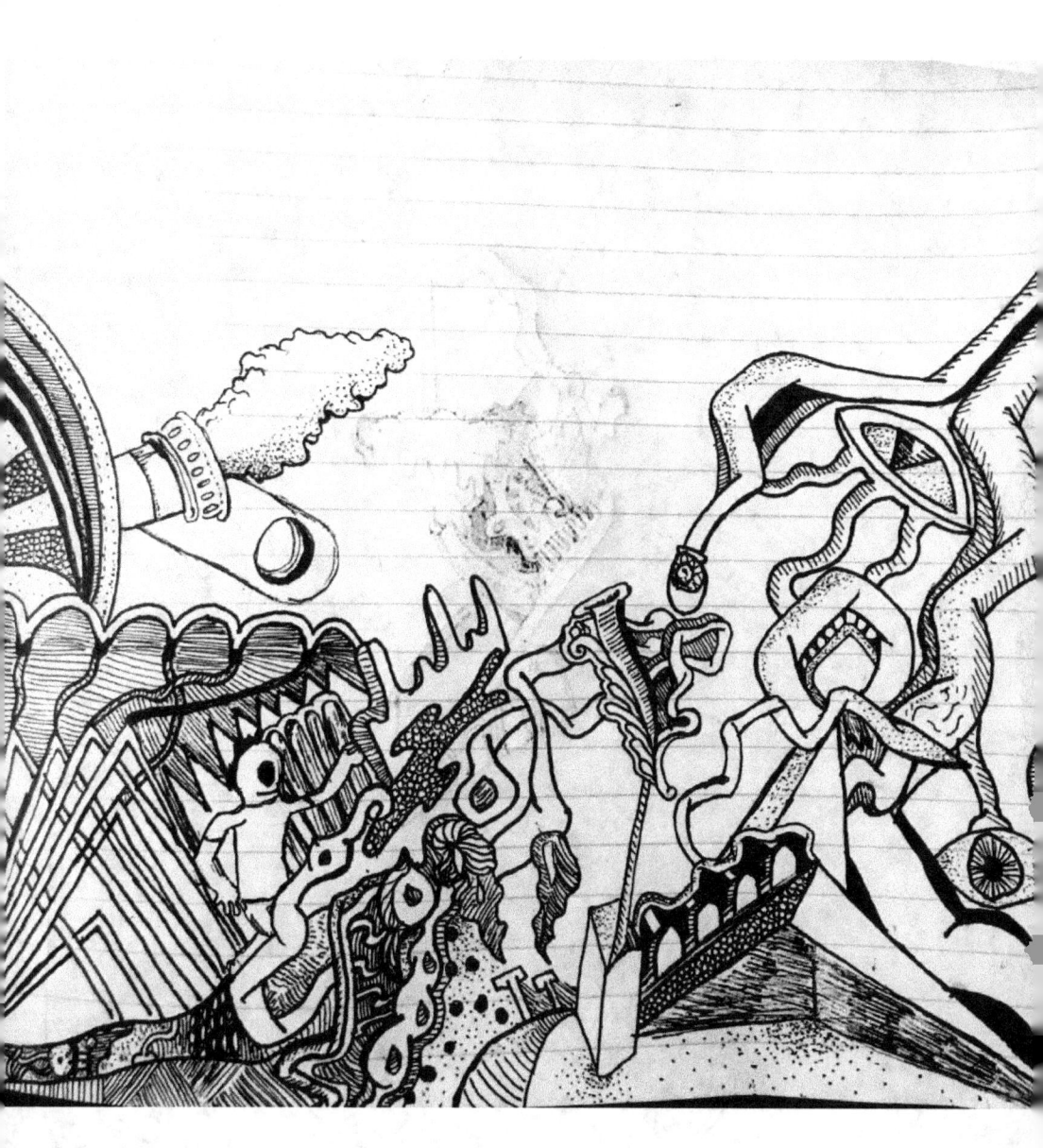

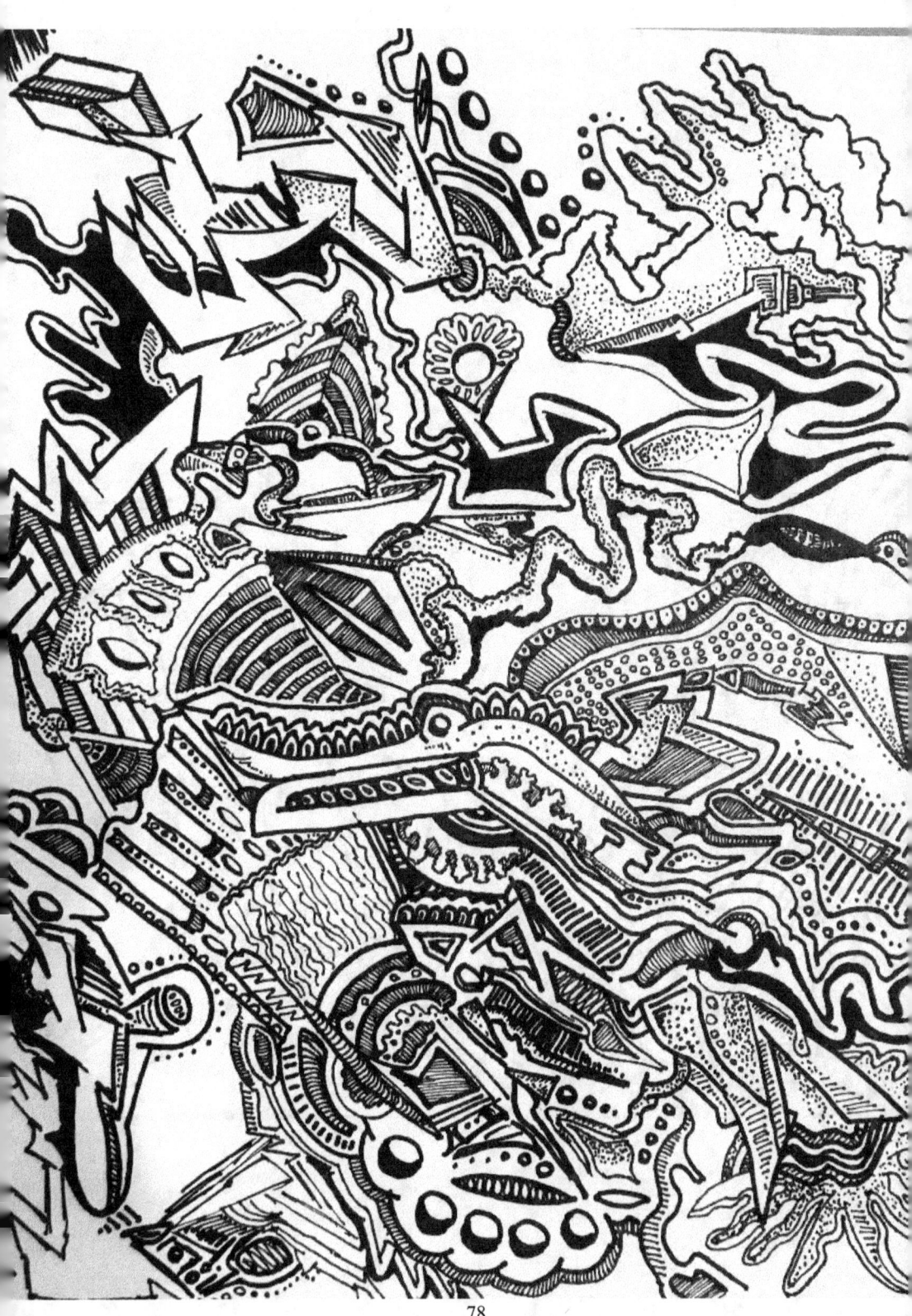

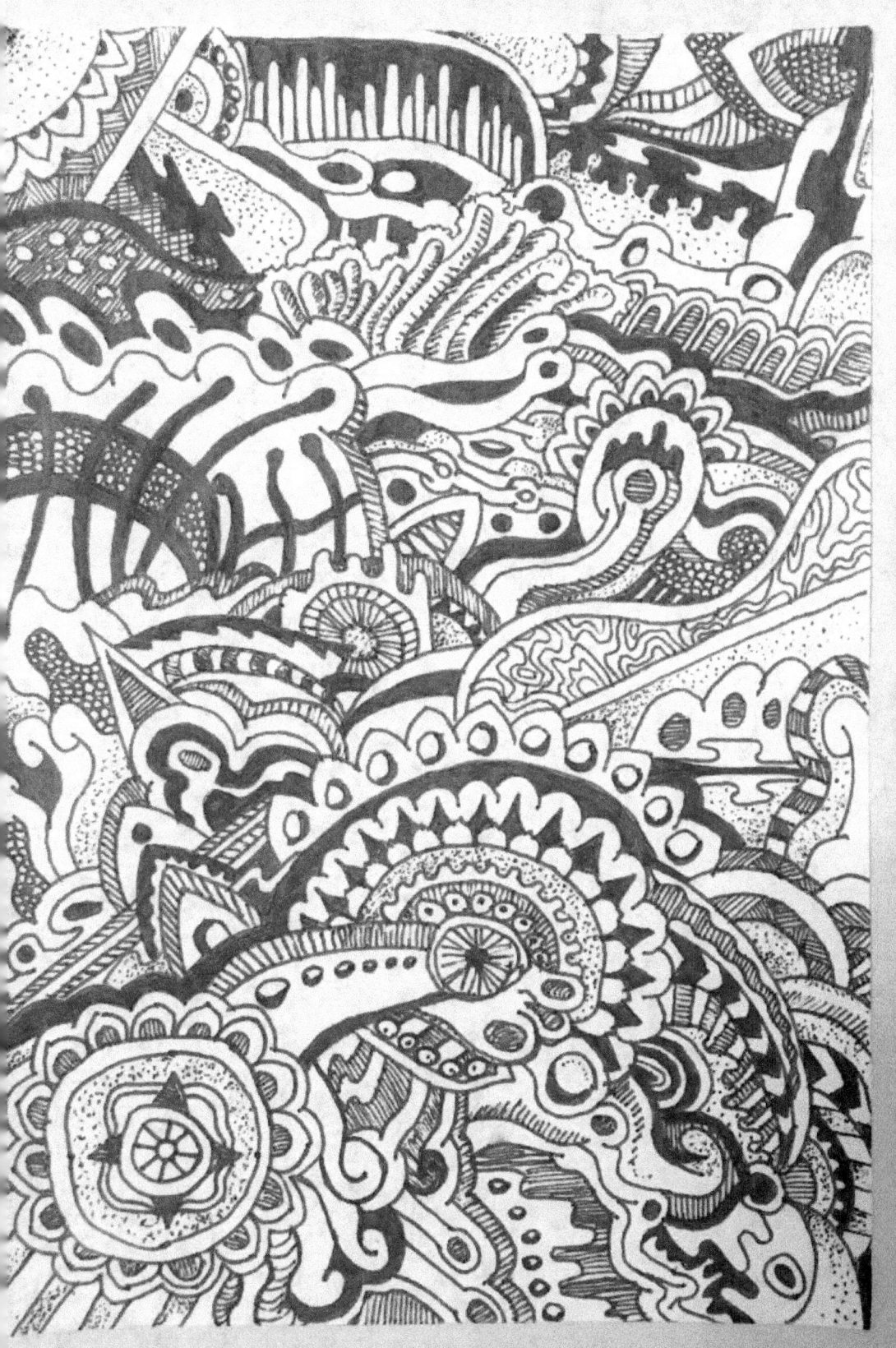

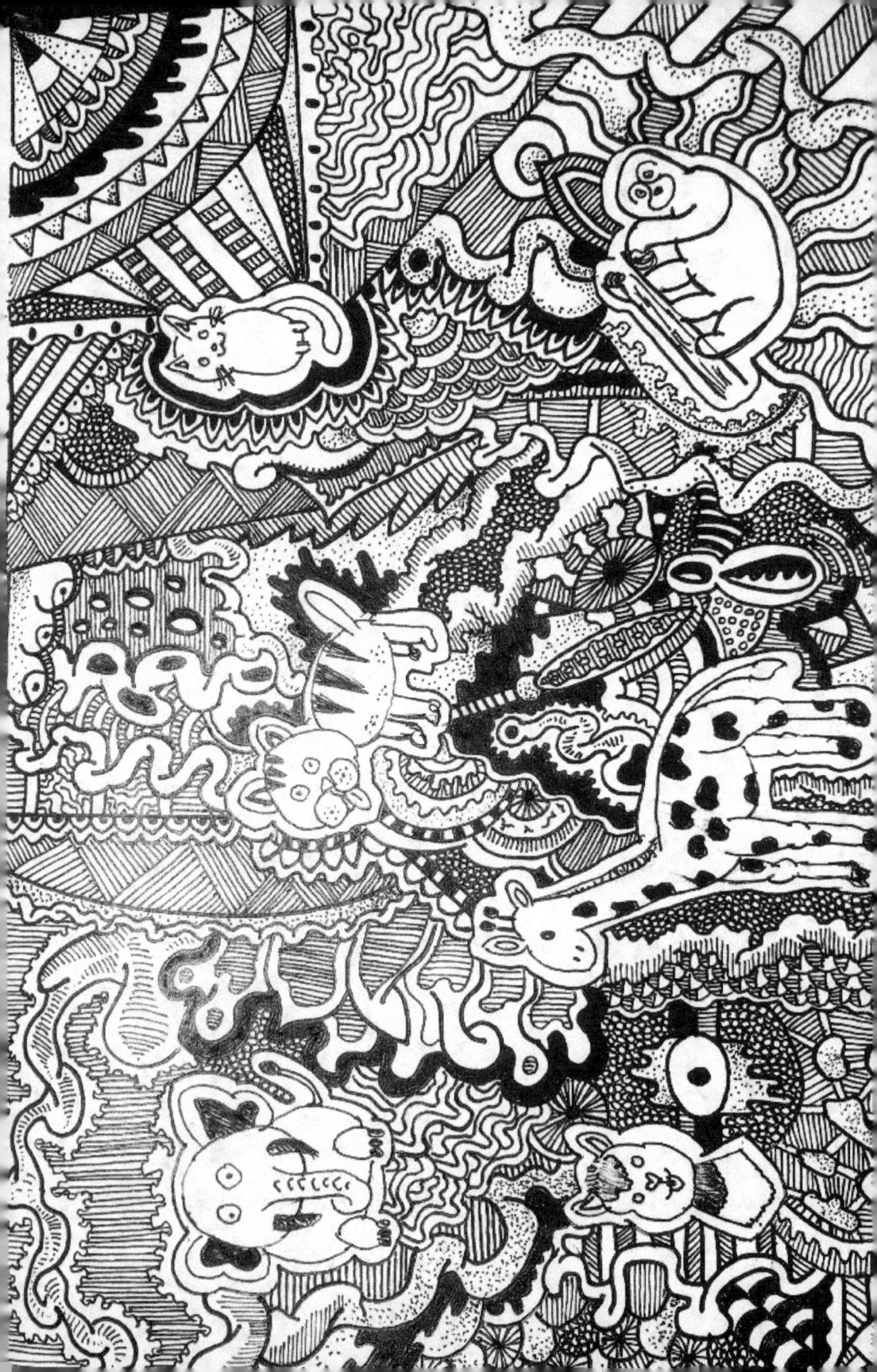

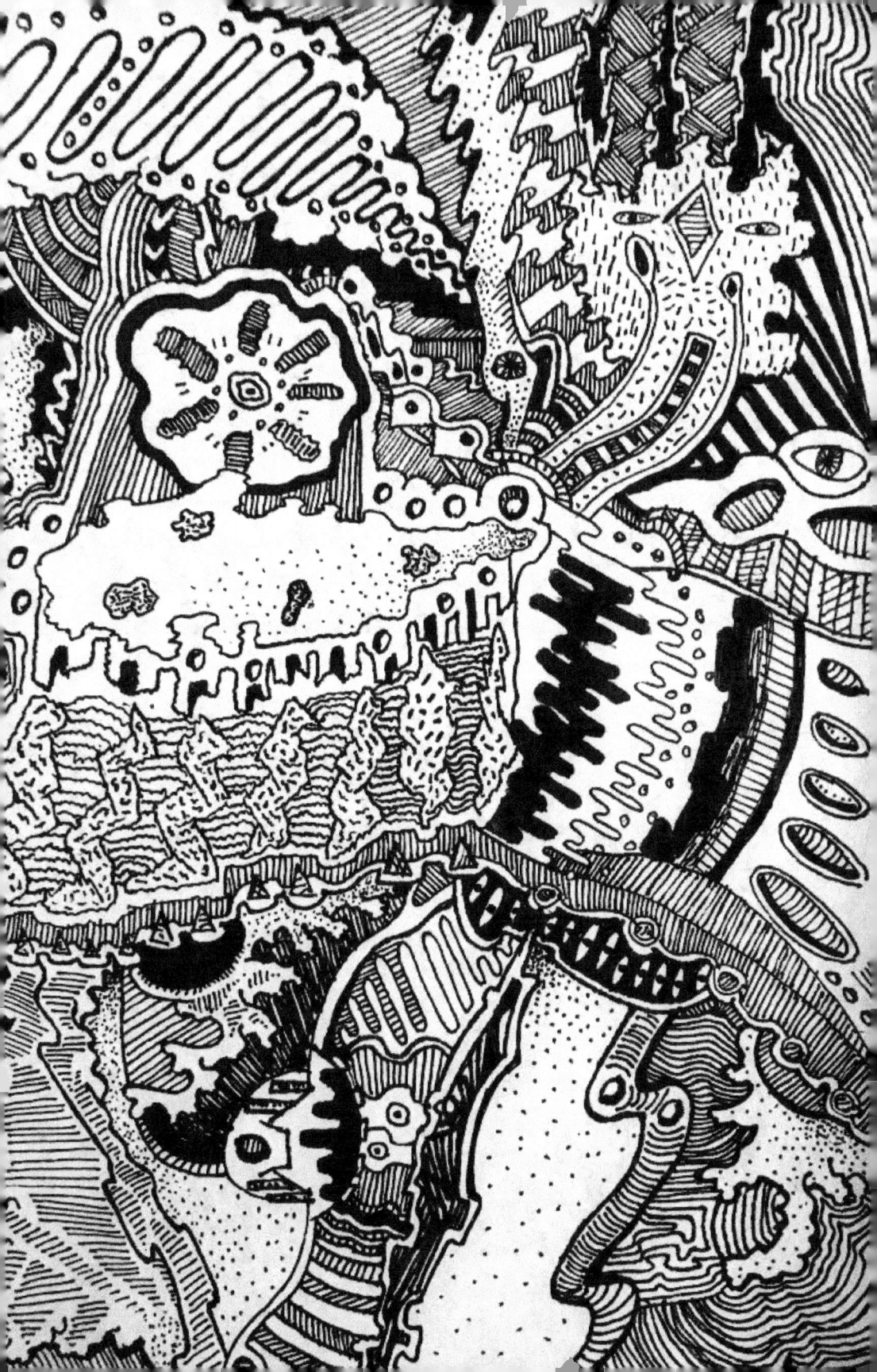

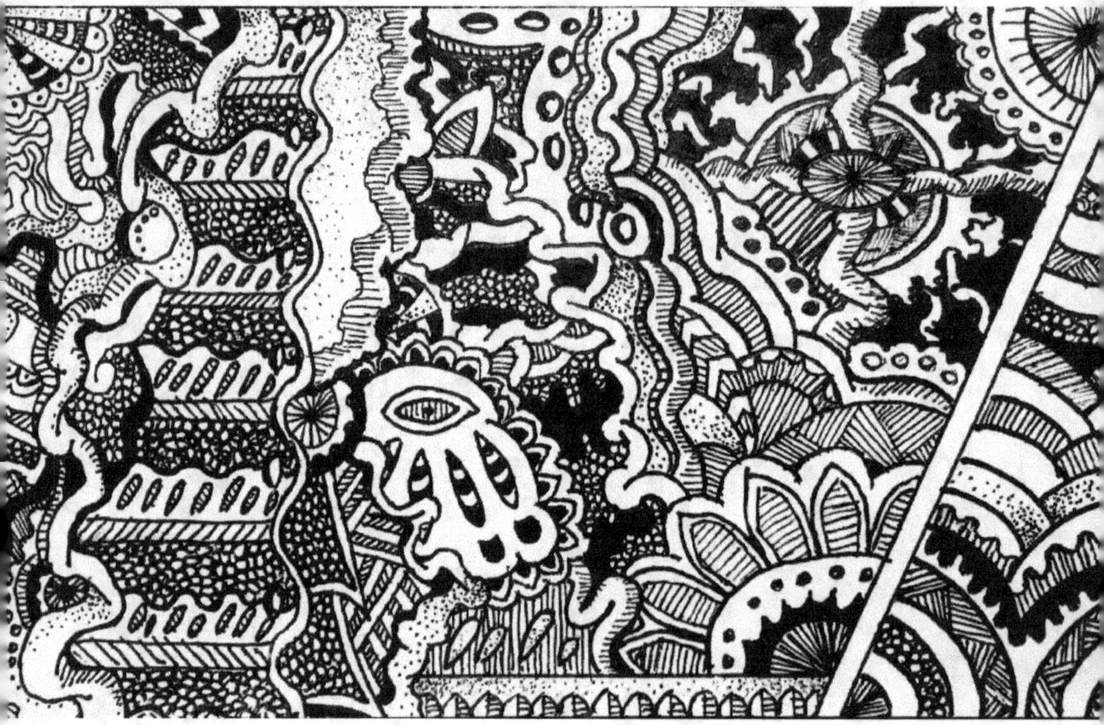

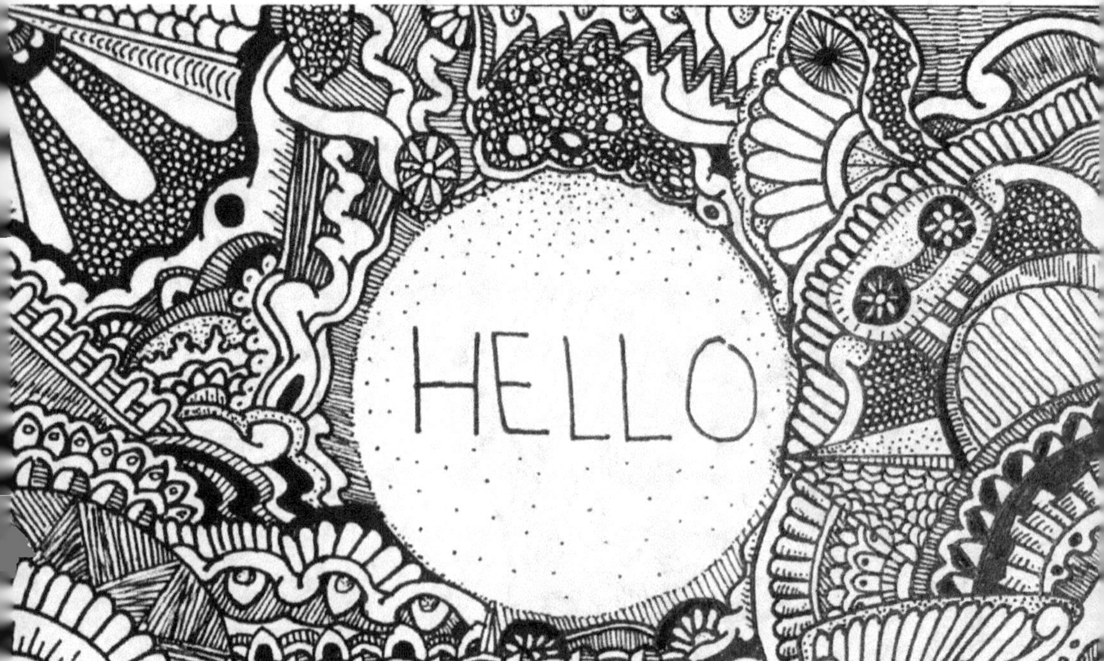

HELLO

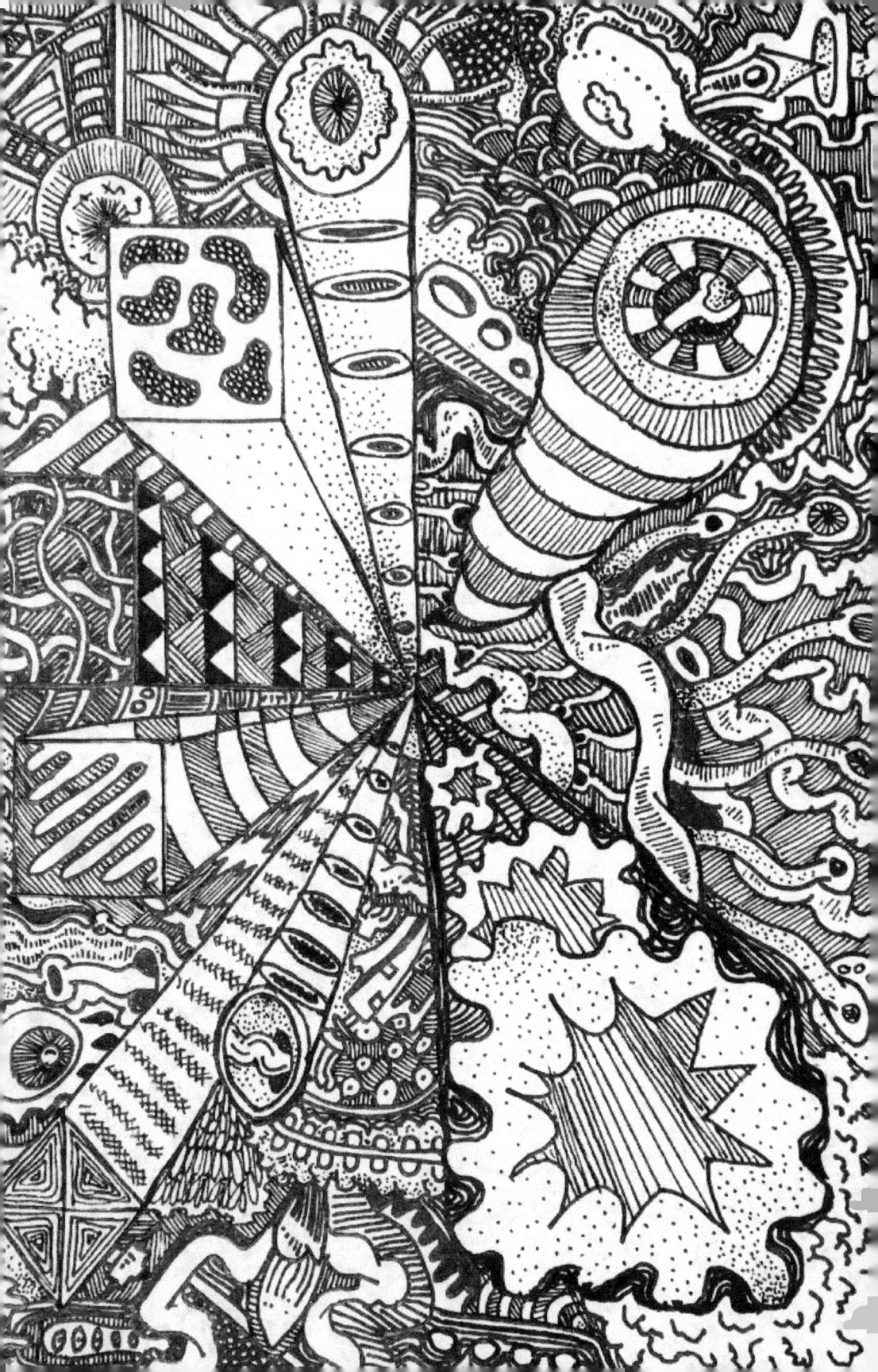

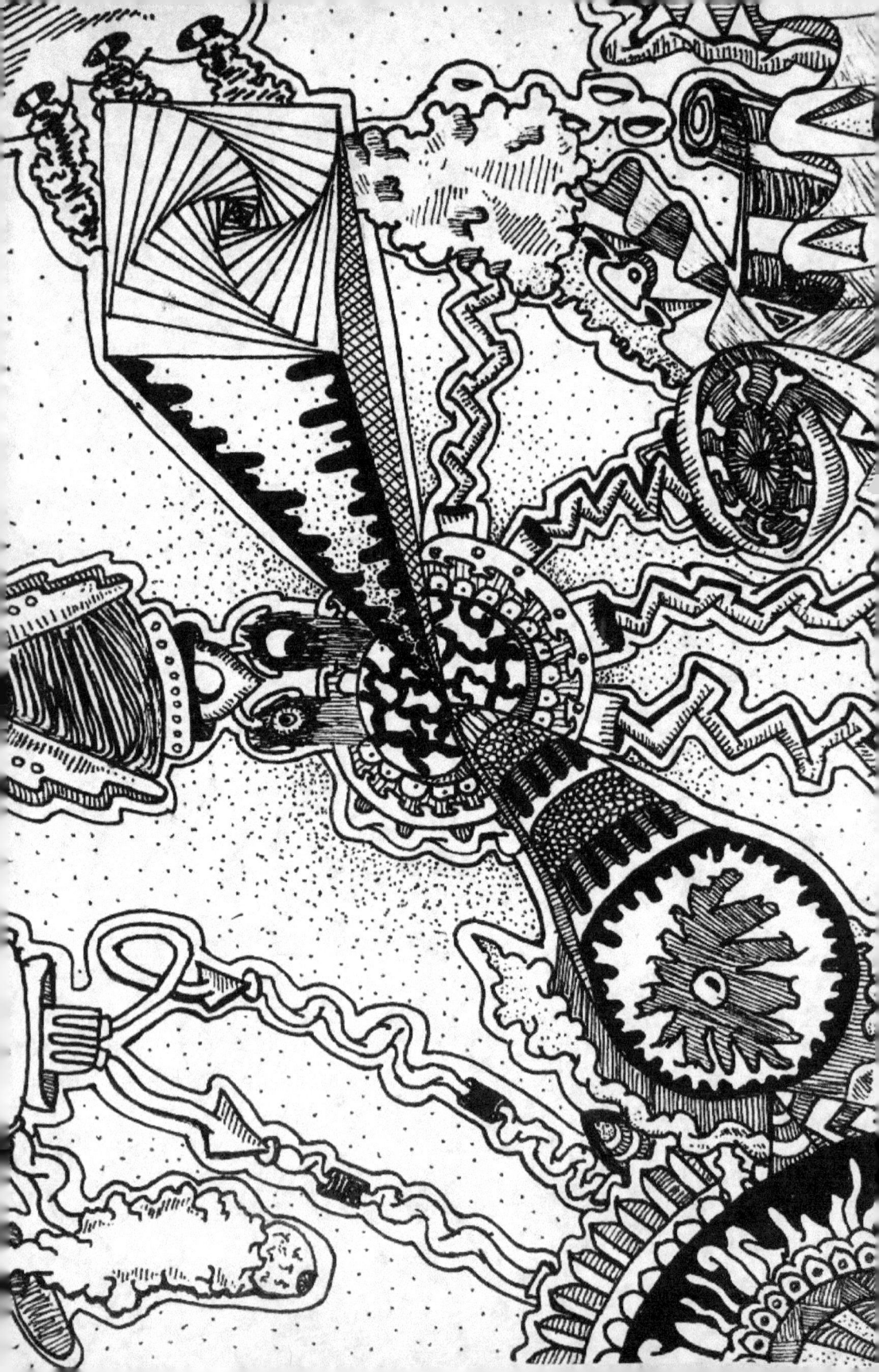

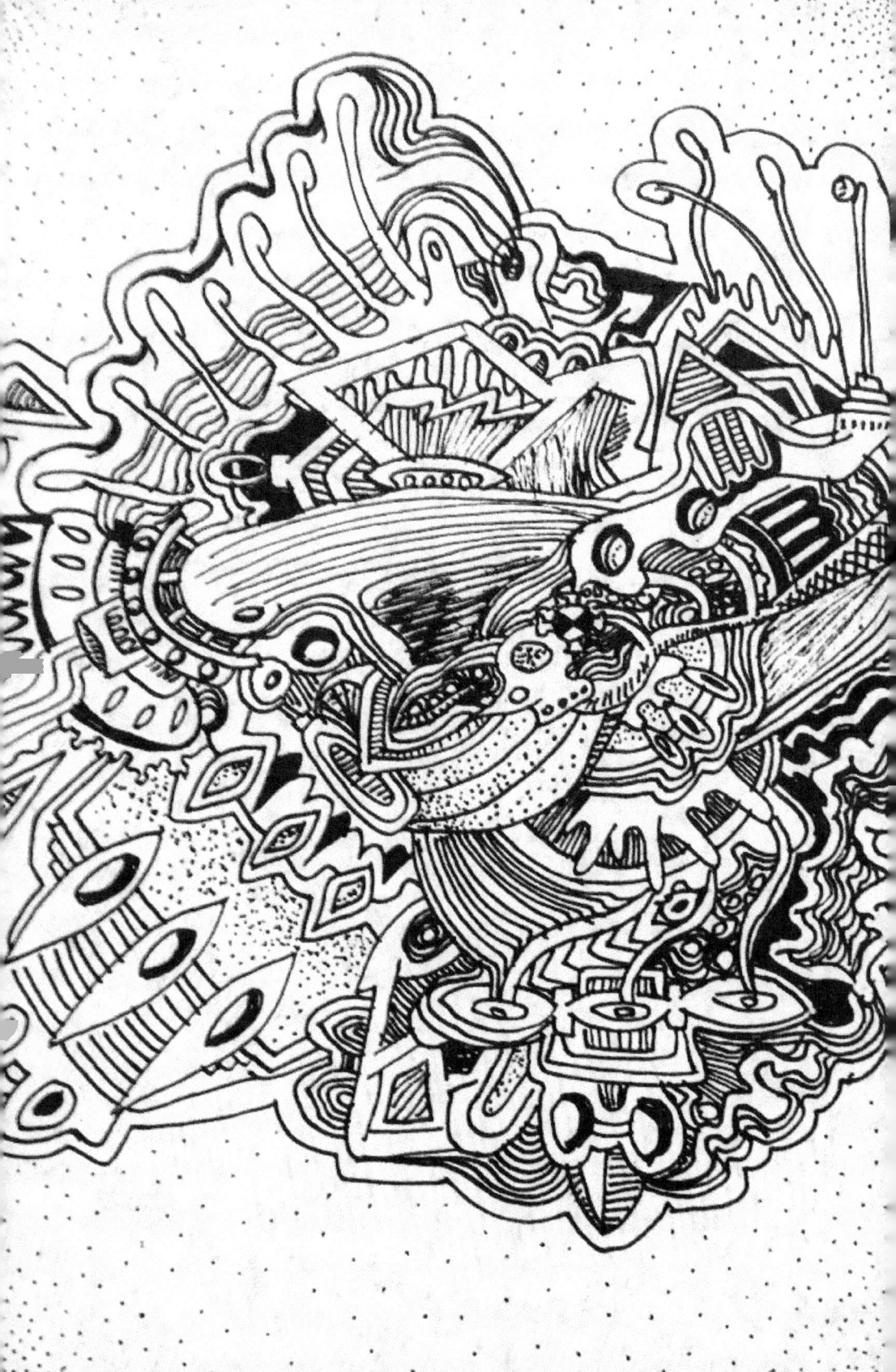

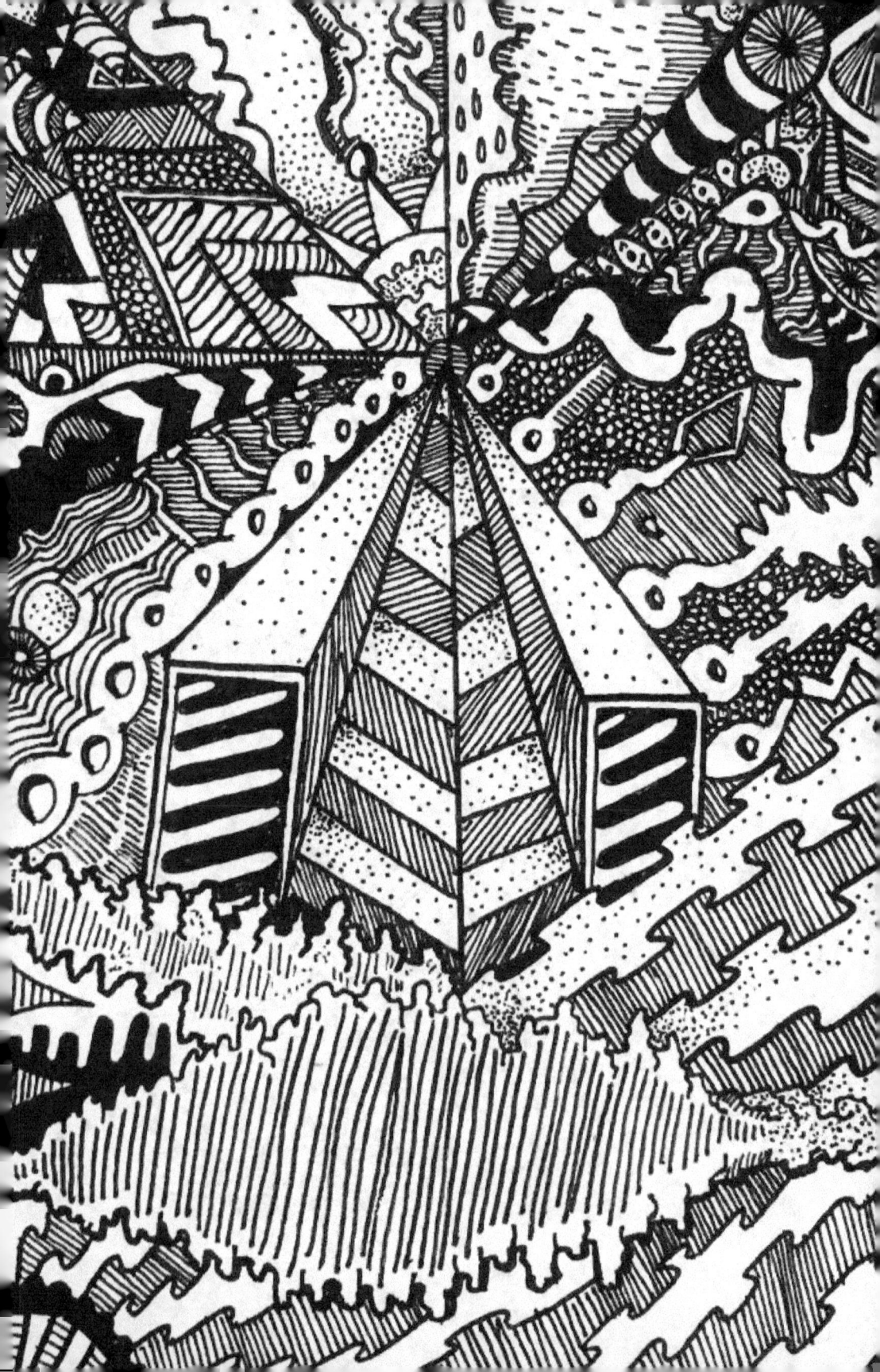

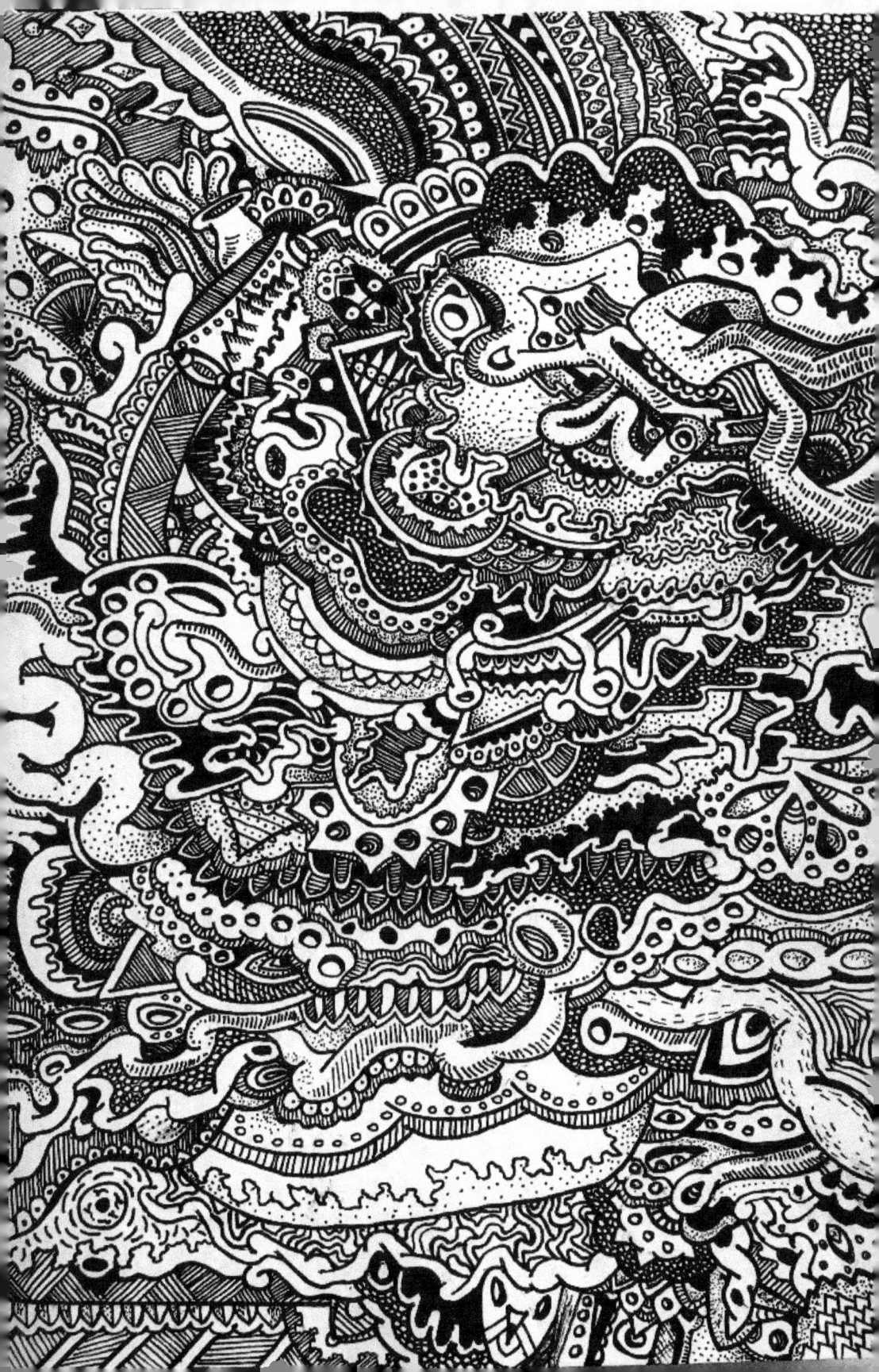

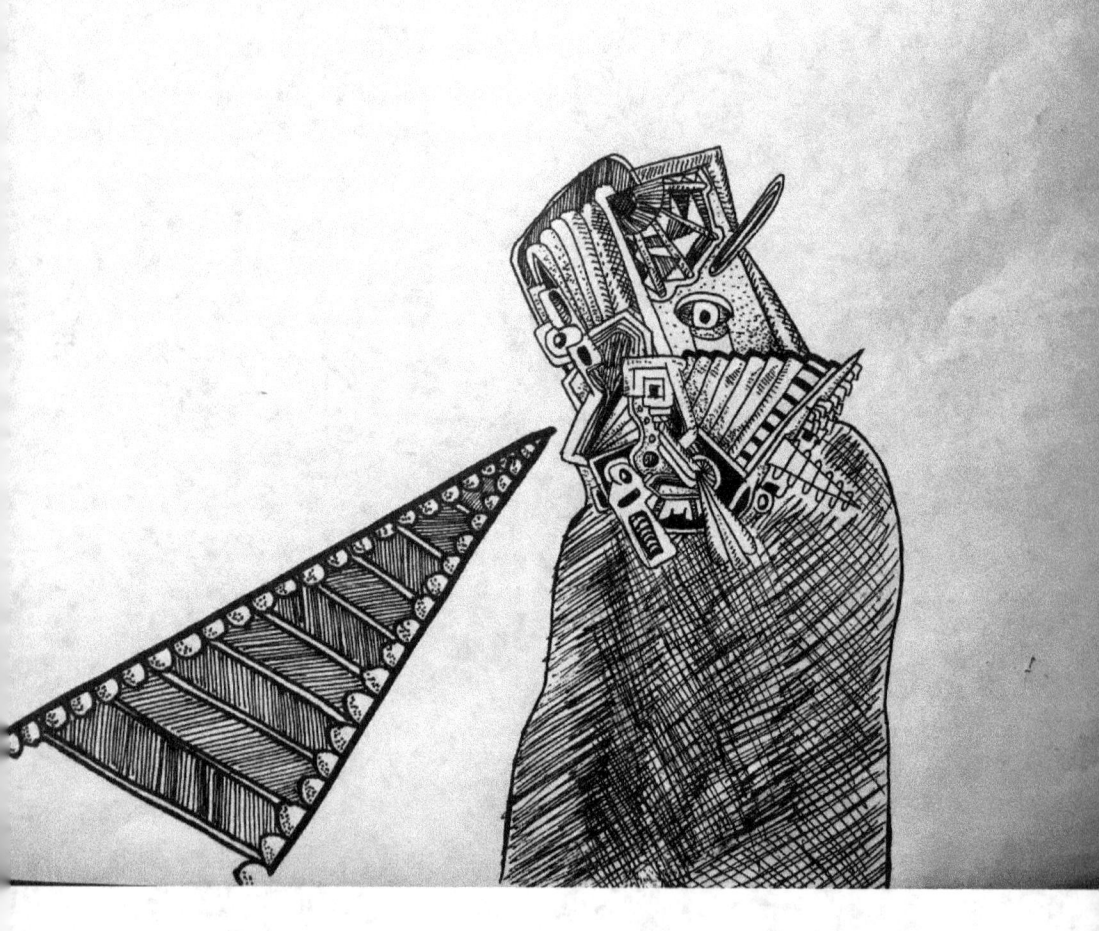

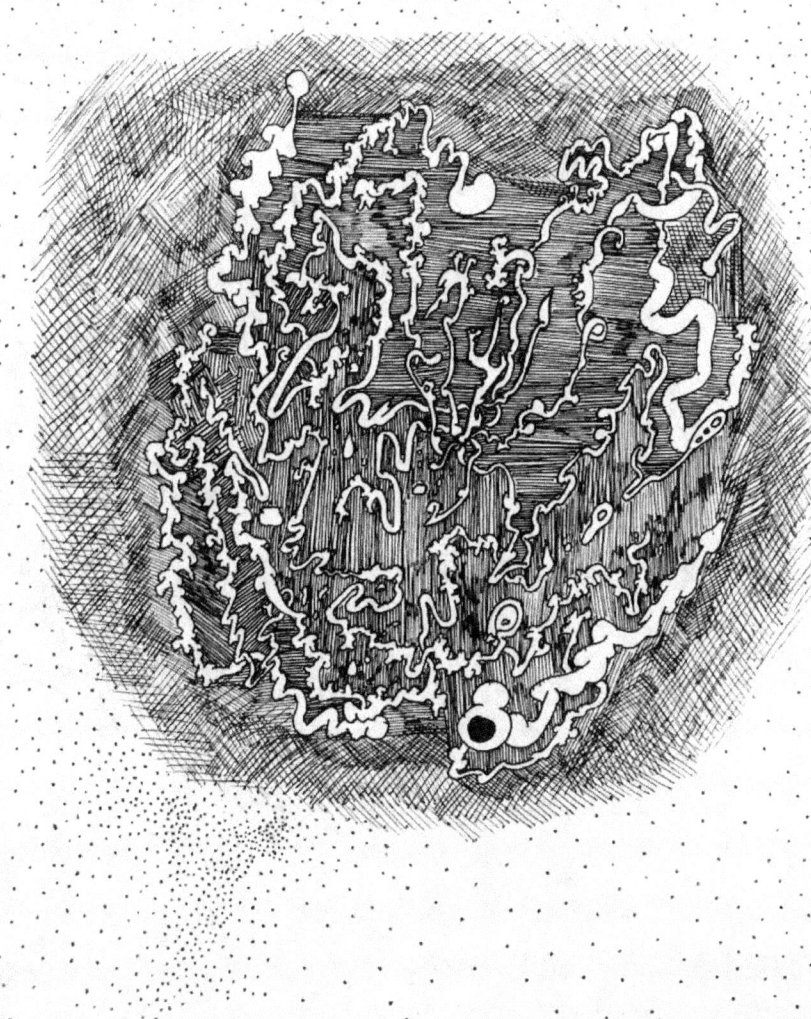

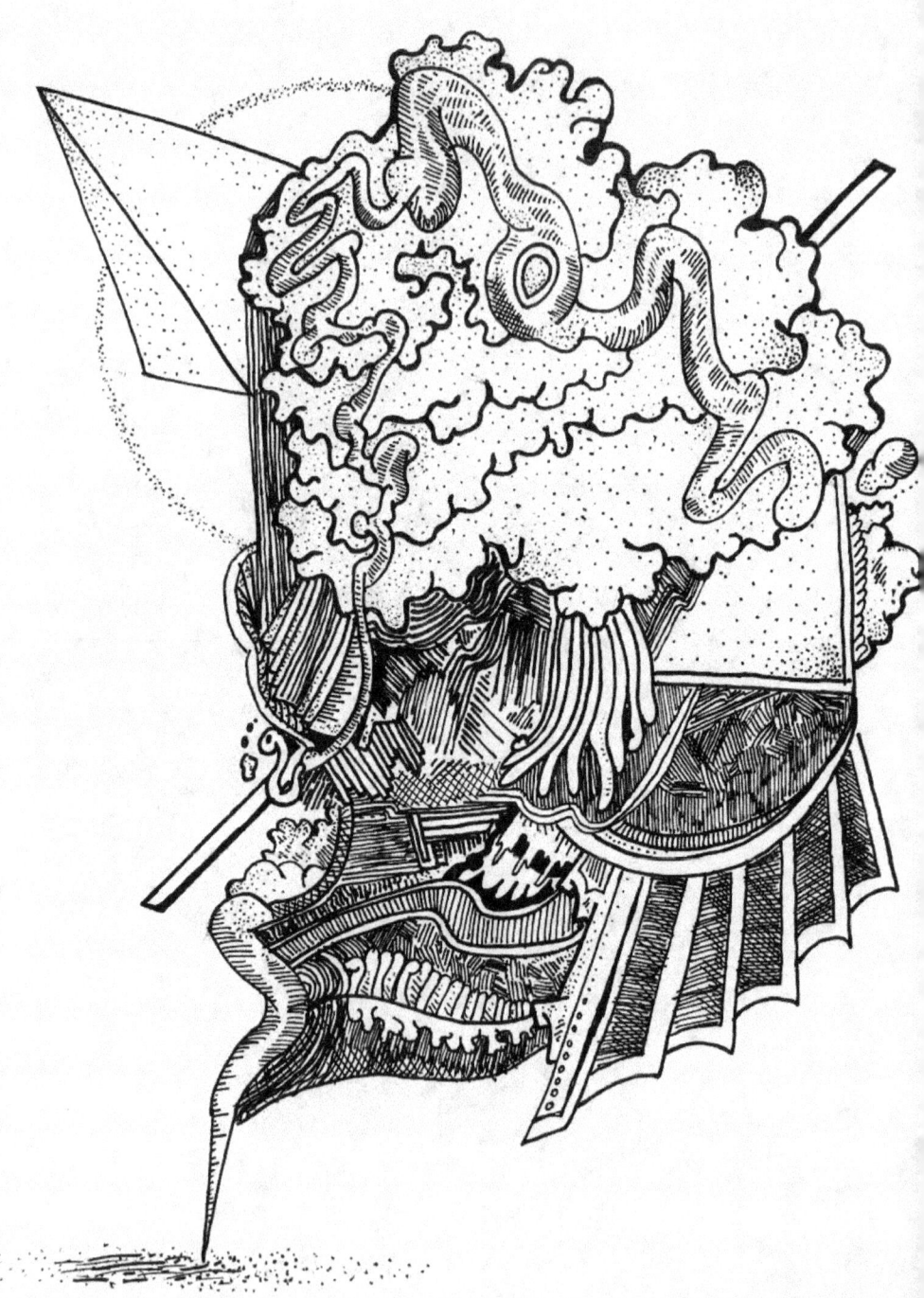

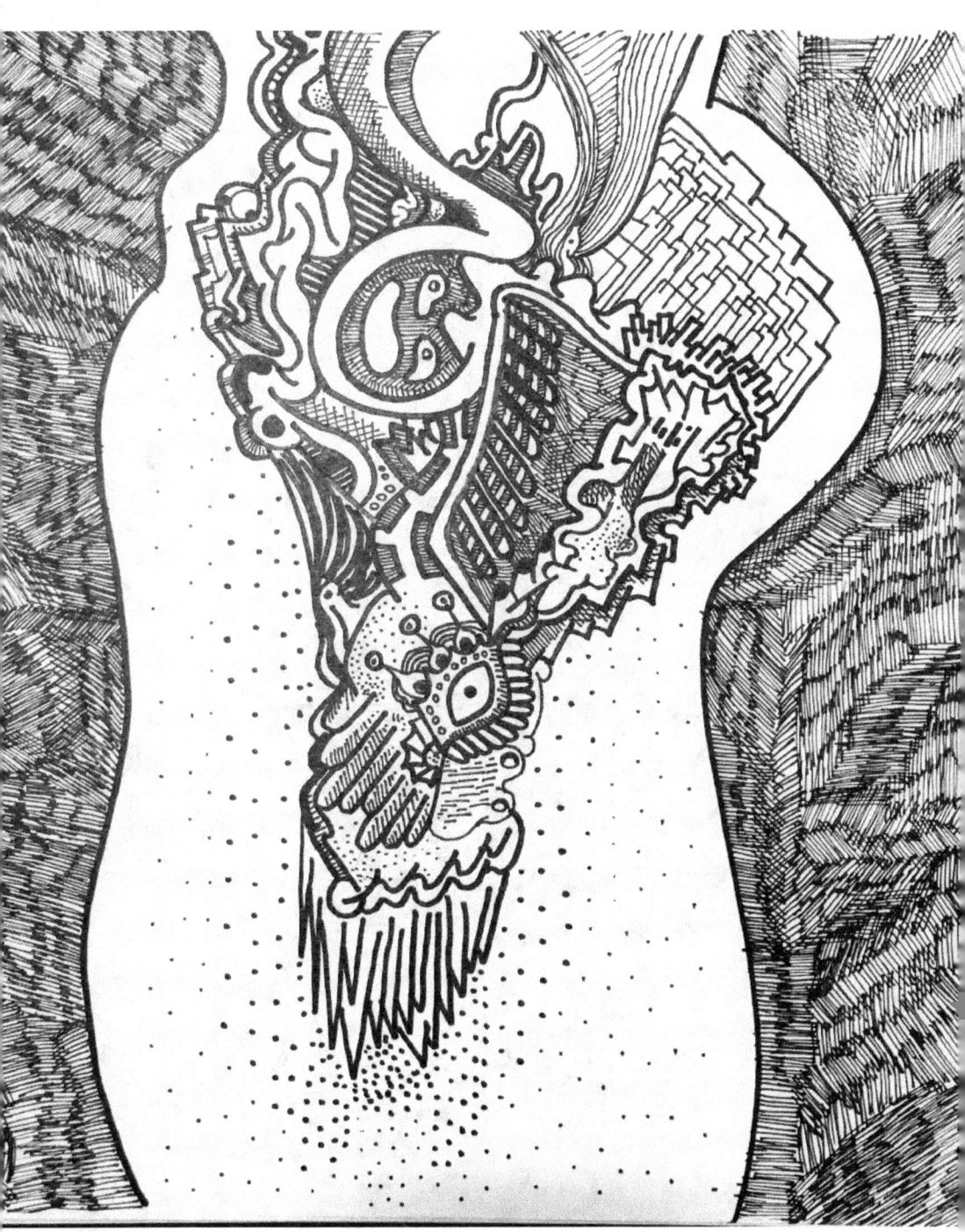

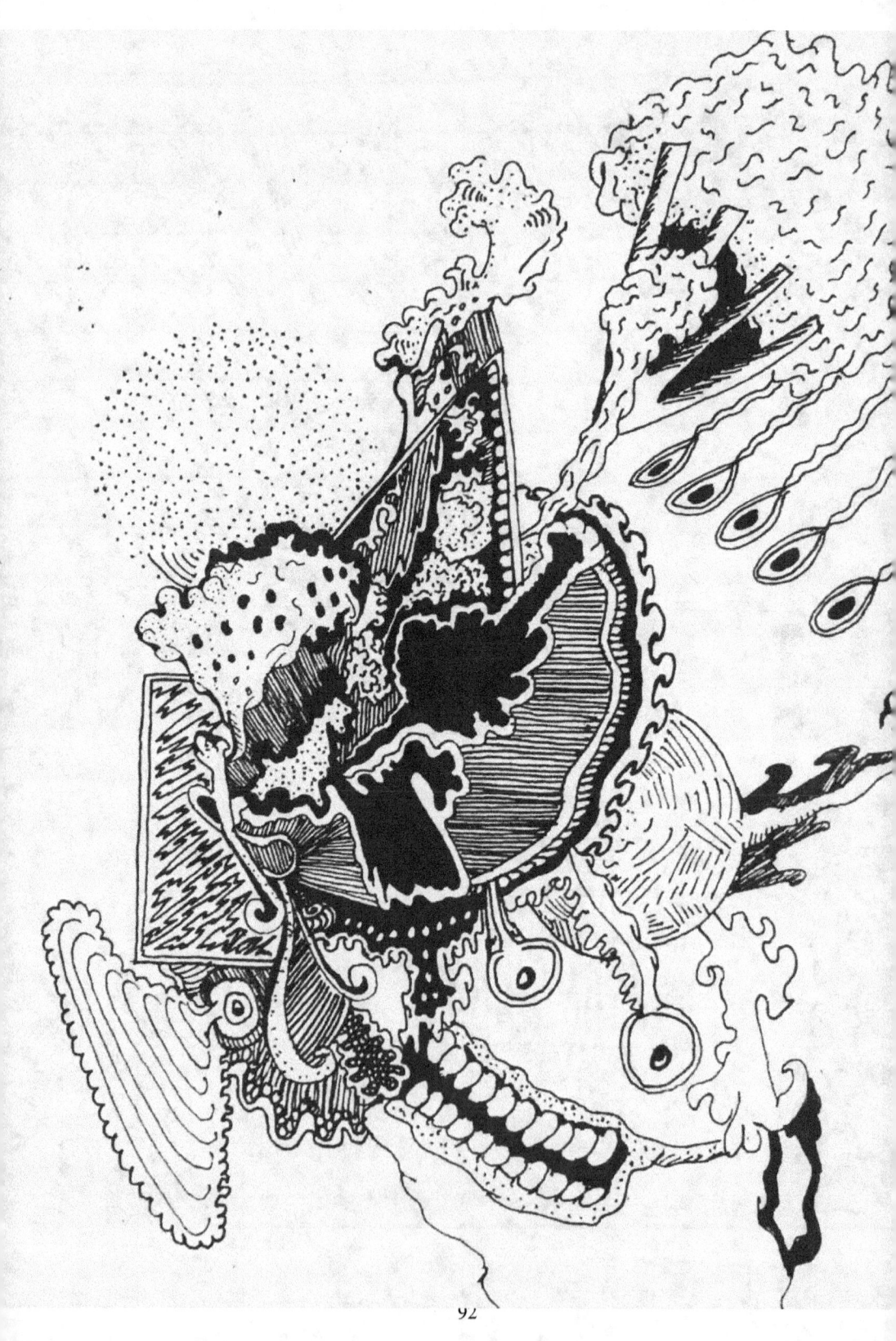

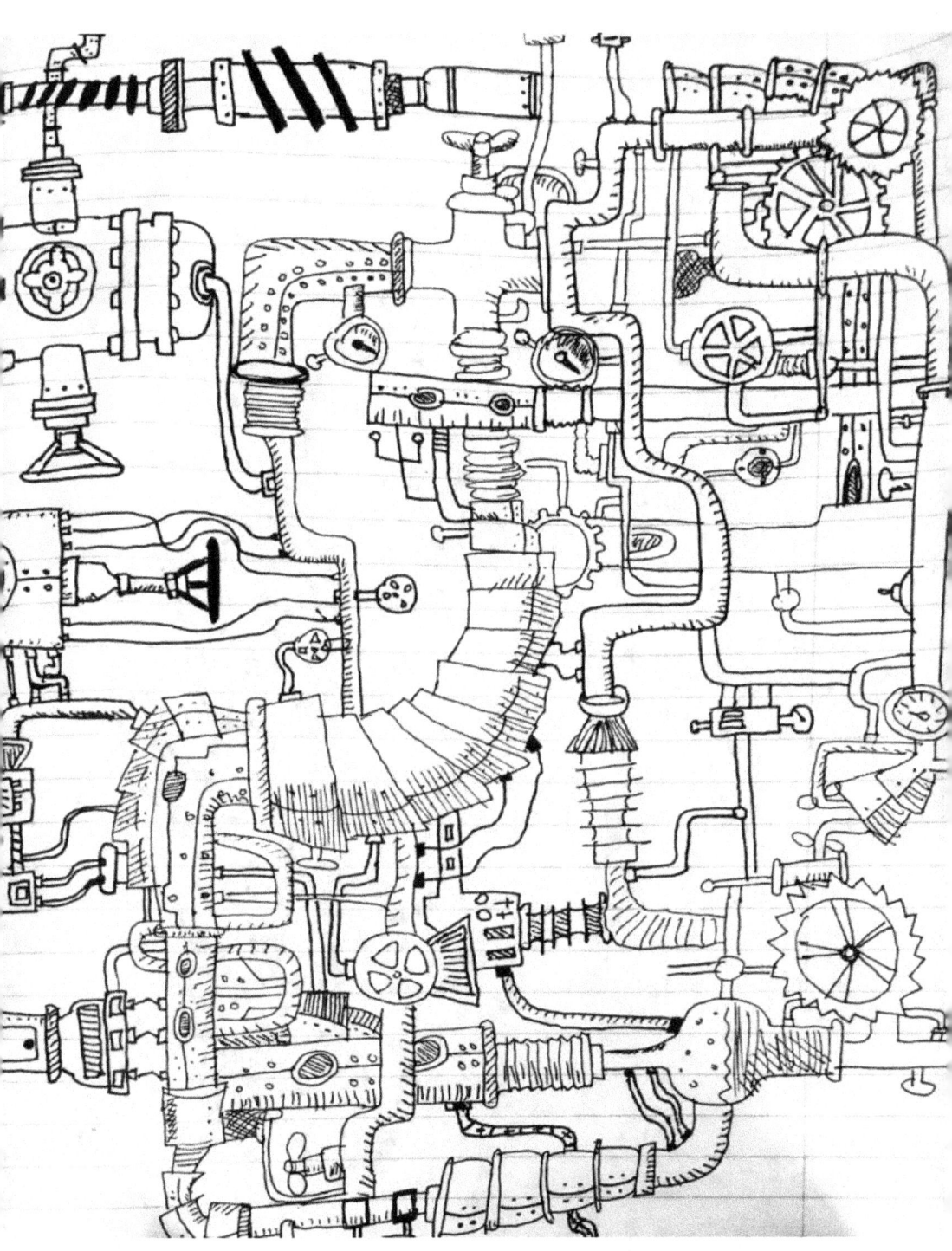

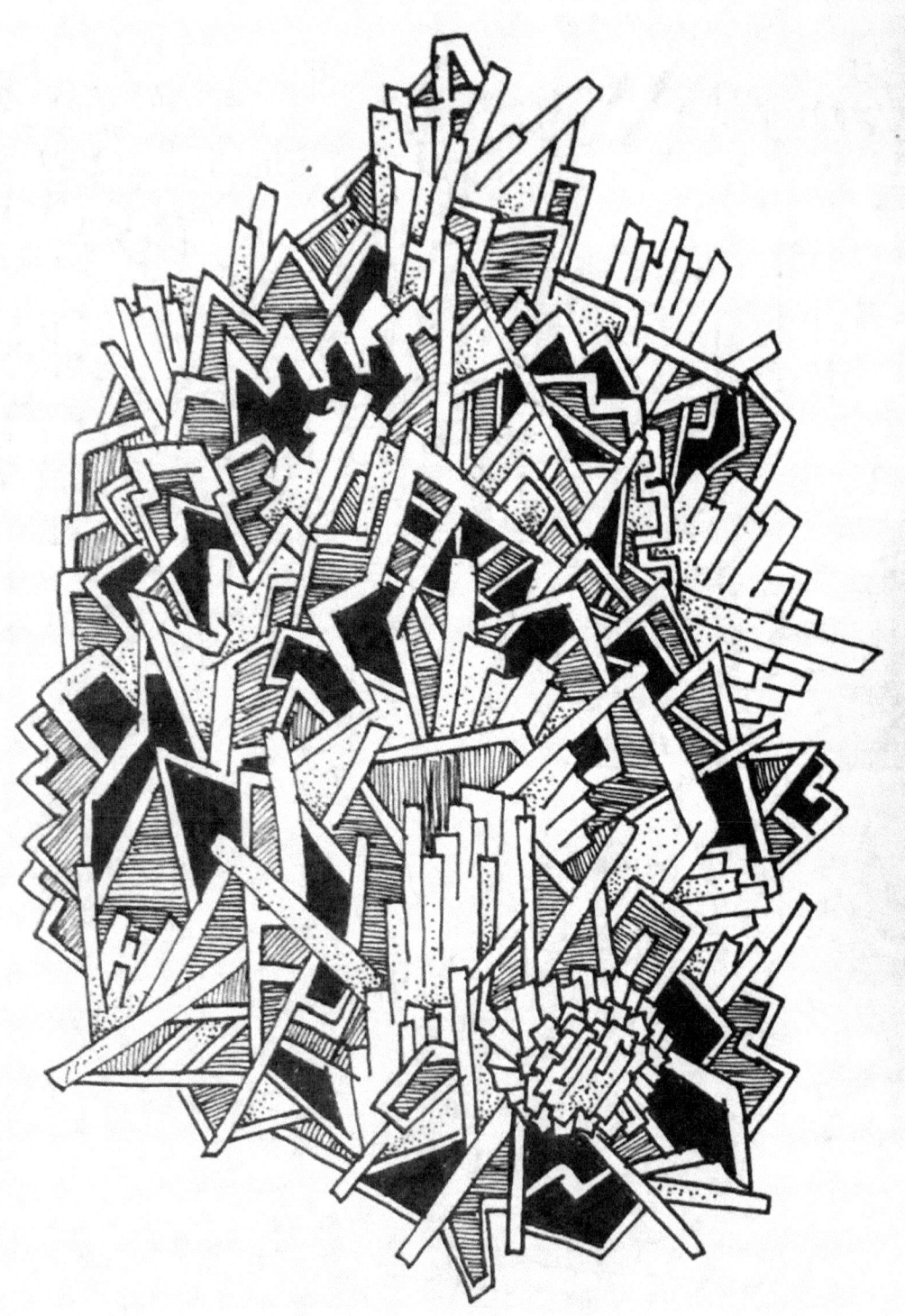

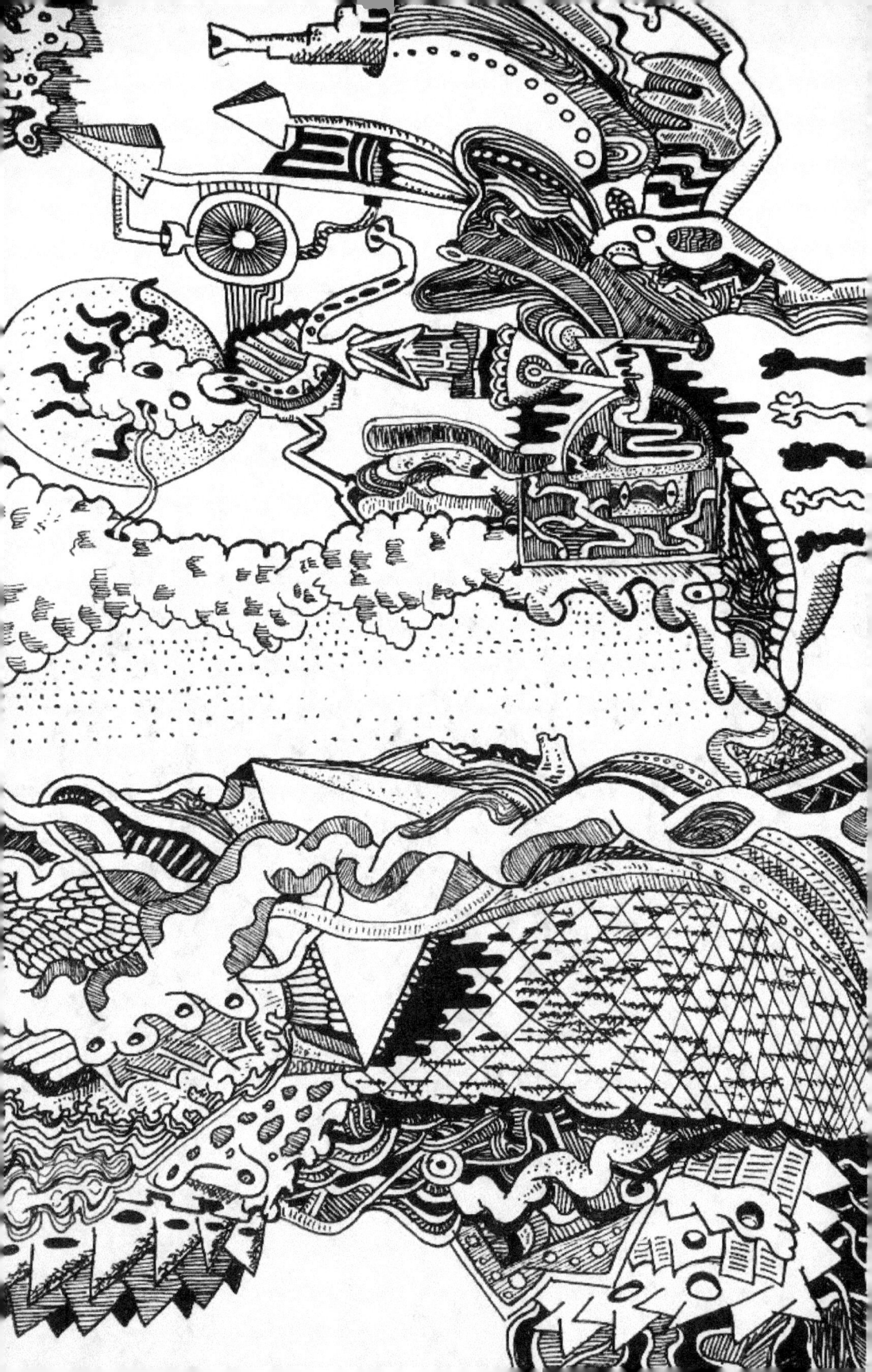

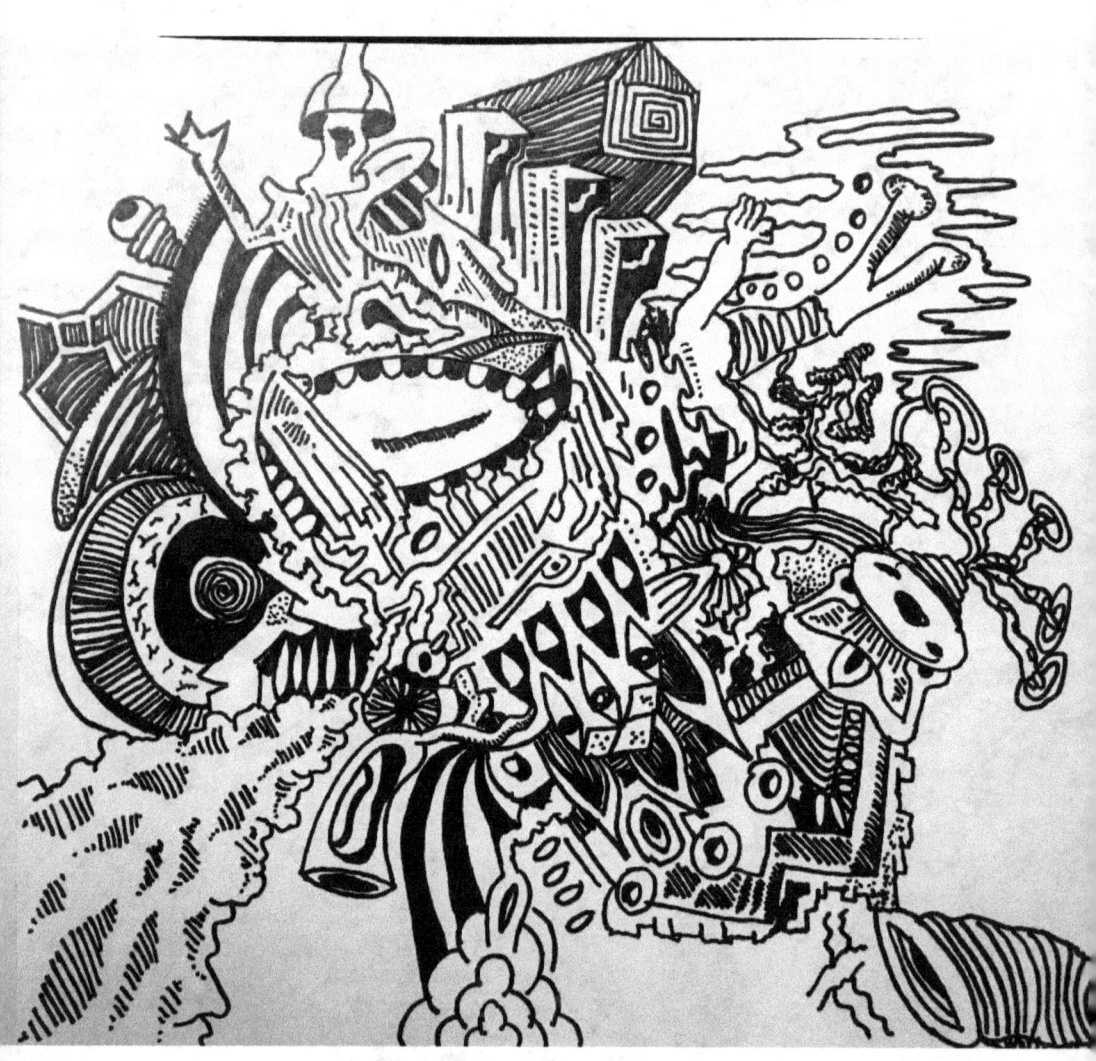

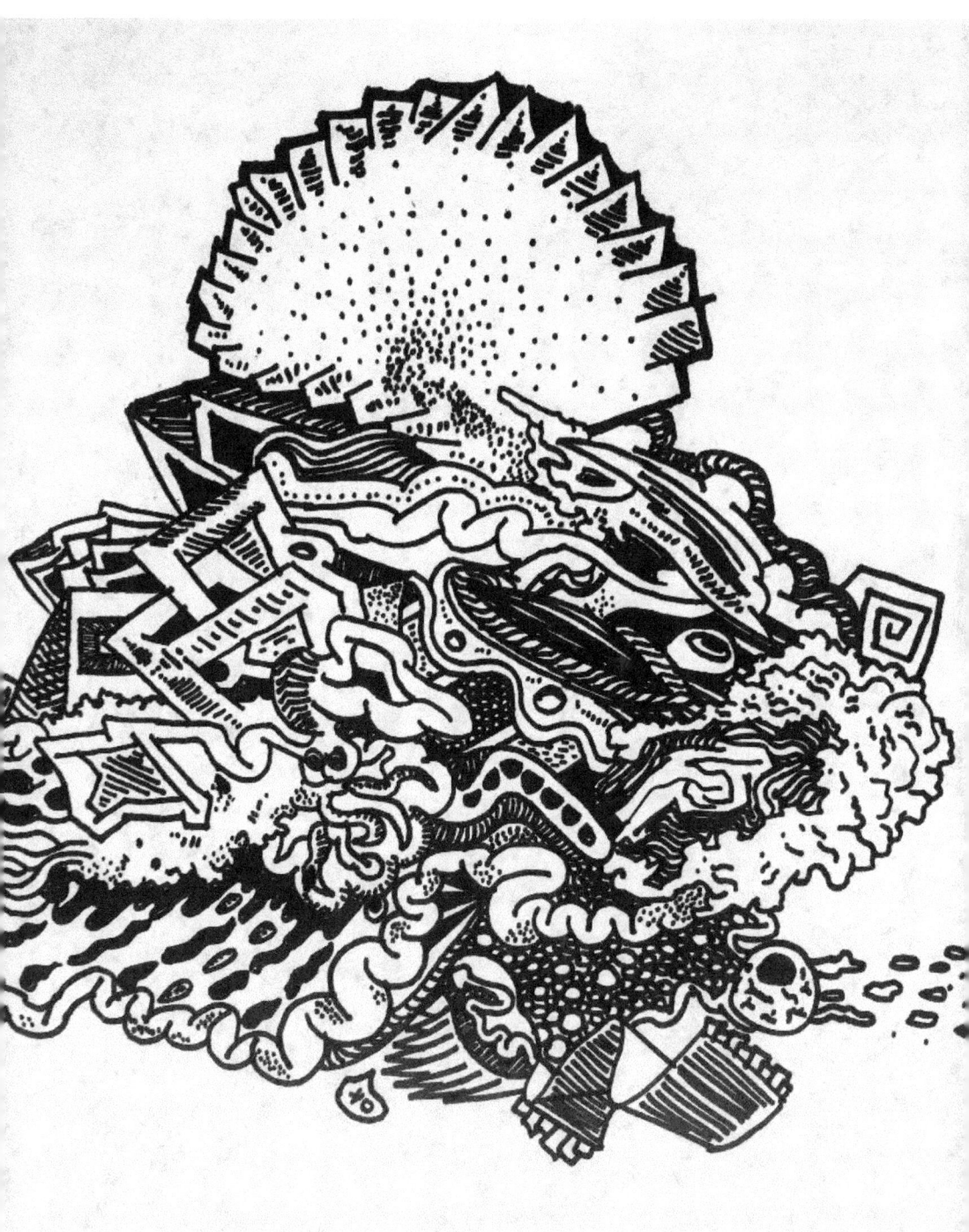

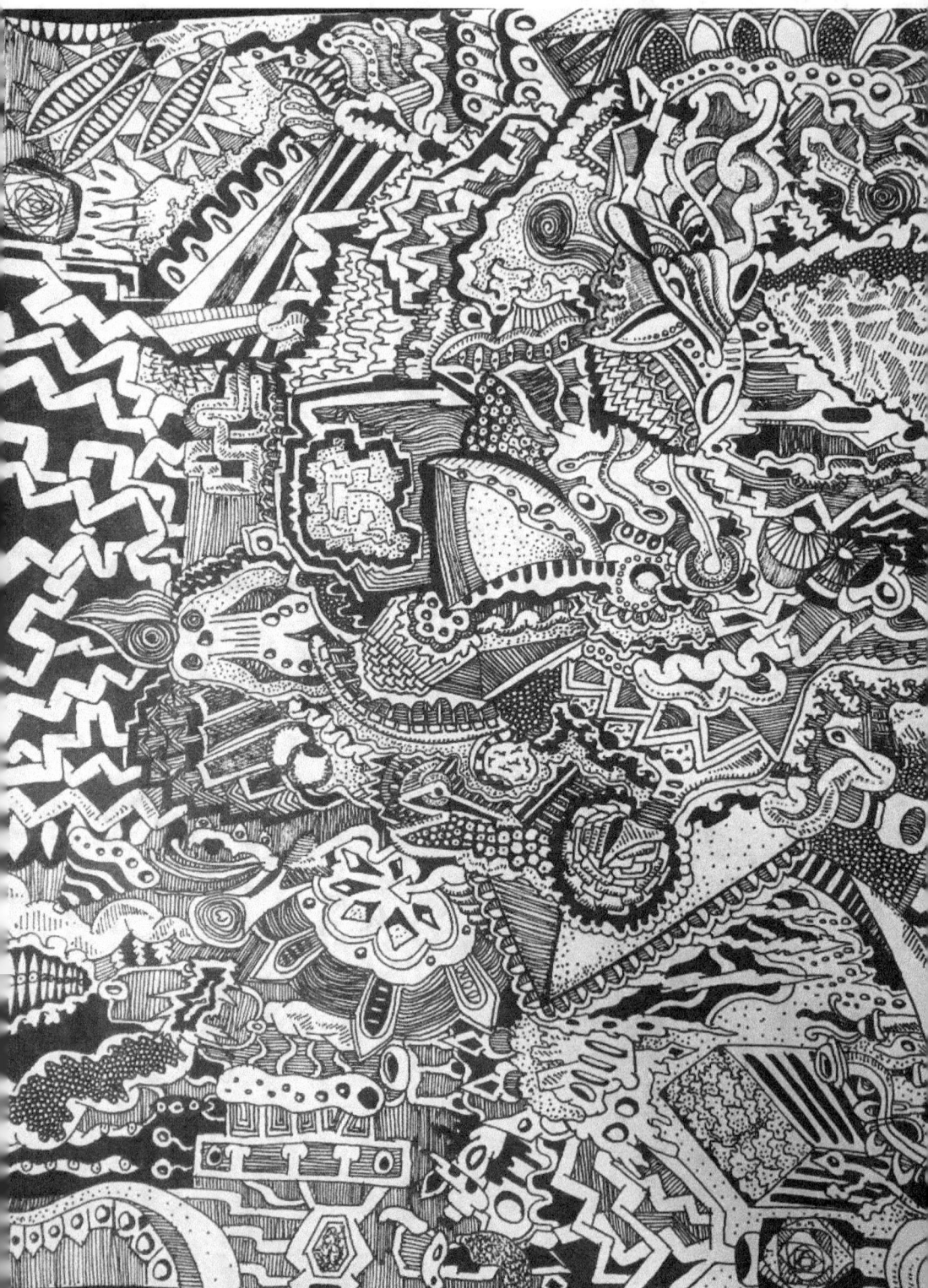

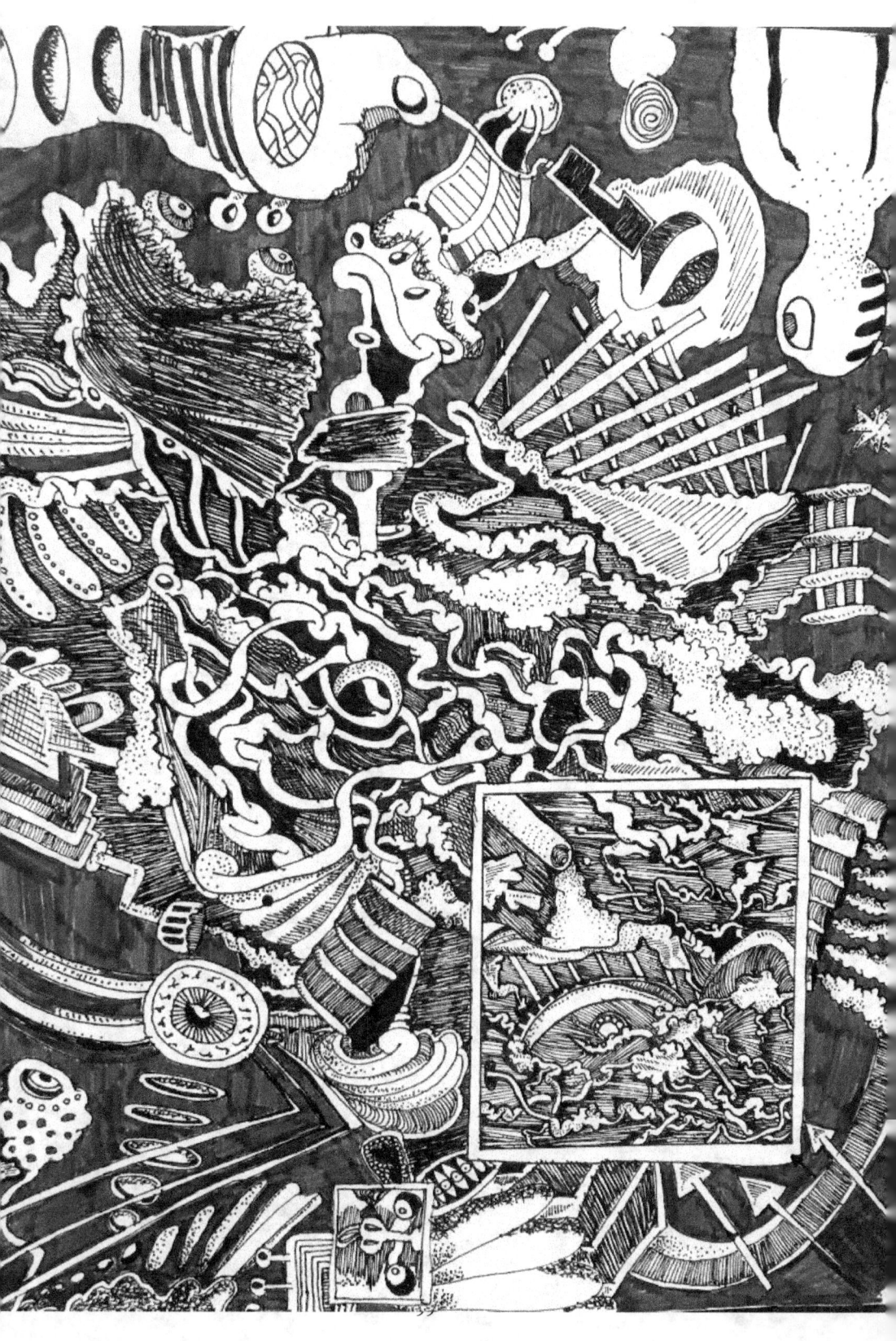

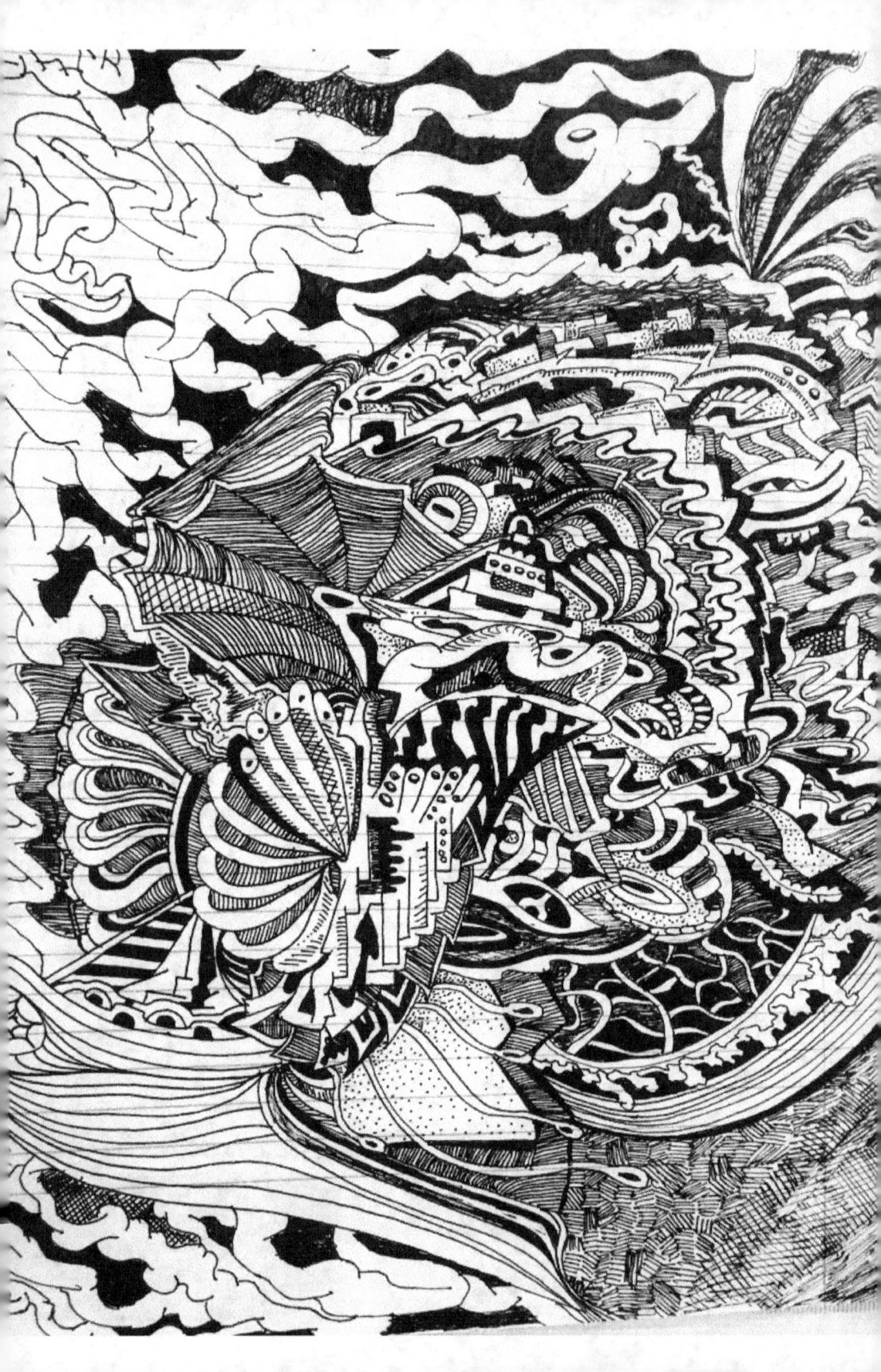

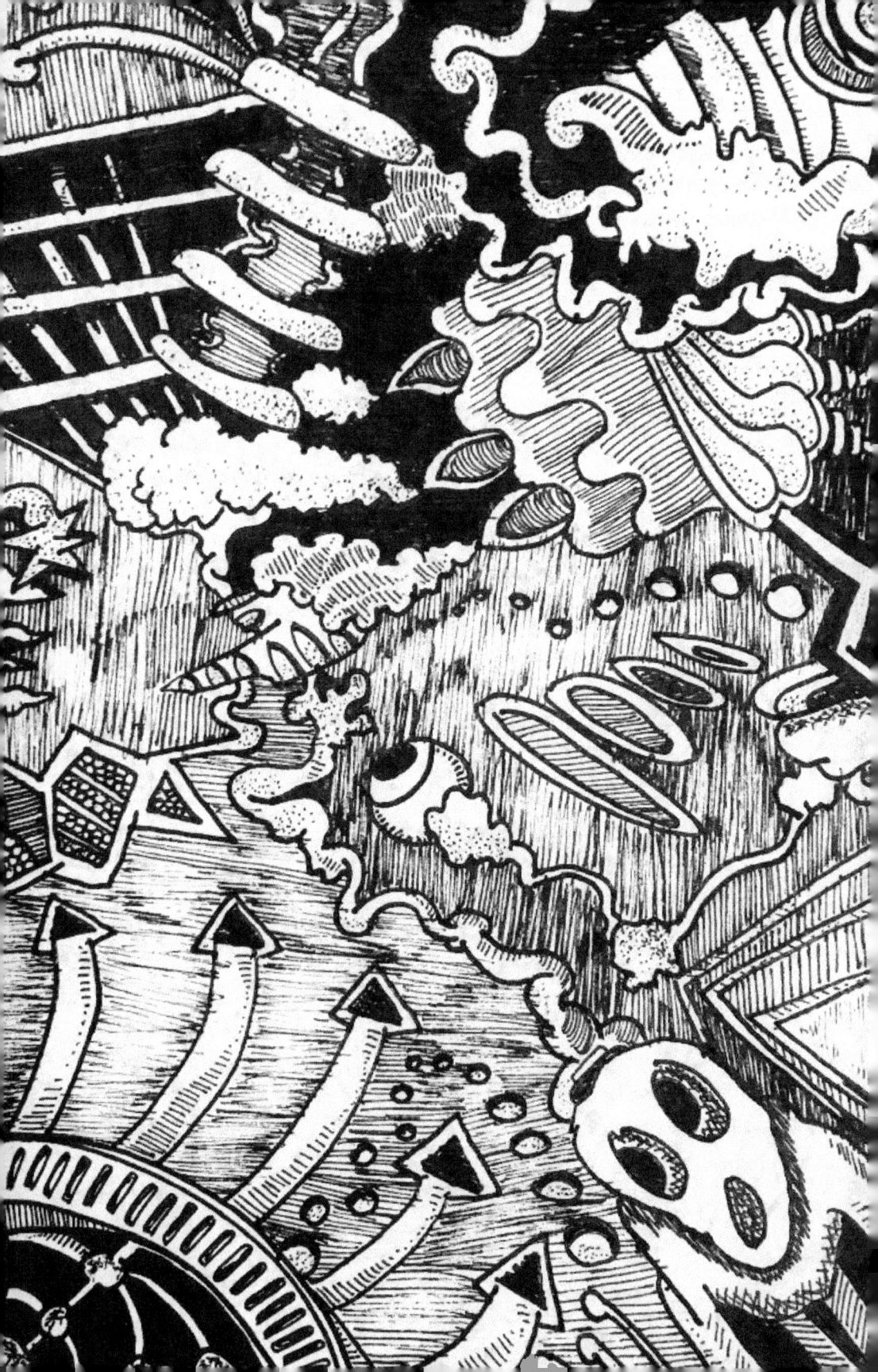

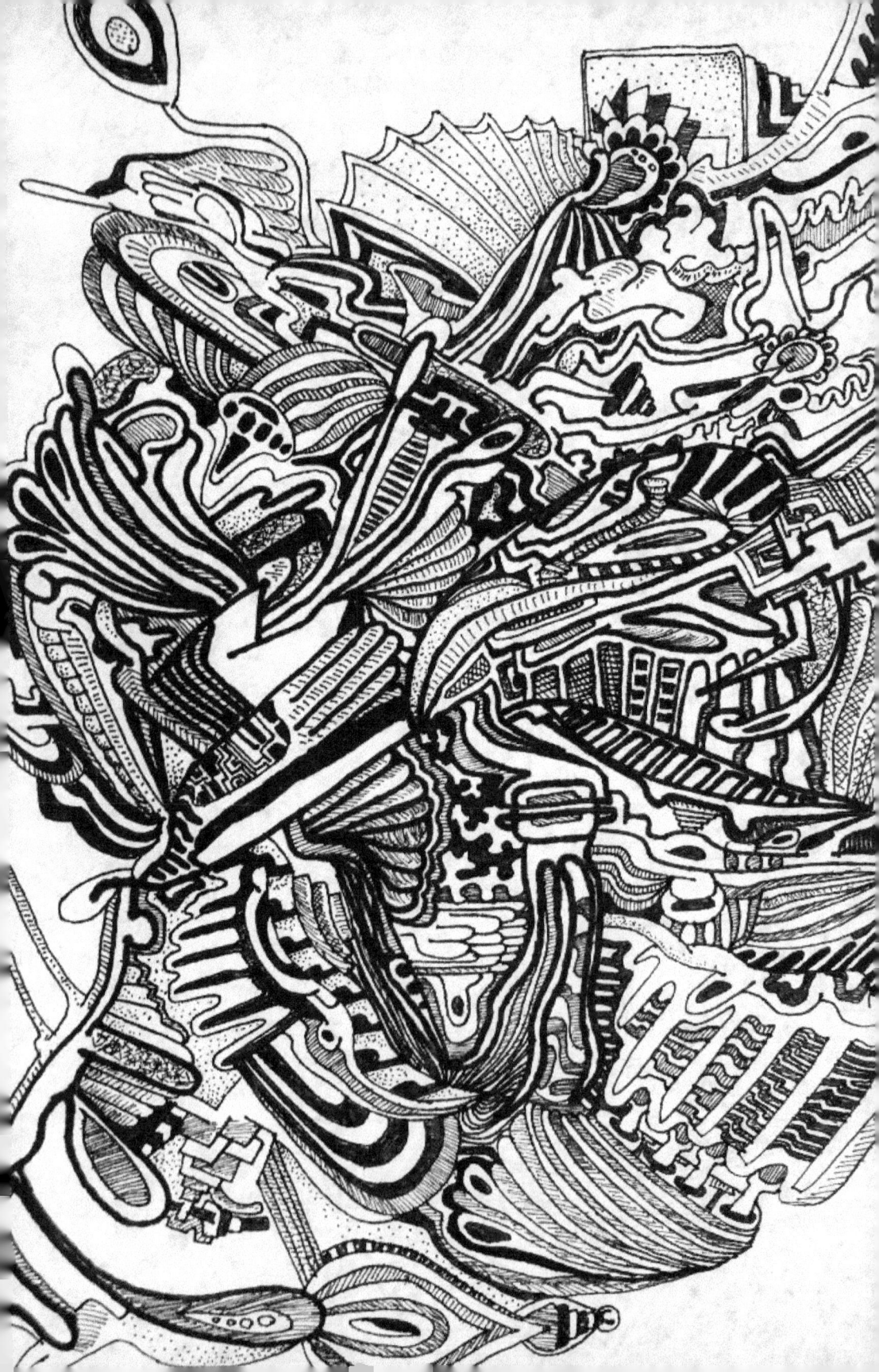

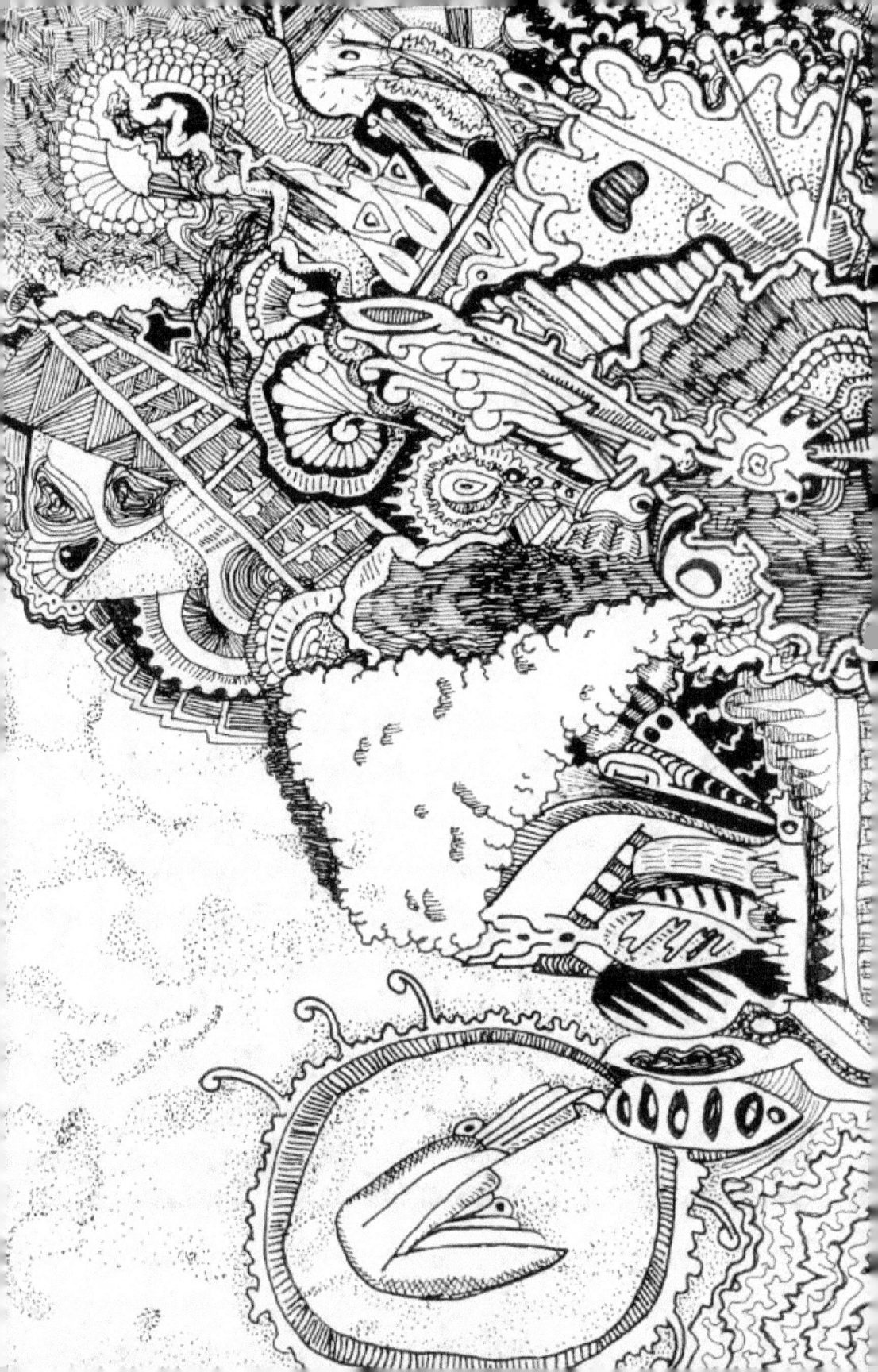

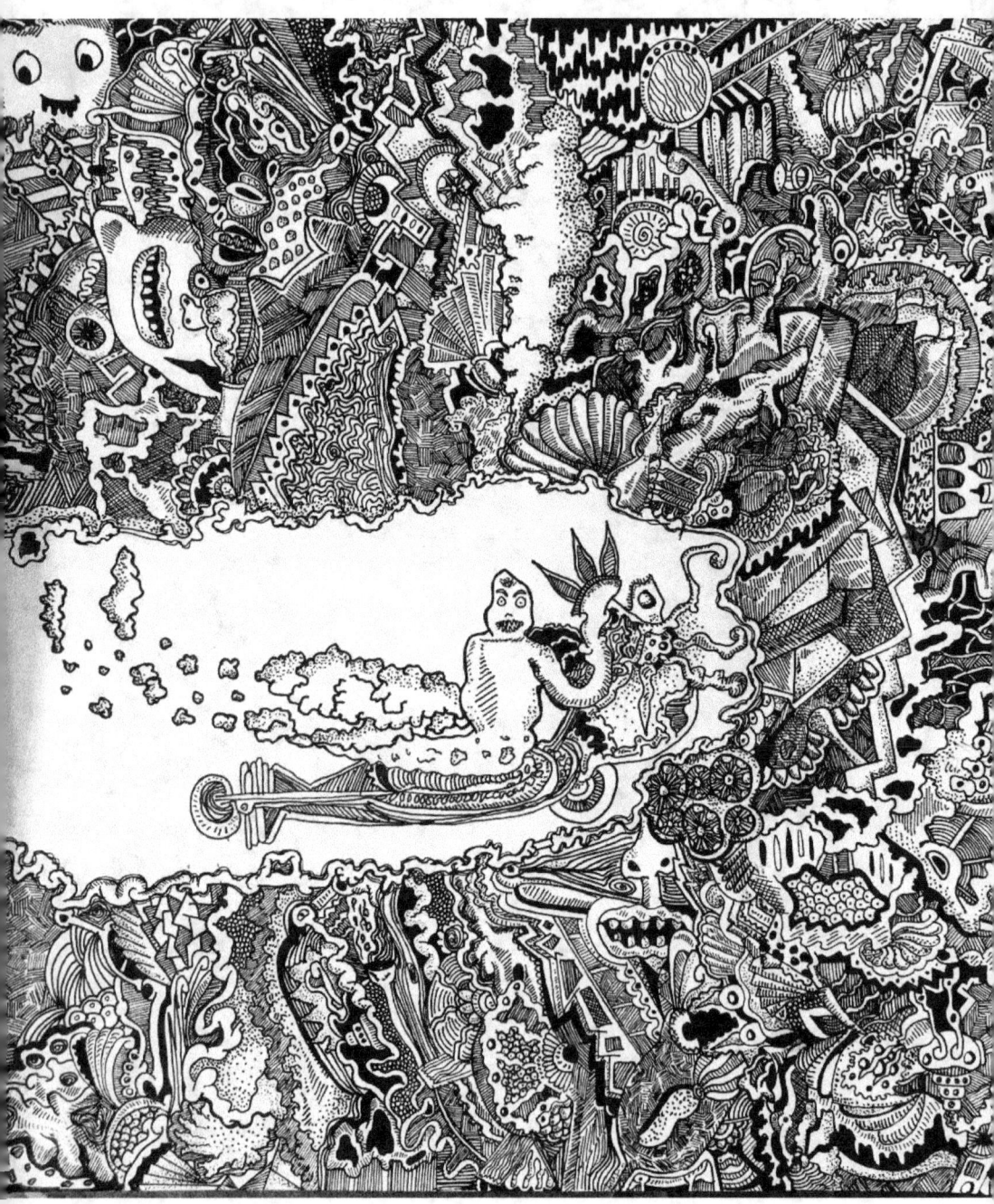

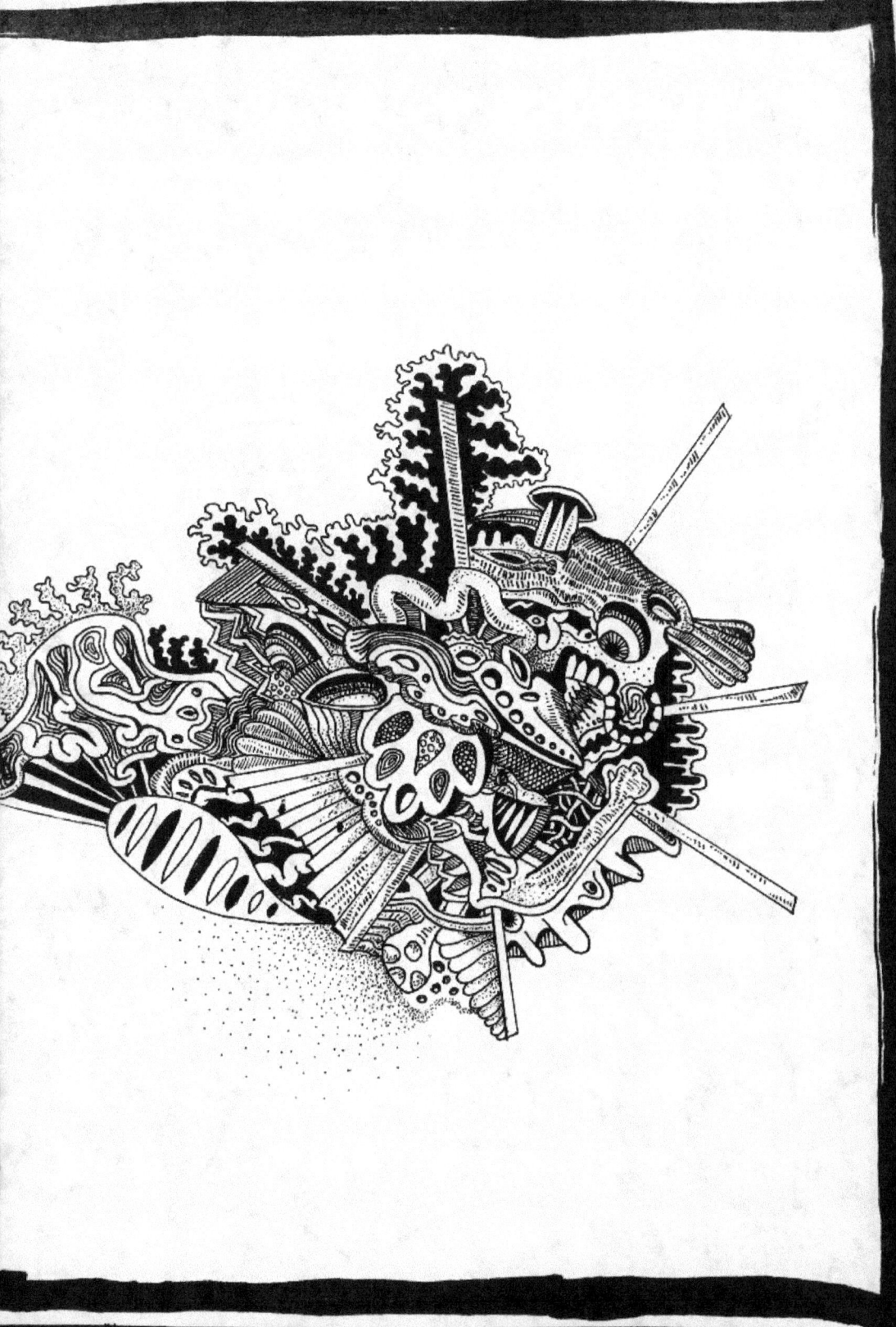

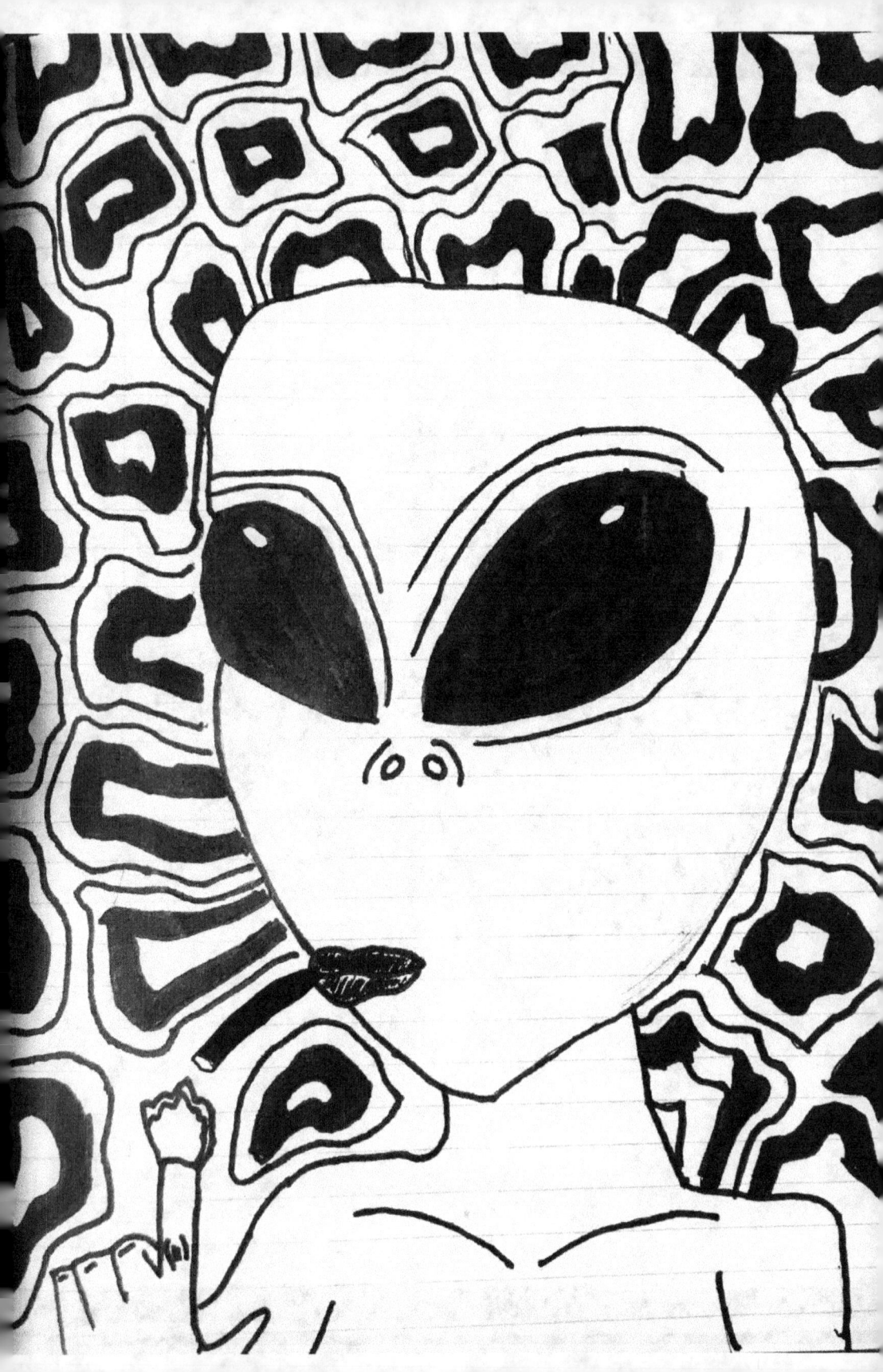

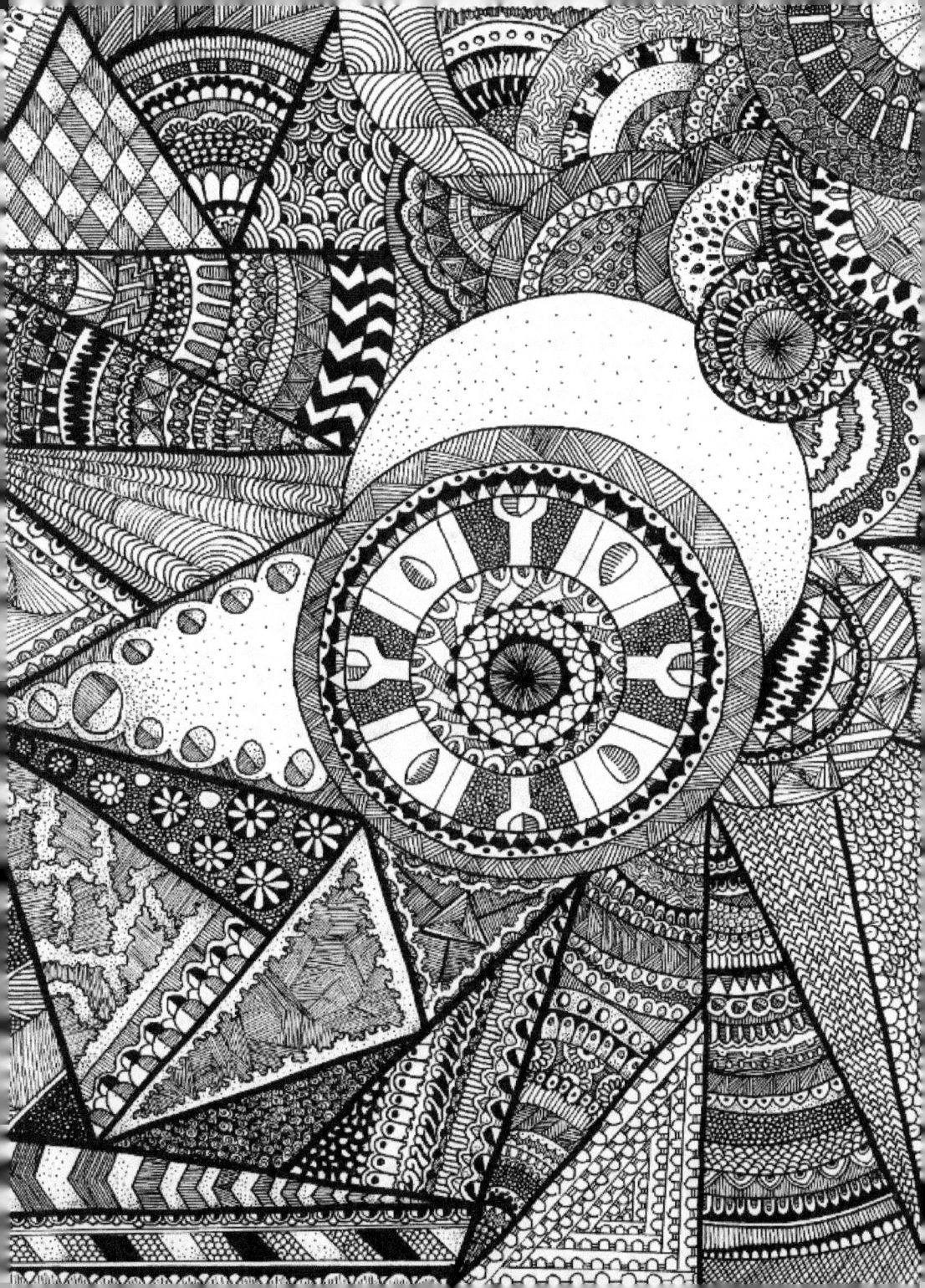

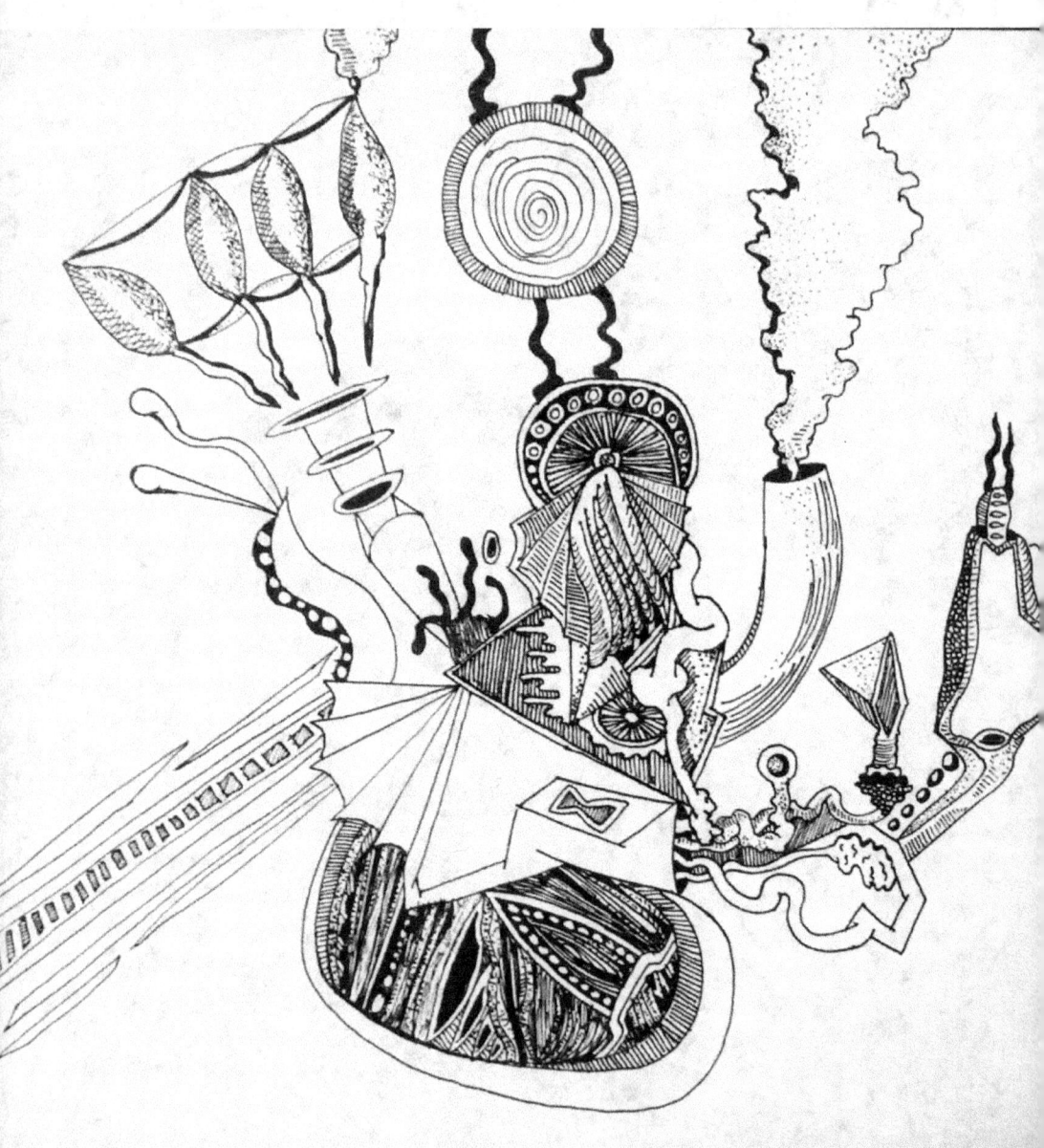

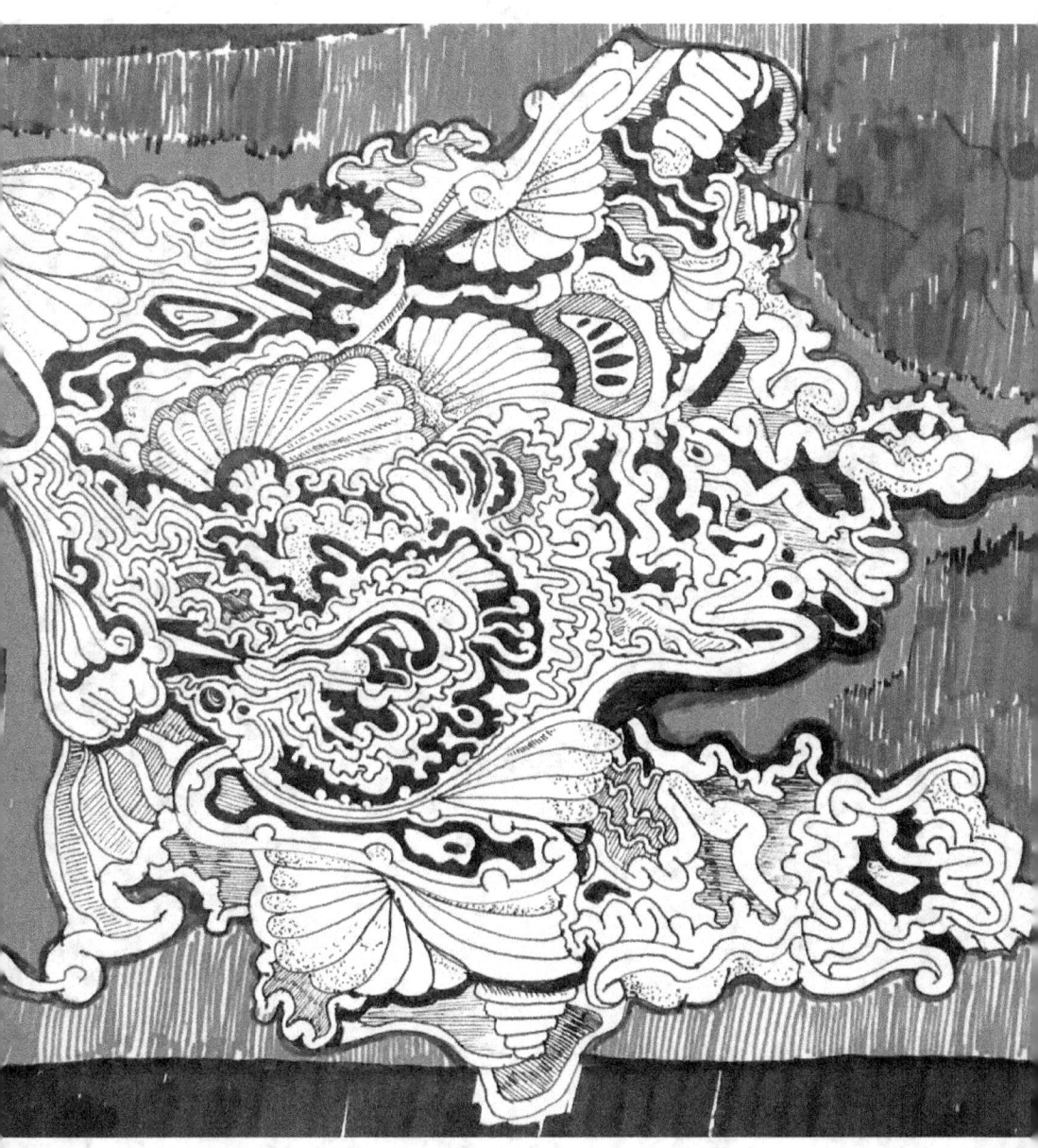

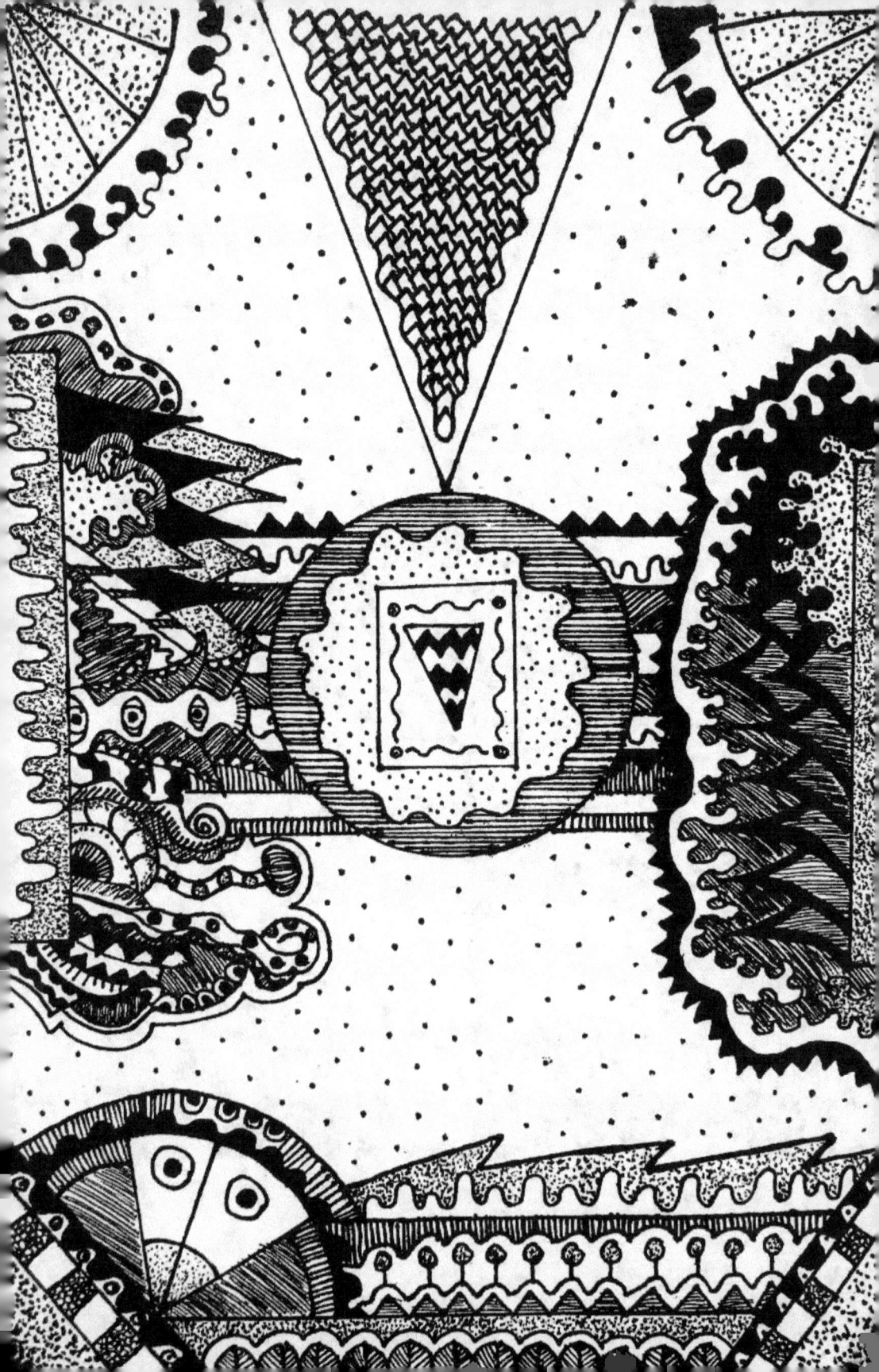

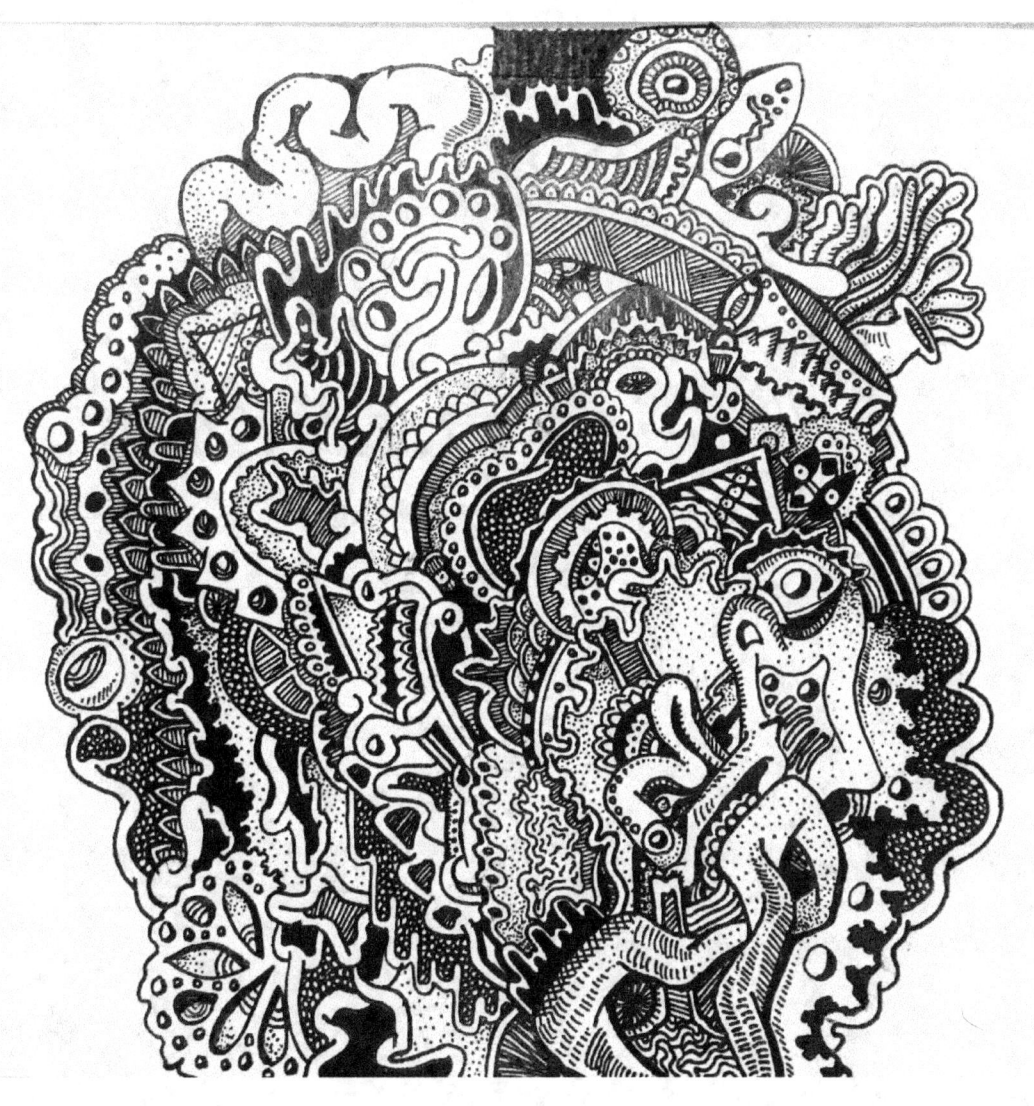

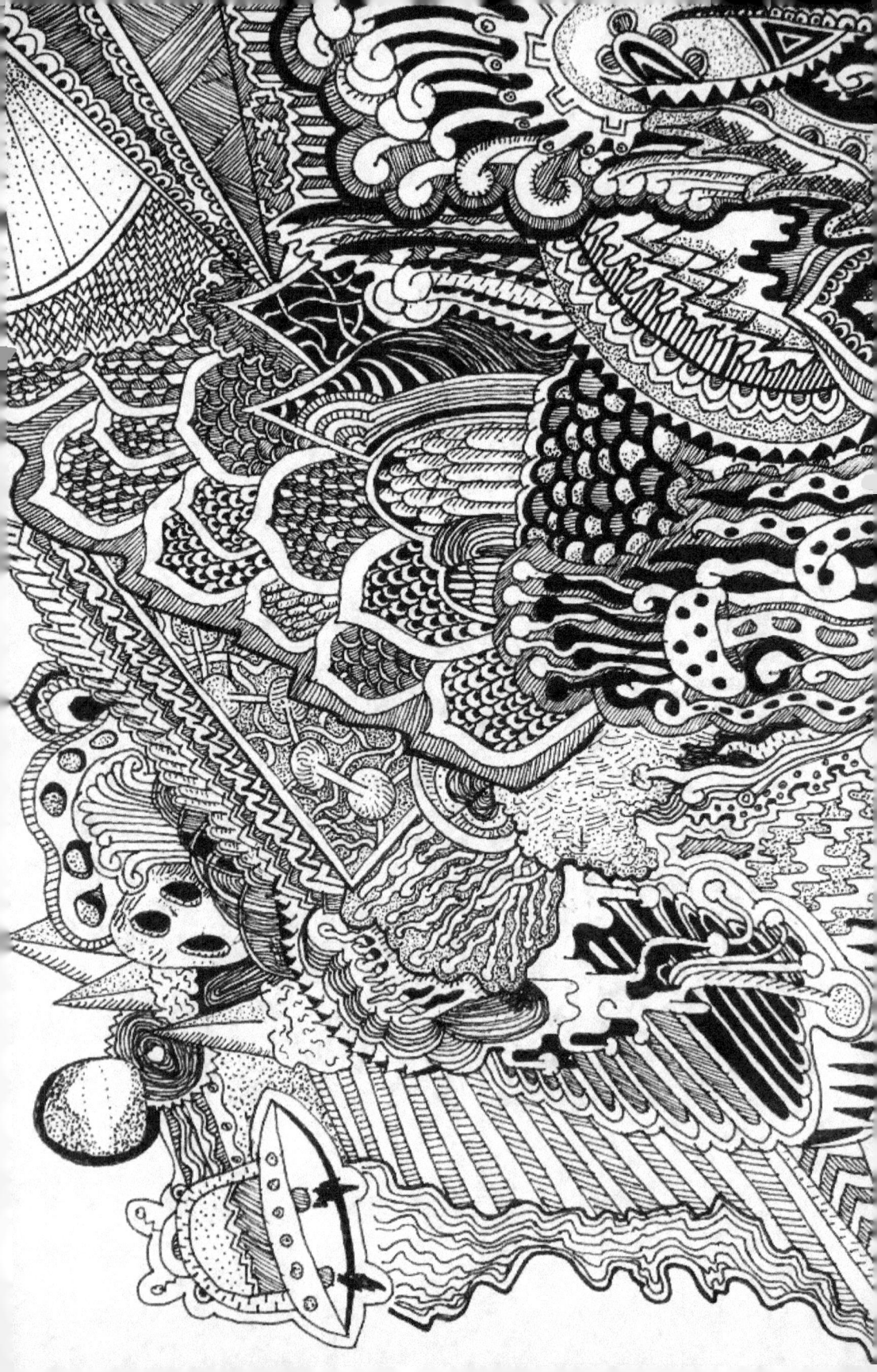

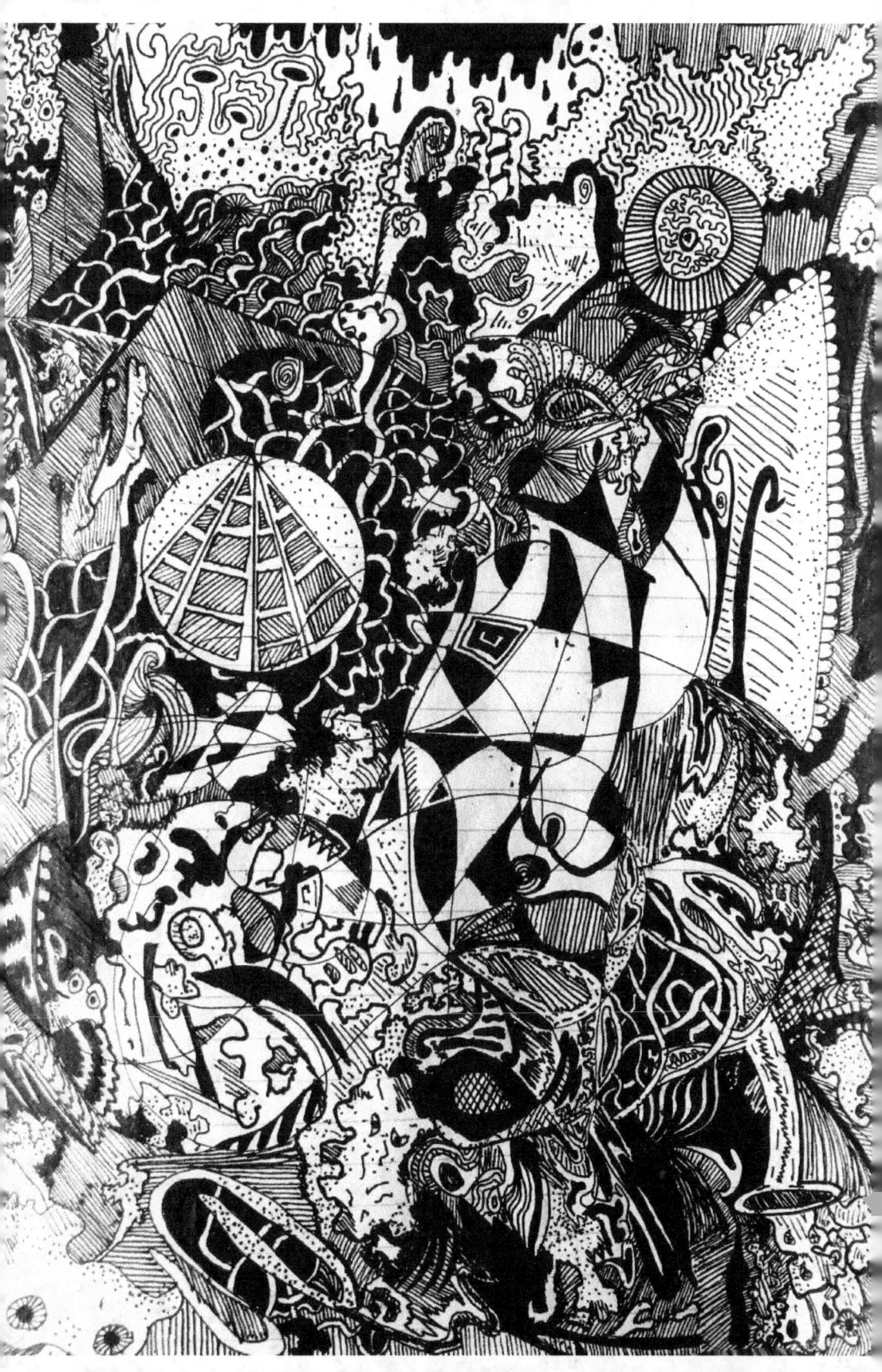

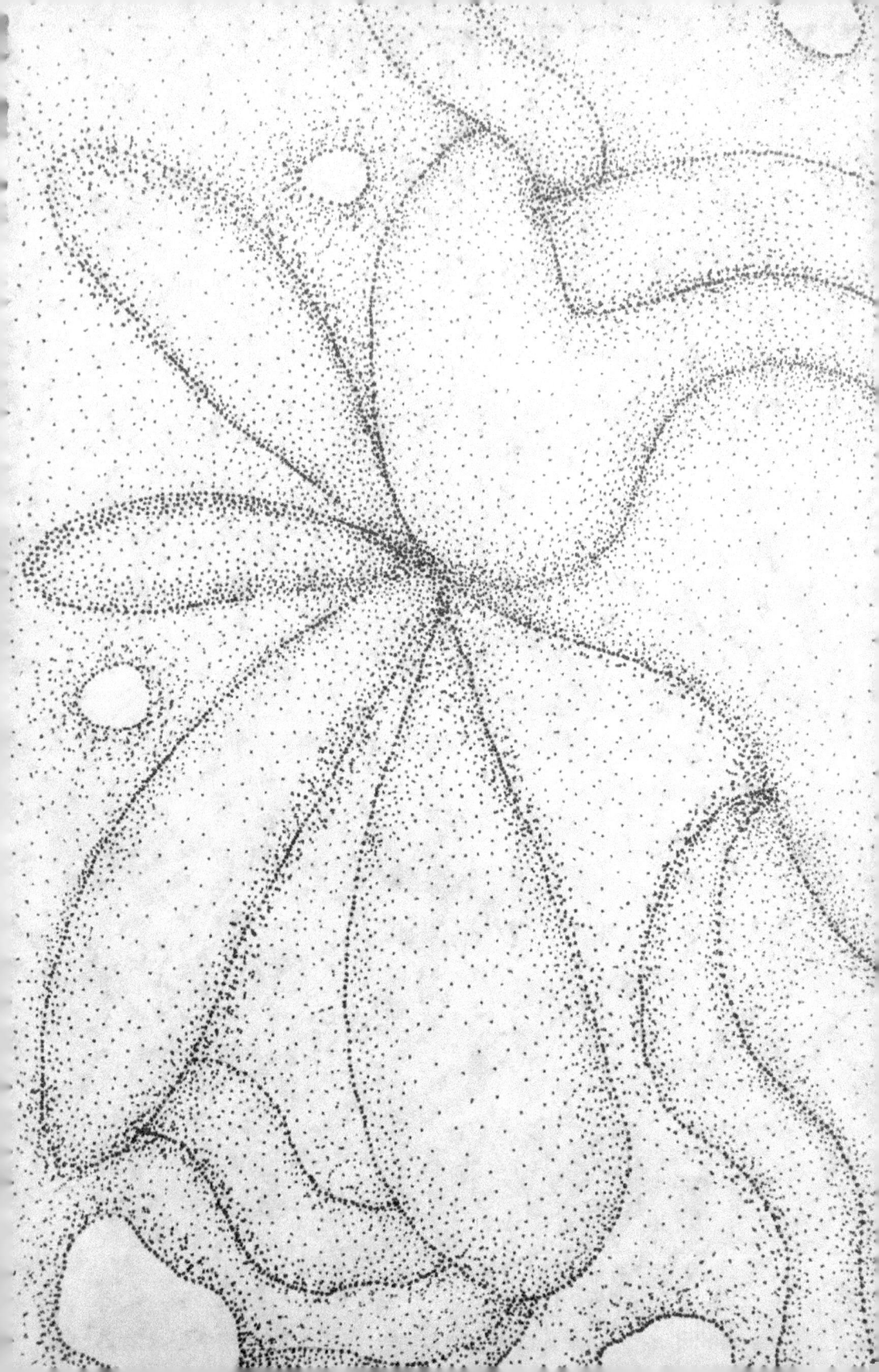

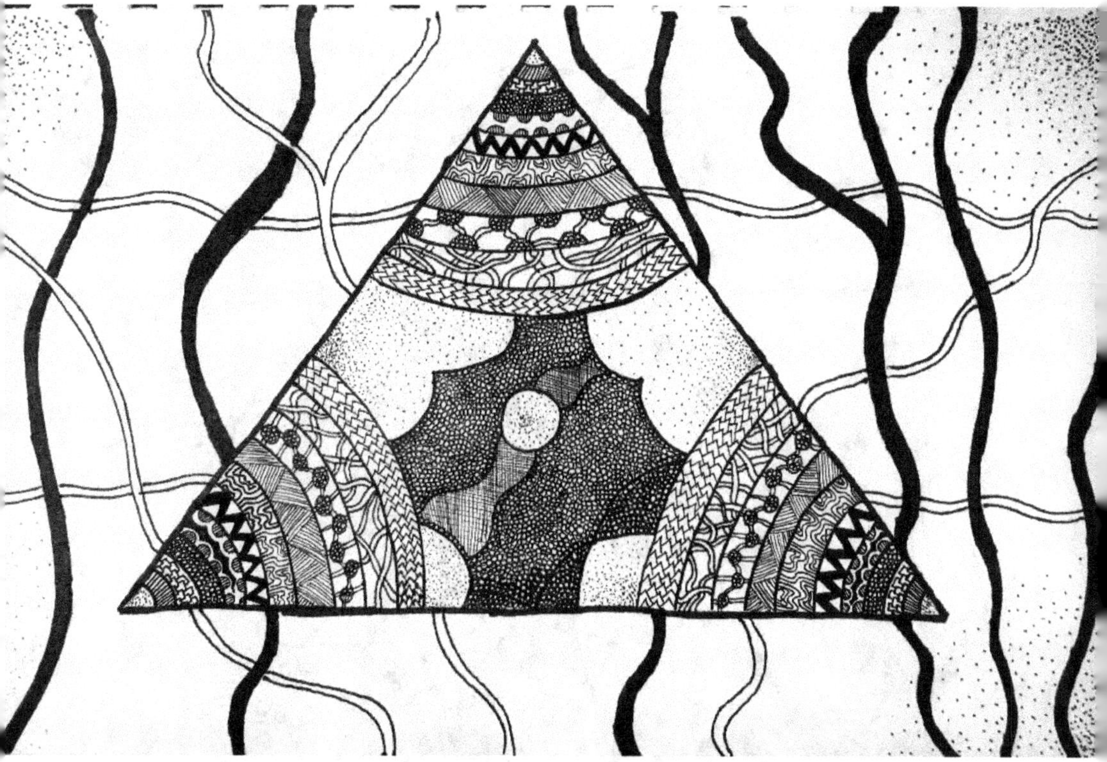

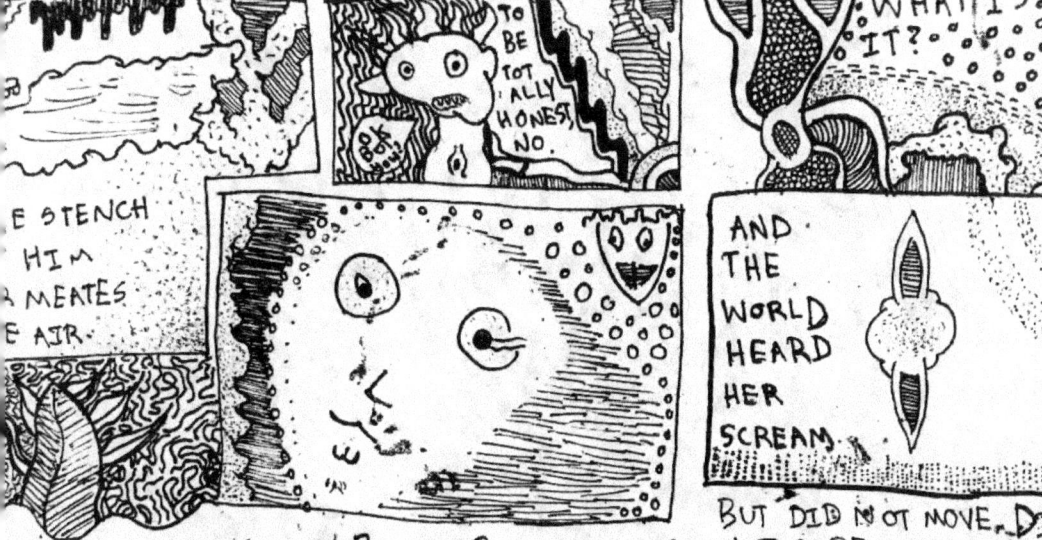

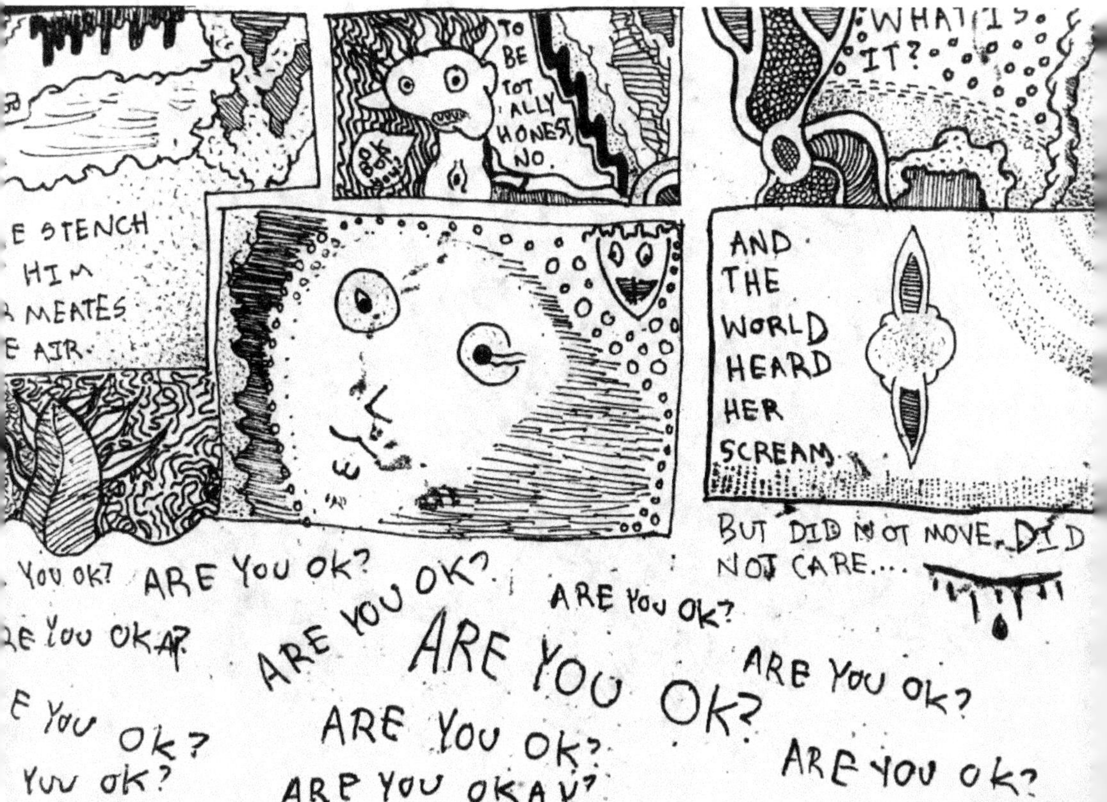

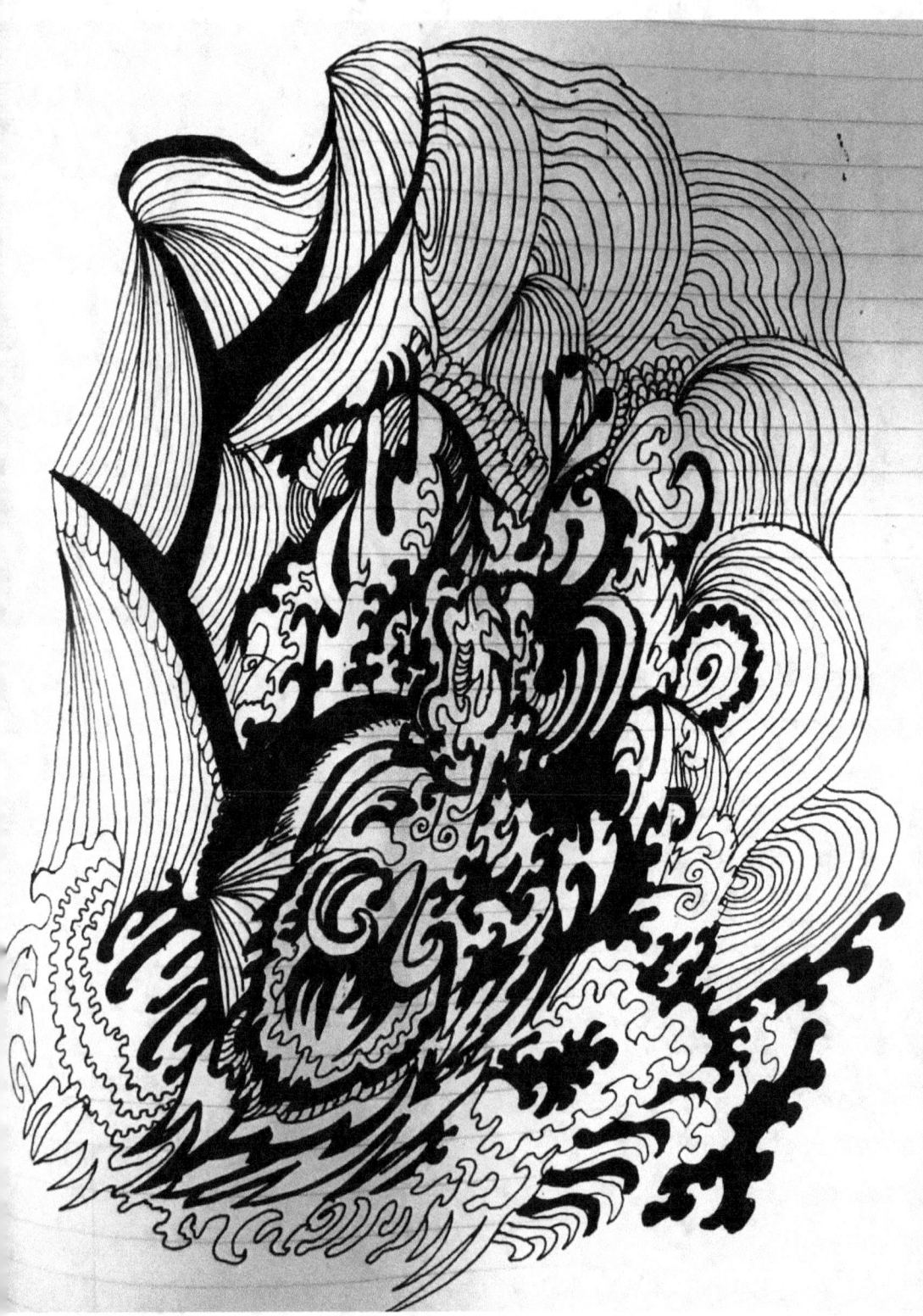

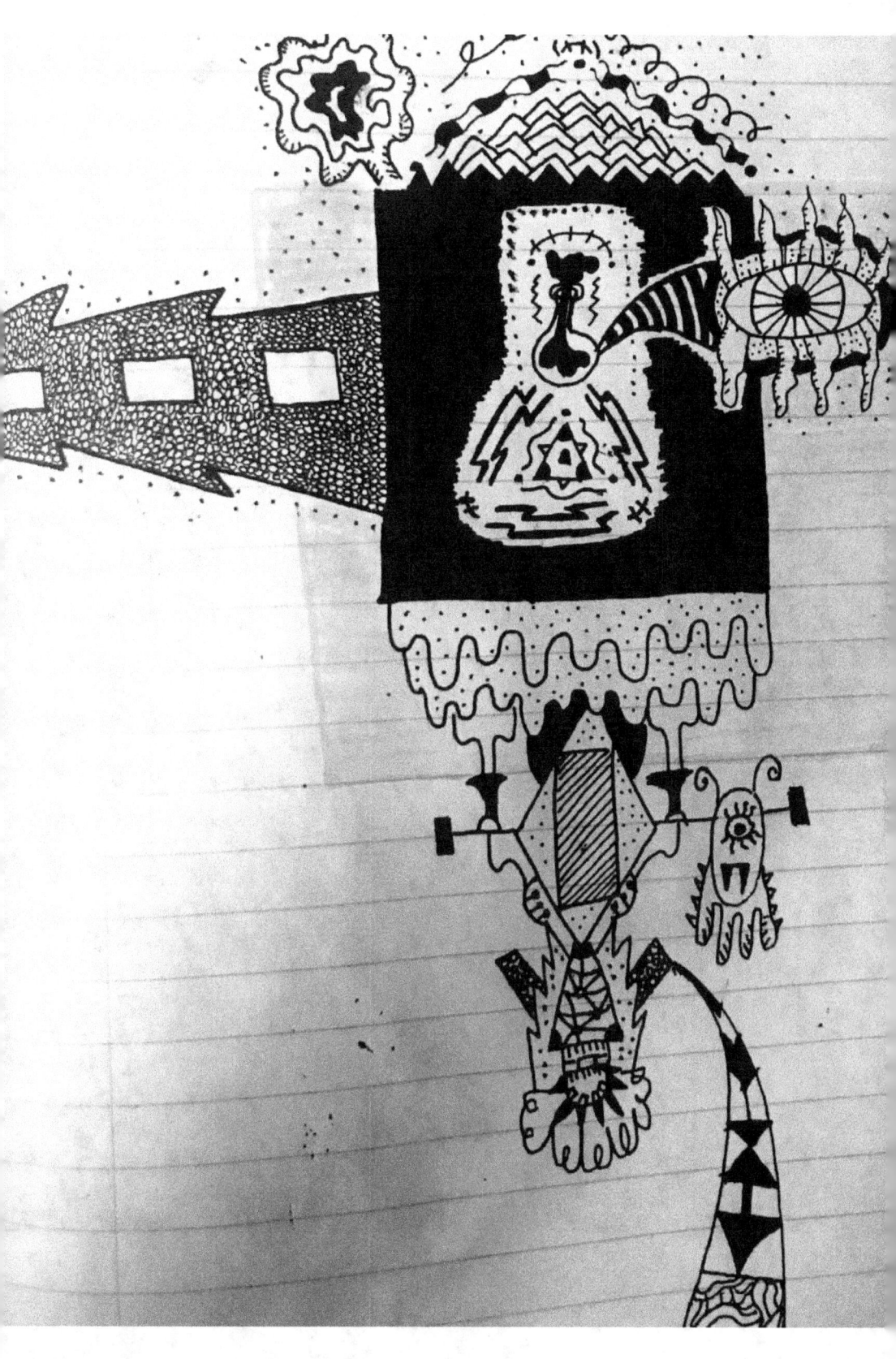

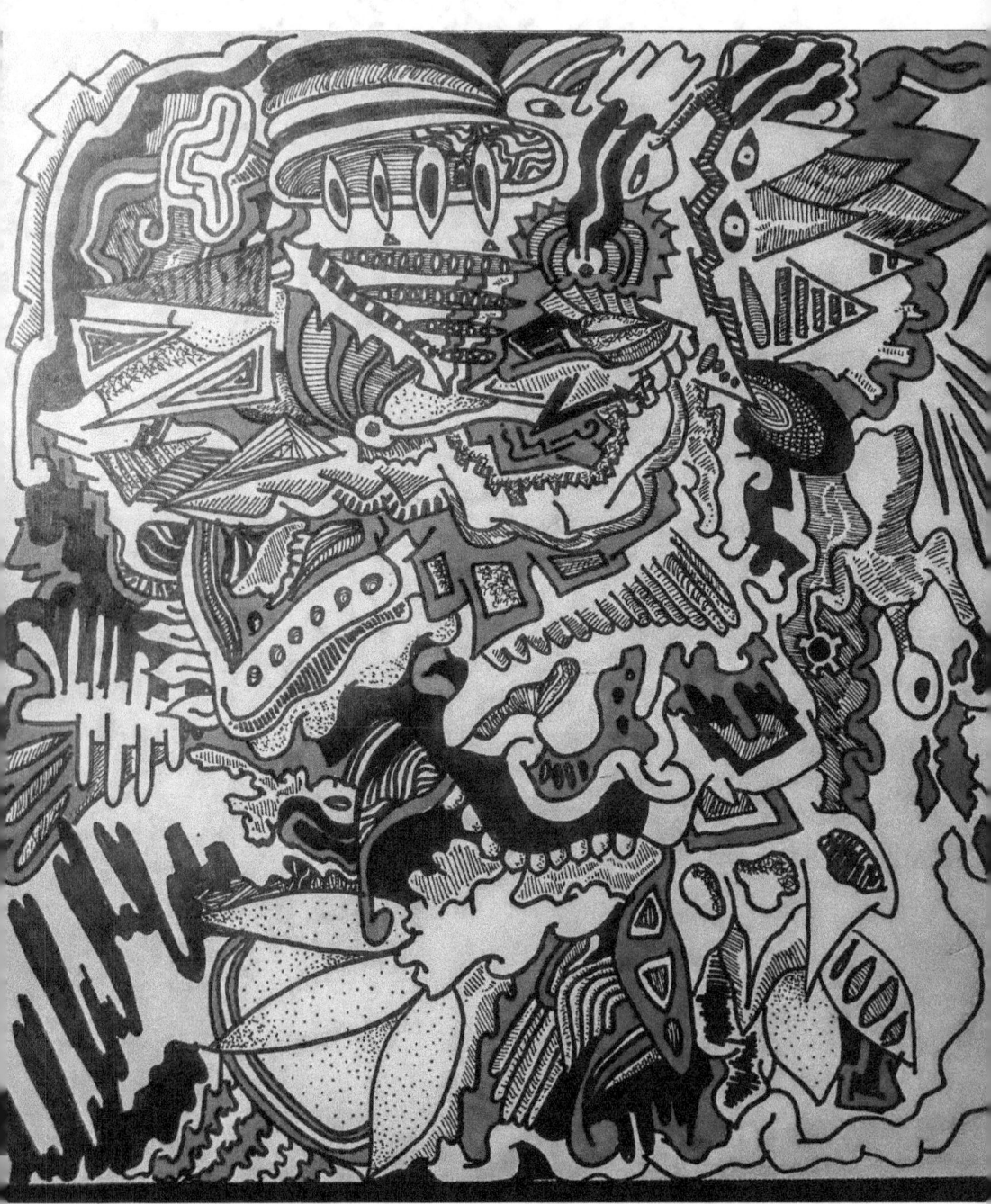

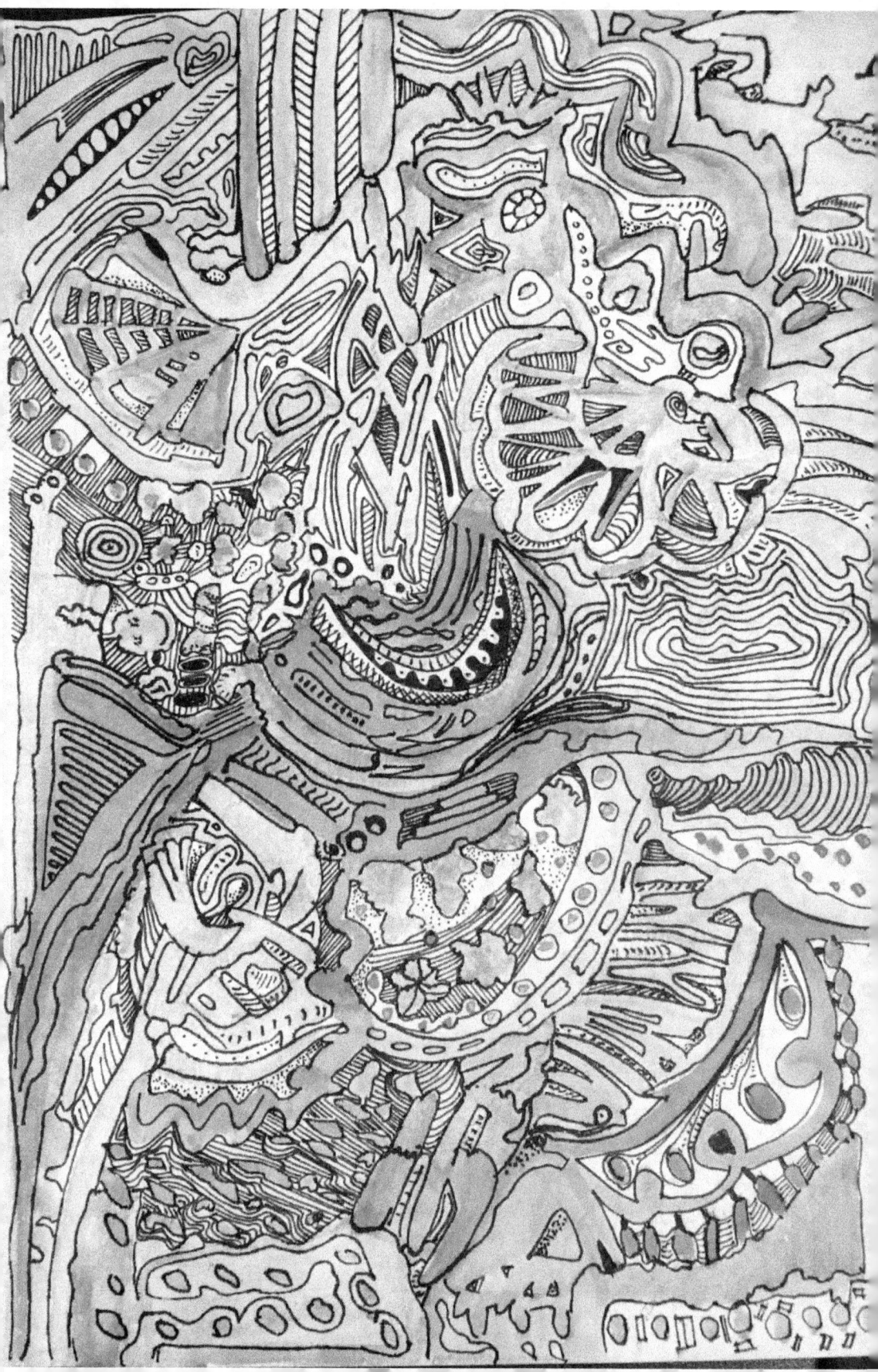

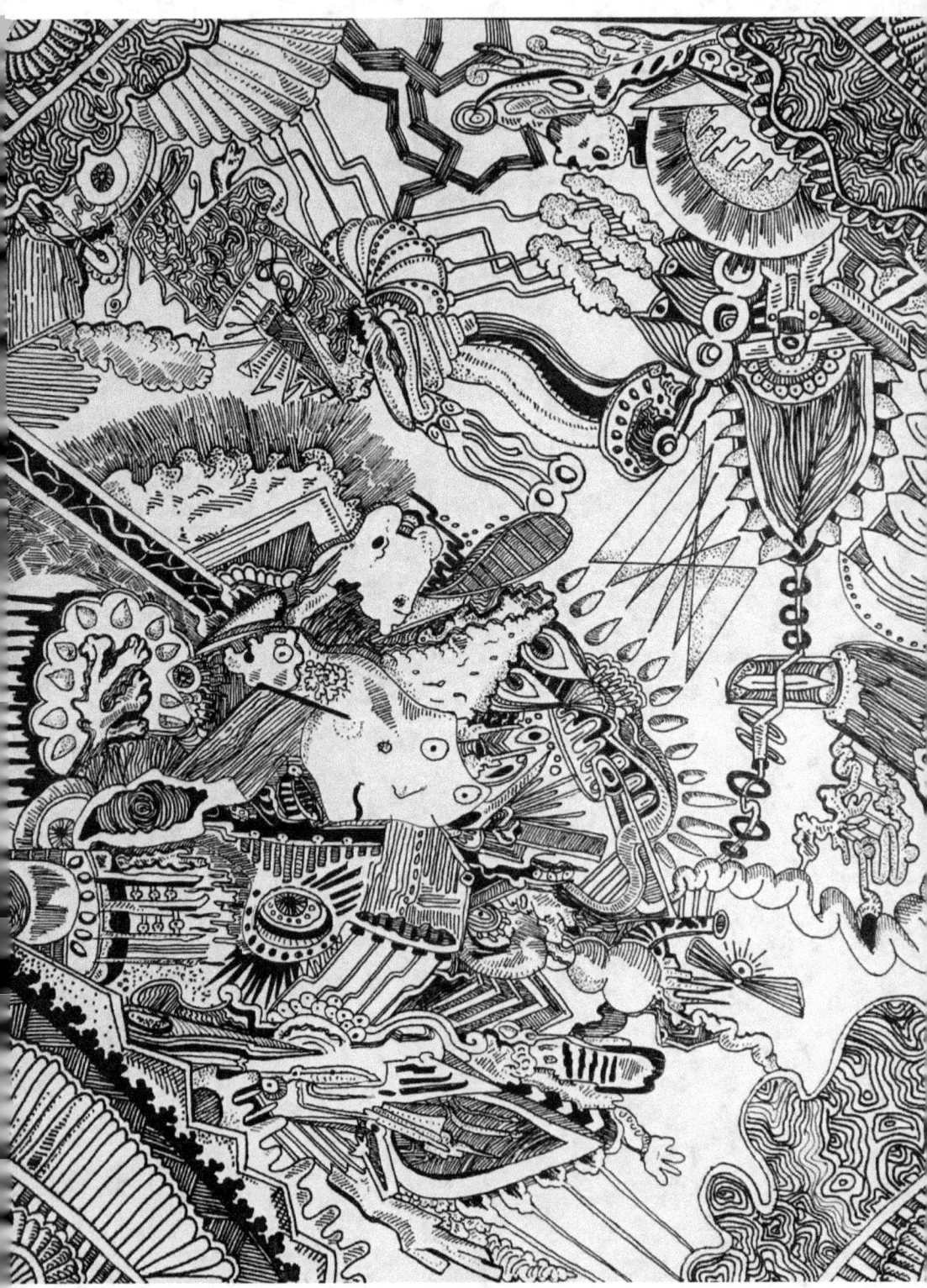

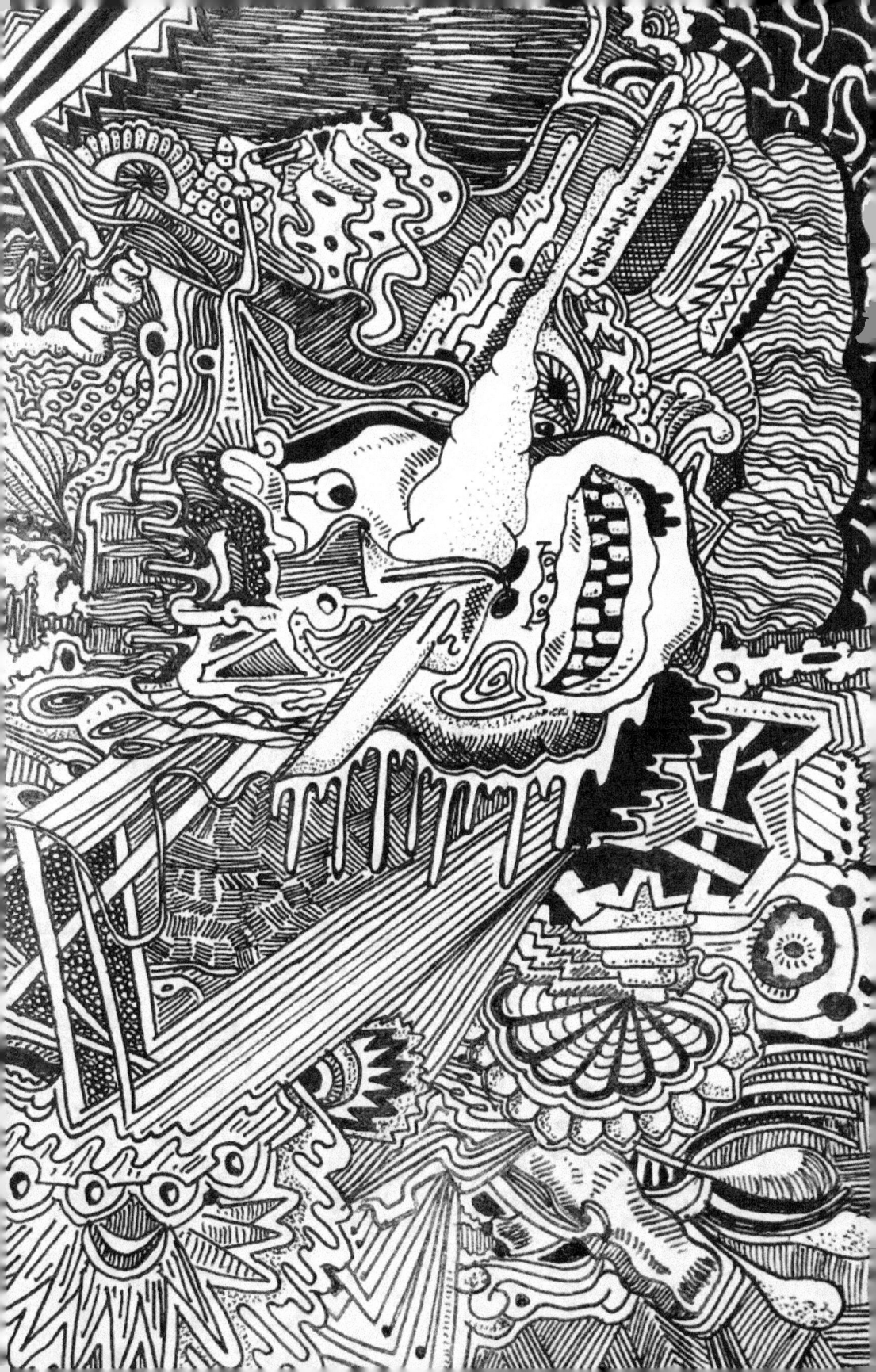

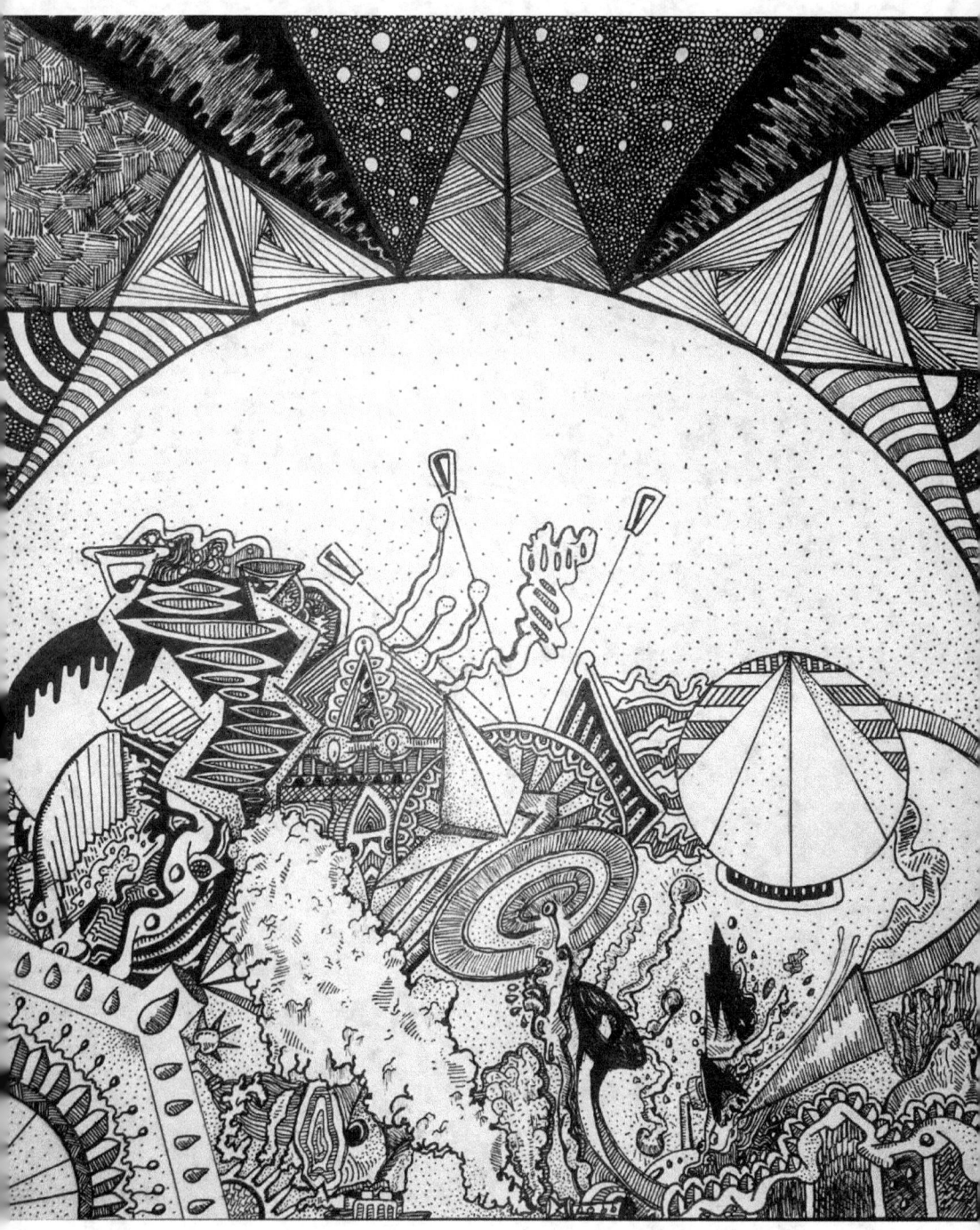